Woodshop Jigs & Fixtures

Woodshop Jigs & Fixtures

SANDOR NAGYSZALANCZY

The Taunton Press

Cover photo: Sandor Nagyszalanczy

Taunton
BOOKS & VIDEOS
for fellow enthusiasts

First printing: 1994
Second printing: 1996
Printed in the United States of America

A Fine Woodworking Book

Fine Woodworking® is a trademark of The Taunton Press, Inc., registered
in the U.S. Patent and Trademark Office.

The Taunton Press, 63 South Main Street, Box 5506, Newtown,
CT 06470-5506

Library of Congress Cataloging-in-Publication Data

Nagyszalanczy, Sandor.
     Woodshop jigs & fixtures / Sandor Nagzszalanczy.
        p. cm.
     "A Fine Woodworking book"–T.p. verso.
     Includes index.
     ISBN 1-56158-073-2
     1. Woodworking tools.   2. Jigs and fixtures.
  3. Workshops–Equipment and supplies.   I. Title.
  II. Title: Woodshop jigs and fixtures.
  TT186.N34   1994   94-15224
  684'.08'028–dc20   CIP

About Your Safety

Working wood is inherently dangerous. Using hand or power tools improperly or
ignoring standard safety practices can lead to permanent injury or even death. Don't
try to perform operations you learn about here (or elsewhere) unless you're certain
they are safe for you. If something about an operation doesn't feel right, don't do it.
Look for another way. We want you to enjoy the craft, so please keep safety foremost
in your mind whenever you're in the shop.

This book is dedicated to my father, Lorant, and my mother, Maria, who never really taught me much about woodworking, but gave me the support and encouragement to pursue my dreams, which has made this book possible.

ACKNOWLEDGMENTS

With any major motion-picture production, the director and star performers provide only a fraction of the talent needed to transform an idea into a box-office spectacle. Likewise, a great many individuals besides myself have helped to make this book possible.

First, I'd like to thank my woodworking friends and colleagues who made direct contributions to this book: Jeff Dale, Michael Dresdner, Steven Gellman, Roger Heitzman, Randy Jenkins, Ken Picou, Paul Silke, Richie Starr and Pat Warner. Special thanks to Mark Duginske for his extensive contributions and technical assistance.

Professionals and technicians who offered information and advice include: Alan Boardman, for advice about clamping forces and fixtures; Jerry Glaser, for recommendations regarding aluminum alloys; Jim Hayden, for technical and practical information about medium-density fiberboard; Jeff Kurka at Woodhaven, for tips on vacuum systems; and Chris Minick at 3M, for generous help and information about glues and adhesive transfer tape.

The following representatives of various companies provided essential product information and assistance: Brad Witt at Woodhaven, Carlo Venditto at CMT, Jon Behrle at Woodcraft, Rob McLaren at Modulus 2000 Machinery, Kenneth Lauzon at De-Sta-Co Clamp, Steve Jackel at Jackel Enterprises, J. Philip Humphrey at Excalibur Machine & Tool, Paul Bruhn at RK Industries, Bob Whitehead at TAP Plastics, Ed Fiantaca at Accurate Technology, and Daryl Keil at Vacuum Pressing Systems.

Finally, I'd like to thank some special people: Ann Gibb, for her eternal patience and endless wellspring of compassion and emotional support; Jodie Delohery, for her sensitive layouts and effusive sense of humor; Vince Babak, for his skillful drawings; Helen Albert, for her production and marketing prowess; and, last but certainly not least, Ruth Dobsevage, the best editor I could possibly hope to work with.

CONTENTS

INTRODUCTION

Finding an effective jig or fixture for a woodworking operation can be as elusive—and as time-consuming—as designing a great piece of furniture or cabinetry. It takes solid woodworking knowledge and some problem-solving skills, with a good dose of inspiration thrown in. Even a moderately complex setup can pose numerous choices: What tool or machine is best for the operation? Should the jig move the wood over the machine or guide the machine past the wood? How does the workpiece need to be referenced and clamped? Should the jig be adjustable? Most of the woodworkers I've met delight in solving challenging jigging problems. But if inspiration fails to strike, the task can quickly become tedious. And the feeling that you're reinventing the wheel each time you try to create a jig or fixture can be downright maddening.

That's how I felt more than 15 years ago when I started out as a naive but ambitious woodworker with no formal training, except a university degree in design theory. As I struggled to figure out what jigs were best for each task, I sought advice: I spoke with experienced colleagues and read every shred of literature I could find on the topic: do-it-yourself journals, woodworking magazines and books, even metalworking and machinist's texts. While I learned about a great many different jigs and fixtures, no single source covered the topic very thoroughly. Hence, every time I needed to build a new jig for a particular task, I had to remember which book or journal contained a particular jig that might provide a useful insight into getting that job done. I often wished I could buy one book that covered all the bases, but it seemed unlikely that a single source could contain the vast array of jigs and fixtures needed for custom woodworking.

In an attempt to make it easier for me to find specific bits of information, I spent many evenings cataloging hundreds of different jig and fixture designs, both from published sources and from my own shop journals, in which I had recorded my personal innovations. Gradually, a pattern started to emerge. In different sources, I kept running across the same fundamental components (such as fences and templates), mechanisms (like eccentric cams and detents) and construction strategies (for example, fitting threaded inserts for adjustable components). Regardless of how simple or complex a jig or fixture I needed to build, these basic elements seemed to provide the means for creating them. It then occurred to me that a book that treated these elements comprehensively might be most useful to woodworkers.

Following this approach, each chapter in this book focuses on a category of basic elements: fences, carriages, tables, stops, templates and fixtures (jigs orient and control the motion of the tool or workpiece, fixtures position the work and secure it during machining). These elements, used alone or in combination, provide the building blocks you'll need for developing and building devices for practically any situation, whether you make furniture, cabinets, musical instruments, wooden boats or stairways. I purposely didn't organize the chapters around specific machines, such as "Jigs for the Bandsaw," as other jig and fixture books do. That approach is just too limiting, since most jigs can be used for more than one operation or with more than one tool. I find it's more productive to assemble basic elements and develop a jig to work with whatever tool you do own, rather than deciding you can't do something because you don't have a particular tool or machine.

I have chosen not to include dimensions for most of the jigs featured in this book, no doubt to the chagrin of many readers who are beginning woodworkers. The whole point of building your own jigs and fixtures is to make them suit your own tools and machines and the particular tasks you encounter. It wouldn't be helpful for me to tell you exactly how big or small to make a jig. In most cases, proportions aren't critical, and are flexible over a fairly wide range. Extreme adaptations of the jigs and fixtures in this book will call for common sense and perhaps a little experimentation, but shouldn't require major research. In cases where the dimensions or shape of a particular part is essential for good performance, that information is provided.

While the book contains many simple jigs for the beginner, ready to be lifted directly from the page and built, I've also attempted to present ideas for more complex jigs that should be useful to advanced woodworkers and professionals as well. Hence, I've included material on some high-tech systems, including pneumatic clamping devices and digital electronic measuring instruments, which in recent years have become more affordable for medium-sized and even small woodshops.

Another purpose of this book is to acquaint you with the extensive collection of materials, special hardware and fasteners available to jig builders. These help make shop-built devices more accurate, safer and easier to build. Many items, such as FasTTrack and Incra Miter Sliders, are specially designed for use in woodworking jigs. Others, such as taper pins and universal hold-down clamps, are borrowed from the metal machinist's trade. Some items, such as threaded inserts, quick-release toggle clamps, hand knobs and studded handscrews, come in a confusing array of types. Therefore, I've attempted to review specific hardware items, as well as give information on installation and construction techniques, to help you to make better decisions about what to use when and how. I've also included a chapter on building and using jigs safely, including a discussion on how to incorporate dust control. An extensive Sources of Supply section at the end of the book lists catalog suppliers for every hardware item and device mentioned in the text. I've endeavored to make this list as complete and accurate as possible and to include only items that I use in my own jigs and fixtures or that I tried out in the course of writing this book. However, I cannot vouch for all items from all suppliers, and I do not personally endorse any of the products included in this section. Therefore, caveat emptor—let the buyer beware.

This book is a distillation of the ideas collected from many resources, including strategies garnered during a decade and a half of my own woodworking experience and methods learned from my woodworker colleagues and authors I had the pleasure of working with during my 6½-year stint as an editor for *Fine Woodworking* magazine. Some of the jigs described have been adapted for woodworking from the field of metalworking, a field I worked in for many years before becoming a woodworker. While I can claim that a handful of the jigs and fixtures in this book are original creations, I consider most of the designs shown to be reiterations of age-old devices. Just like the wheel or the bow and arrow, most basic jigs weren't invented at one time by a single woodworker, but rather over centuries by scores of clever individuals who faced the same woodworking problems that have challenged us since Noah built the ark. In instances where I've gleaned a particularly unique or innovative jig from a colleague, I give credit to that person.

As the ancient proverb says: "If you give a man a fish, he'll have supper; if you teach a man to fish, he'll never go hungry." Similarly, I believe that cultivating an extensive knowledge of basic jigging elements and strategies will go a long way toward helping you come up with exactly the right custom jigs and fixtures to meet all your needs, and make woodworking a more creative and pleasurable pursuit. Even if you're a veteran woodworker who has been building jigs for decades, I hope my book provides you with some fresh insights and perhaps even a few surprises that will spark your creativity and prompt you to reconsider the way you approach your work. If you're just starting out, I hope this book will be the catalyst that helps get you started and guides you through the confusing maze of jigging ideas that abound in conventional woodworking lore and literature.

CHAPTER 1

Fences that Guide

Most billiard players preparing to attempt a particularly tricky shot have wished that a divine hand would graciously descend and direct the wayward gyrations of their ball and guide it into the pocket—surreptitiously, of course. Fences serve this divine purpose for the woodworker: They guide boards or wooden parts in a controlled way across a machine's table and into the blade, cutter or abrasive. Without a fence, everyday woodshop tasks such as ripping and shaping would be dangerous or impossible to perform accurately. That is why many tools come with fences as standard equipment—the table saw and jointer are obvious examples. Fences are also useful for guiding portable tools, such as routers and saber saws, and usually come as optional accessories. But there are many occasions where a standard fence needs to be augmented or replaced by a shop-built alternative. Many custom woodworking jigs require shop-built fences that are sturdy and easy to set to enable the jig to perform quickly and accurately.

A fence is any device that maintains a fixed distance between a workpiece and the tool while one or the other moves to perform the operation. Since much woodworking is done with straight-edged boards, most fences guide workpieces in a straight line. But as we'll see in this chapter, curved fences are also useful for guiding round parts or parts with concave or convex edges for many shaping operations. Fences are typically used on the tables of stationary tools to guide stock past

Fences guide the workpiece along a predictable path into a blade, cutter or abrasive. This box-beam-style extension fence (pp. 17-18) fits over the bandsaw's standard rip fence and aids in cutting long stock.

the cutter or blade, or to locate stock for an operation, such as when boring a straight row of holes on the drill press. Fences used on portable tools provide guidance while the tool is moved past the workpiece. There are also situations in which it's better to secure the fence directly to the workpiece than to the tool. At the end of the chapter, I'll also deal with fences that are part of more elaborate fixtures that support and orient the workpiece, such as a box jig for fluting table legs that has fences that guide a router.

In jig building as in other aspects of woodworking, safety should always be a concern. Fences and other jigs and fixtures are a lot safer to use if they incorporate guards (see pp. 208-213) and hold-downs (see pp. 213-220).

Parallel Fences for Bladed Tools

Circular-bladed tools, such as the table saw and bandsaws fitted with wide blades, require a fence that not only guides the workpiece a fixed distance from the blade, but also keeps the work parallel to it (see the sidebar on the facing page). The most basic fence is just a straight board or strip of plywood clamped to the machine's table. A clamp-on fence is also useful as a secondary fence—an extra guide for operations where you need to contain the workpiece on two sides to keep it from creeping away from the main fence, as when cove cutting on the table saw.

If your saw table isn't big enough to mount a fence, say, for crosscutting a full sheet of plywood, you can clamp a strip of straight wood to the underside of the workpiece instead; this fence will ride against the end of the machine table during the cut. Another occasion for mounting a fence to the workpiece is when you want to rip a straight edge on a big, rough waney-edged plank too heavy to maneuver over the jointer. A straight board tacked on top with drywall screws (see the photo at left) acts as a temporary fence and rides against the saw's regular rip fence.

The only problem with most simple clamp-on fences is that adjusting and readjusting them precisely for different cuts can be very tedious. That's why every new table saw comes with a parallel-locking rip fence of some kind. But there are many circumstances in which it's desirable to have a separate, custom-made fence that can be attached to the table without much fuss and allow operations that the regular fence doesn't permit, such as an angled fence for cove cutting or a wooden fence you can bury the blade into for rabbeting.

A handy way to get a straight, square edge on an irregular plank is to screw a strip on top. This strip 'fence' rides against the saw's rip fence as the plank's other edge is trimmed off straight.

When cutting wood on a table saw, a good portion of the sawblade occupies the kerf just behind the cut. If the fence used to guide stock past the blade — a stock rip fence or shop-made fence jig — isn't mounted correctly, the rear edge of the blade can contact the sides of the kerf, at best causing tearout, at worst causing dangerous kickback (at its rear edge, the blade teeth will lift the stock up and throw it back at the operator).

For standard rip cuts, a fence must be mounted so that it is parallel to the blade. If you're clamping a wooden fence bar to the saw table, check for parallel by measuring between the fence and both the front and rear edges of the blade. Do this with the saw unplugged and the blade raised to maximum height. Many woodworkers prefer a slightly greater distance at the back of the blade, say an extra 1/64 in., to allow the cut piece next to the fence a little clearance. If you're clamping a fence, such as the basic utility fence described below, to the front edge of the saw table, or mounting it to standard rip fence rails, you may discover that the blade and edge of the table aren't perpendicular. You can temporarily compensate by shimming one end of the fence's crossbar. But ultimately you should remedy the problem by realigning your saw's blade (including the arbor, trunions and cradle) to the saw table, a procedure too complex to get into here, but well described in Mark Duginske's book: *Mastering Woodworking Machines,* available from The Taunton Press.

You must also take care when doing tricky table-saw operations, such as cove cutting, which require a fence to be mounted at an angle to the blade. First, always set up the fence forward of the blade (angling toward the right rear corner of the saw). In that position, the force of the blade will press the workpiece tighter against the fence. Second, clamp a secondary fence on the other side of the workpiece, to keep it aligned and running true (It will be ruined if it wanders away from the main fence.) Finally, when cove cutting — or during any other table-saw operation — use featherboards and/or wheeled hold-downs and safety guards at all times (see pp. 208-220). In addition to preventing tragedy, they'll also improve the quality of your cuts.

Basic utility fence

One of the simplest ways to make a fence that is adjustable, yet remains parallel to the blade is to attach a crossbar at 90° to a fence bar, to align it and provide a means to attach the fence to the machine table's front edge or guide rails. I've seen at least a half dozen good designs for fences of this kind, many consisting of not much more than two straight-grained pieces of hardwood joined at a right angle. While parts can be permanently pinned together with couple of dowels or screws, I designed my utility fence, shown in the the drawing on p. 9, to be adjustable. For standard parallel work, a taper pin set through the angled brace into the crossbar locks the fence at 90° (for more on taper pins, see p. 194). With the pin removed, the fence bar can be locked at any angle using the hand knob. This is a useful feature for cove cutting because you can set the bar at the desired angle yet move the fence back and forth to change the location of the cove on the workpiece without affecting the fence angle (which determines the cove profile). A smaller version of this fence can be used on the band-saw; the angle adjustment can be used to set the fence to accommodate blade drift.

To construct the utility fence, size the fence bar long enough to overhang the machine table by a few inches at either end and cut the crossbar about 12 in. to 16 in. long. The angle brace is a piece of plywood or MDF cut to the shape of a truncated right triangle, its long leg one-third to one-half as long as the fence bar. A curved slot is routed in the brace for the angle adjustment (the center of the radius is the pivot bolt). Carriage bolts are used for the bar/crossbar pivot and the angle locking bolt (a hand knob tops the angle bolt). With this fence—or any other fence, for that matter—the bottom edge of the bar's face should be chamfered slightly to prevent sawdust and debris from accumulating that would keep the workpiece from bearing flush against the fence bar.

The best way to secure the utility fence to your machine depends on the guide rails. On machines without rails, you can simply clamp both ends of the crossbar to the front lip of the machine table. A faster alternative to C-clamps is to use quick-release plier clamps, such as De-Sta-Co model 462). You could also mount two quick-release toggle clamps, such as the De-Sta-Co model 317-U, on the underside of the crossbar to clamp to the lip of a cast-iron machine table. If your table saw has tubular guide rails for its standard rip fence, you can cove-cut the underside of the crossbar to fit the rail. An L-shaped strip, as shown at bottom left in the drawing on the facing page, is also cove cut and locks to the underside of the rail via a carriage bolt and winged hand knob.

The wooden utility fence is great for rabbeting, since you don't have to worry about the blade hitting a metal fence bar. To prepare the fence for rabbet cuts, first clamp the back end of the bar down and raise the spinning sawblade up into it. For repetitive rabbet cuts that require the same setting, you may wish to screw a cleat to the underside of the fence that registers it in the saw's miter slot. If you are cutting large panels and have problems with the back end of the fence bar lifting or deflecting, clamp it down or add a rear hold-down, as shown at bottom right in the drawing.

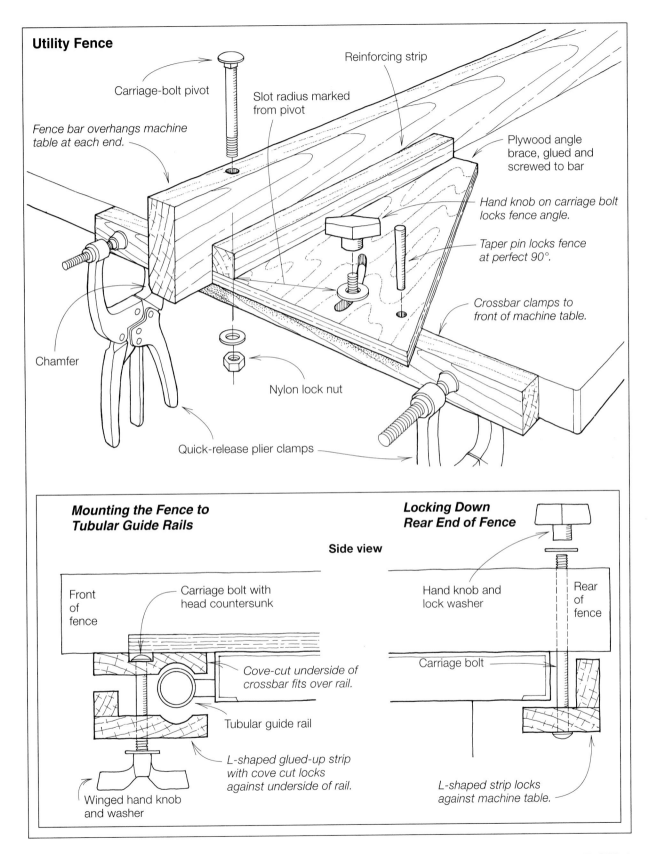

Utility Fence

Carriage-bolt pivot

Reinforcing strip

Slot radius marked
from pivot

*Fence bar overhangs machine
table at each end.*

Plywood angle
brace, glued and
screwed to bar

*Hand knob on carriage bolt
locks fence angle.*

*Taper pin locks fence
at perfect 90°.*

*Crossbar clamps to
front of machine table.*

Chamfer

Nylon lock nut

Quick-release plier clamps

Mounting the Fence to
Tubular Guide Rails

Locking Down
Rear End of Fence

Side view

Front
of
fence

Carriage bolt with
head countersunk

Hand knob and
lock washer

Rear
of
fence

*Cove-cut underside of
crossbar fits over rail.*

Carriage bolt

Tubular guide rail

*L-shaped glued-up strip
with cove cut locks
against underside of rail.*

Winged hand knob
and washer

*L-shaped strip locks
against machine table.*

Sliding-wedge fence

For jobs that require a fence that stays parallel, yet adjusts with great precision over a narrow range, such as sawing small parts to precise dimensions or hollow-chisel mortising, a sliding-wedge fence, such as the one shown in the drawing below, is a good choice. This fence works on a principle you probably remember from your high-school geometry class: If you have two right triangles with the same angles and you slide them together along their hypotenuses, their long sides will remain parallel.

The jig requires three long right-angle wedges cut at the same angle. The acute angle isn't critical—anything from 8° to 30° will work (smaller angles yield a finer degree of adjustment). Scale the length of the wedges to your application; they should be one-half to two-thirds

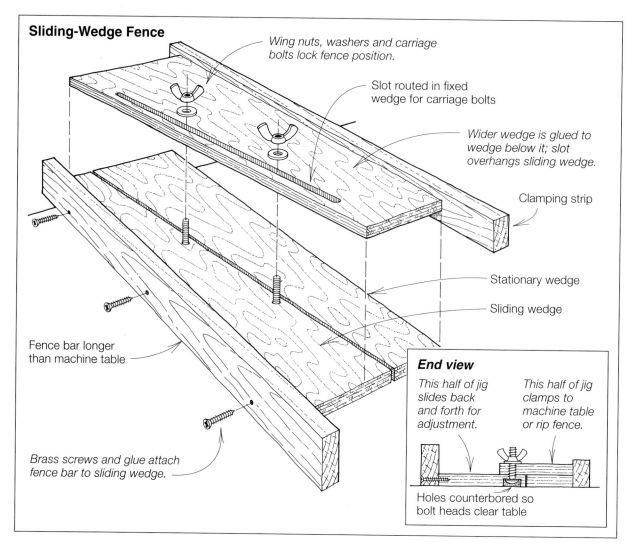

Sliding-Wedge Fence

Wing nuts, washers and carriage bolts lock fence position.

Slot routed in fixed wedge for carriage bolts

Wider wedge is glued to wedge below it; slot overhangs sliding wedge.

Clamping strip

Stationary wedge

Sliding wedge

Fence bar longer than machine table

Brass screws and glue attach fence bar to sliding wedge.

End view

This half of jig slides back and forth for adjustment.

This half of jig clamps to machine table or rip fence.

Holes counterbored so bolt heads clear table

the length of the fence bar. For a table saw-size jig, I cut the three wedges 24 in. long with a 12° angle (using a tapering jig on the table saw, as discussed on pp. 53-54). One of the wedges should be about 1¼ in. wider than the other two.

Start by routing a slot in the wider wedge, parallel to and near the hypotenuse edge. Now glue this wedge atop one of the other wedges, then glue and screw this assembly to the clamping strip, as shown in the drawing. After drilling two holes near the edge of the hypotenuse of the remaining wedge, glue and screw the long leg (not the hypotenuse) of this wedge to the fence bar. The drilled holes are for carriage bolts that will ride in the slot in the wider wedge. The bolts keep the two halves of the jig together and lock down fence settings.

A sliding-wedge fence can be clamped down to the machine's table or screwed to a stock rip fence, or the jig's clamping strip can extend below the wedges for a press fit into a miter-gauge slot. To set the fence, slide the fence bar forward or back, then tighten the wing nuts. To save having to measure blade-to-fence distance each time, you can locate frequently used settings by marking a perpendicular line across the hypotenuses. If you're more ambitious, you could mark graduations along the hypotenuse to create a scale for measured settings.

For hollow-chisel mortising on a drill press, I fitted a small sliding-wedge jig with a taller L-shaped fence bar as shown in the photo at right, and mounted the whole thing to a plywood base clamped to my drill-press table. An adjustable hold-down secured with machine screws through the fence keeps the mortising chisel from lifting the stock. Such a fence could also be incorporated into a more complex jig, such as the rail-guided mortising carriage described on pp. 62-63.

Fitted with a tall, L-shaped fence and an adjustable hold-down (screwed on from the back), a sliding-wedge fence is mounted to the drill-press table. The fence allows accurate parallel adjustment for hollow-chisel mortising various thicknesses of stock.

Fixed-Dimension Fences

While infinitely adjustable fences allow a full range of settings, they are not always the most convenient to use. They are time-consuming to set and are subject to small variations when you try reset the fence to the same measure (which is why it's usually best to rip all members that are to be the same width at one time). Furthermore, whenever you set a fence using a cursor and scale or tape measure, there's always the risk of accidentally setting it to the wrong measurement. Because there are a great many operations that call for setting the fence to exactly the same position time after time, you can save yourself a lot of trouble by building a fence that doesn't require setting: a fence that allows only one distance between it and the blade.

Taper-pin plug-in fence

A plug-in fence is precisely aligned and mounted directly to the surface of a machine table. The quickest way to do this is simply to drill holes through the fence bar, then drill and tap corresponding holes in the machine's table for bolts. If you don't want to drill holes in your cast-iron machine's table, make an auxiliary top that will fasten over the table (see p. 76), and use threaded inserts in that. For jobs that require very precise fence placement, I use taper pins instead of bolts (see p. 194).

Plug-in fences are useful a great number of other tools besides bladed machines. For example, I use a plug-in fence as an accessory to my router table for end-slotting stock, as shown in the drawing below. The jig's two fence bars keep the stock in line as it is pushed into the kerfing bit.

Taper pins alone are more than enough to secure small fence bars. For large fences (or if you just don't trust taper pins alone) you can drill and tap holes for one or two bolts to lock the fence down. If your plug-in fence is for a shop-built stationary-table tool that has a solid wood or plywood top, such as a router table, you can make your own wooden taper pins from a dense hardwood, like maple (teak pins might be even better, since the pins would be self-lubricating). The right degree of taper for small to medium-size wooden pins is about .025 in. per in.

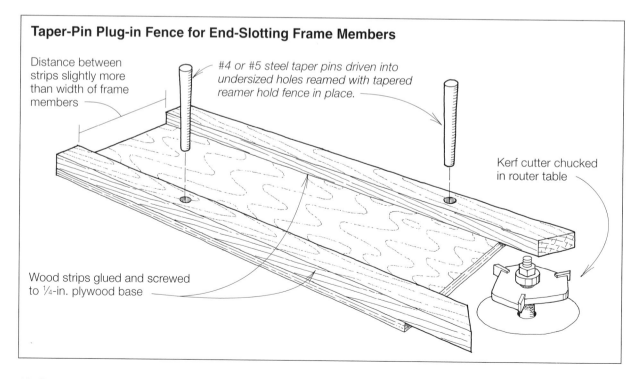

Taper-Pin Plug-in Fence for End-Slotting Frame Members

Distance between strips slightly more than width of frame members

#4 or #5 steel taper pins driven into undersized holes reamed with tapered reamer hold fence in place.

Kerf cutter chucked in router table

Wood strips glued and screwed to ¼-in. plywood base

Miter-slot fence

The miter slot on most saw tables is a good place to locate a fixed-dimension fence (see the photo at right). This is simply a fence bar with a wood strip on the bottom that's sized to press snugly into the slot—$\frac{3}{8}$ in. by $\frac{3}{4}$ in. on most machine tools. By carefully sizing the width of the bar and mounting the strip off center, the slot-mounted fence becomes reversible, providing two different cutting setups with one jig. (By the way, by adding another set of tapered holes, a taper-pin fence can also be made reversible. A miter-slot fence is especially handy when you need the fence face to be flush with or overlap the blade, allowing rabbeting without mounting an auxiliary face to the regular rip fence.

Bench-hook fence

The bench-hook fence is especially good for machines with small worktables. This fence, shown in the drawing below, is shaped like the bench hook used by modelmakers and jewelers, which hooks over the edge of a workbench, providing a lip that allows small work-pieces to be hand held for crosscutting. The bench-hook fence has two lips: One acts as a fence bar to guide the workpiece; the other aligns with the edge of the stationary tool's table. C-clamps or plier clamps (or screws on a wood table) hold it in place. Because both lips are parallel, a bench-hook fence can be used with bladed machines, like small table saws or accessory-table-mounted saber saws, as well as rotary-motion machines, like router tables and drill presses. (When this fence is used with saws, the blade must be parallel with the edge of the saw table that the fence rides against, as described in the sidebar on p. 7).

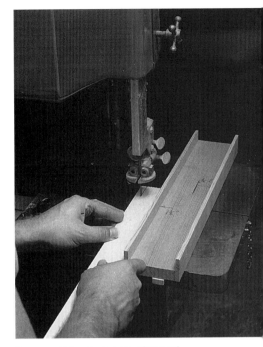

A reversible rip fence plugged into the miter-gauge slot of the bandsaw allows parts to be ripped to either of two precise widths (the fence can be turned around in the slot) without the tedium of setting an adjustable rip fence for each cut.

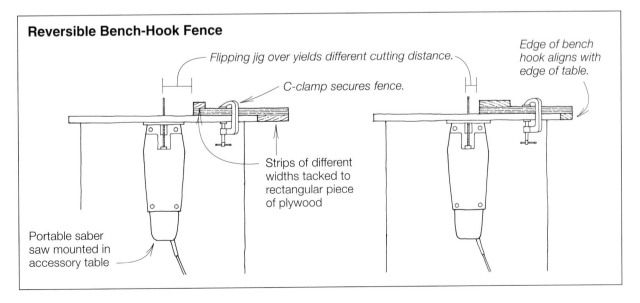

Reversible Bench-Hook Fence

Flipping jig over yields different cutting distance.

Edge of bench hook aligns with edge of table.

C-clamp secures fence.

Strips of different widths tacked to rectangular piece of plywood

Portable saber saw mounted in accessory table

Bench-hook-fences consist of a piece of plywood with strips tacked to opposite faces at each end. By tacking on strips of different widths on each face, as shown in the drawing on p. 13, the fence becomes reversible, yielding two settings from each fence. Bench-hook fences are so easy to make that you can easily construct a separate one for each one- or two-step operation. They're especially good for multiple-cut operations, such as making complex-pattern moldings.

Tambour-slat fence

When you need to make multiple cuts or mill grooves at regular intervals, such as for pigeonhole dividers in a desk carcase, here's a fixed-dimension fence that will save you the time and trouble of having to reset the fence for each cut. The tambour-slat fence, shown in the photo below, is a variation on the practice of putting a row of strips of identical width between the fence and the workpiece. A strip is removed after each cut, hence all cuts are evenly spaced. The tambour-slat fence merely makes this job safer, since the slats are held together with a canvas backing. After the end slat is clamped down (or screwed

A tambour-slat fence can be used on the table saw for cutting evenly spaced dadoes on a carcase side without resetting a rip fence for each cut. The edge of a slat guides the cut; then the slat is flipped back and another slat guides the next cut.

to a rip fence) to space the first cut correctly, the tambour is simply "rolled up" a slat at a time for each successive pass. You can vary the spacing by making the slats different widths or by folding back more than one slat at a time.

Assemble the tambour strip just as you would a regular canvas-backed tambour door. Start by cutting out slats of identical widths and laying them edge to edge, face down on a plywood or particleboard base. A frame tacked atop the base aligns the slats and allows them to be pressed tightly together with opposing pairs of wedges (you can see a photo of this setup on p. 160). Then, coat the backs of the slats with a thin, even layer of white glue and apply a piece of thin duck canvas (6-oz. fabric weight works well) over the surface—it doesn't have to cover edge to edge. Use a veneer roller or printer's brayer to work out any bubbles, and press the canvas flat.

Pivoting Fence for Rotary Tools

Rotary machines, such as shapers, drill presses, spindle sanders, and router tables, do not require fences that adjust and lock in parallel fashion. Although any of the fences described so far in this chapter can be used with rotary machines, it is also possible to create fences for rotary tools that pivot for fence-to-bit adjustments. Most of these shop-made fences use a pivot bolt of some kind. You can also create a pivoting fence using special hardware, such as FasTTrack (see p. 197).

A basic pivoting fence, shown in the drawing on p. 16, has a fence bar that pivots atop a base. Once the fence is set as desired, the bar is locked down with a hand knob on a carriage bolt fitted through a hole in the bar and an arced slot routed through the base. The base is clamped or bolted to the stationary machine table. Edge strips on the underside of the base can be fitted to help align the fence to the table-top. If the pivoting fence is for a shop-made machine with a wood or composite-material tabletop, you can mount the fence permanently, but you'll either have to rout an arc in the top for the fence's lock-down bolt or use a C-clamp or plier clamp to secure the end of the bar.

Construction of a simple pivoting fence requires a base, usually ¾-in. plywood or MDF, with a carriage-bolt pivot pin fitted from underneath. Laminating the fence bar from two thicknesses of ¾-in. plywood or sawing it out of 8/4 stock will make it heavy enough for most small-shop applications. However, if a recess must be cut into the face of the fence for bit or drill-chuck clearance, you might need to reinforce the area behind the cutout or make the bar thicker to prevent deflection. The arced slot in the base can be routed with a circle jig like the one shown in the photo on p. 65. The pivot hole in the fence base is used as the pivot point to swing the circle jig fitted with a router and straight bit.

In use, fence settings that need to be repeated can be marked with a pencil line struck along the bar face to aid resetting later. For greater accuracy, you can add detents that position the fence bar (see pp. 120-121). If you find hand-setting the bar on this fence—or any fence for that matter—too finicky, you can incorporate a micro-adjuster, a device that allows the fence bar to be moved controllably in very small increments before it is locked down. Two designs for shop-built micro-adjusters are described in the sidebar on p. 111. Another possibility is to fit a commercially made micro-adjuster, such as the one made by FasTTrack (see pp. 198-199).

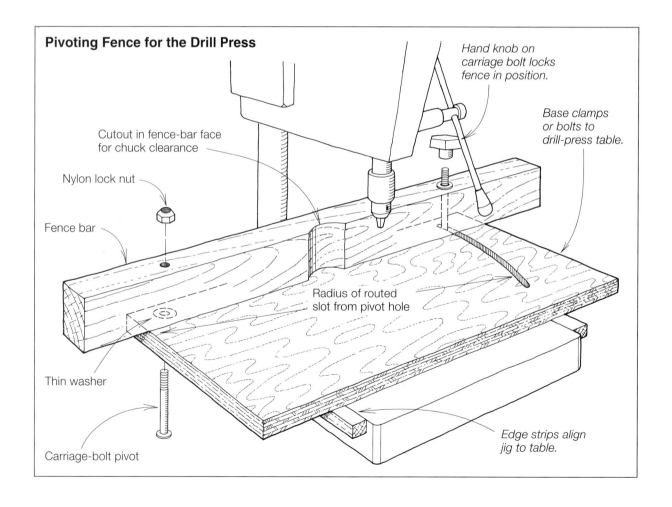

Pivoting Fence for the Drill Press

Hand knob on carriage bolt locks fence in position.

Base clamps or bolts to drill-press table.

Cutout in fence-bar face for chuck clearance

Nylon lock nut

Fence bar

Radius of routed slot from pivot hole

Thin washer

Carriage-bolt pivot

Edge strips align jig to table.

Auxiliary Fences

Probably the easiest way to extend the capabilities of the standard fence on any machine is by attaching an auxiliary fence. An auxiliary fence screws or bolts to the face of another fence, allowing it to handle all sorts of situations, such as cutting exceptionally long, thin or tall workpieces. In each case, the appropriate auxiliary fence will support the work better and guide it with more stability, improving the quality of the cut and making the job safer. Just remember that any auxiliary fence you add changes the fence-to-cutter distance, so you may wish to readjust your fence's cursor if it's fitted with one, to speed up fence adjustment. And an auxiliary fence is almost a must if you expect to get any accurate work done with a miter gauge on a table saw or band-saw. For accurate cutoff work you can add a flip-down stop, as described on pp. 106-107, to the top of a miter-gauge extension fence.

Extension fences

Extending the length and/or height of a standard rip fence is one of the easiest ways to make it more versatile. An extension fence (see the drawing below) is invaluable for controlling extra-long stock or large panels, especially heavy sheet goods, like particleboard. When working with thin pieces, like moldings, it's useful to attach thin pieces of plywood to the bottom of the fence extension where it overhangs the

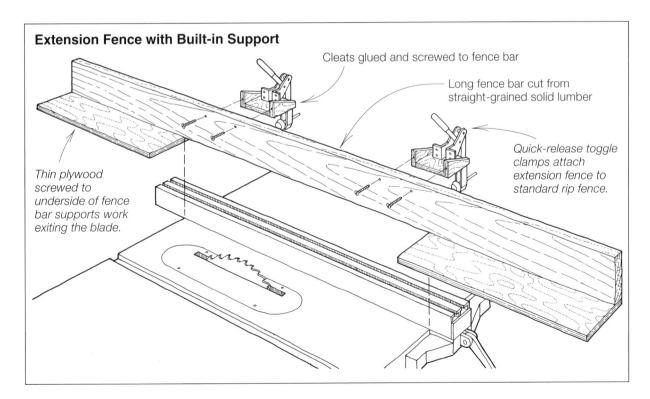

Extension Fence with Built-in Support

Cleats glued and screwed to fence bar

Long fence bar cut from straight-grained solid lumber

Quick-release toggle clamps attach extension fence to standard rip fence.

Thin plywood screwed to underside of fence bar supports work exiting the blade.

machine table front and rear, as shown in the drawing. These act as extension tables to support the spindly molding in front of and behind the table.

You can construct a long auxiliary fence any way that suits you: It could be just a straight board screwed to your rip fence. For a fence that's quicker to fit and remove, glue and screw wooden brackets to the bar and attach quick-release toggle clamps, as shown in the photo below (I used De-Sta-Co model #317U). In addition to fence bars made from vertical-grain Douglas-fir or redwood, I've had good success making fences out of ¾-in. birch plywood covered with a layer of plastic laminate, for a smooth-gliding surface. To stabilize really long workpieces, I made a sort of box-beam extension fence for my table saw out of two plywood strips with small bulkheads between the sides. I made a smaller version for my bandsaw, shown in the photo on p. 5. Leaving the center section hollow allows the extension to fit snugly over a rip fence, and no clamps or screws are needed to hold it firmly in place.

A quick-release toggle clamp mounted to a bracket screwed to the rear side of an extension fence allows the fence to be rapidly fitted to or removed from the table saw's standard rip fence.

Special-profile fences

Although most fences for woodworking typically have flat faces, there's no reason not to give an auxiliary face a profile that better suits the nature of the workpiece and the operation. For example, if thin pieces being ripped on the table saw keep lifting up, a lipped auxiliary fence (see the photo below) will keep the piece flat during cutting. You can also employ a lipped fence for raising one edge of the workpiece to change its angle relative to the saw table, which can come in handy when you're trying to get just the right profile on a piece of stock while cove cutting on the table saw with a tilted blade. Like other auxiliary-fence faces, special-profile faces can be screwed or clamped to stock rip fences or other shop-made fences.

Custom-made special-profile fences are indispensable for cutting or machining odd shapes; you can adapt the face of the fence to support the stock as need be. The drawing on p. 20 shows a decorative crown molding being shaped on the router table using a special-profile fence to support it at the correct angle and guide it past a core-box bit. One part of the fence is cove-cut to mate with a large bead in the molding, which keeps the molding tight against the fence. A featherboard or other hold-down should be used to keep the molding flat on the table (see the photo on p. 215). A special-profile fence can also be used on a

A lipped auxiliary fence, clamped to the saw's standard rip fence, keeps thin stock flat on the saw table during cutting. The lip is a strip of Masonite glued into a dado in the plywood mounting plate.

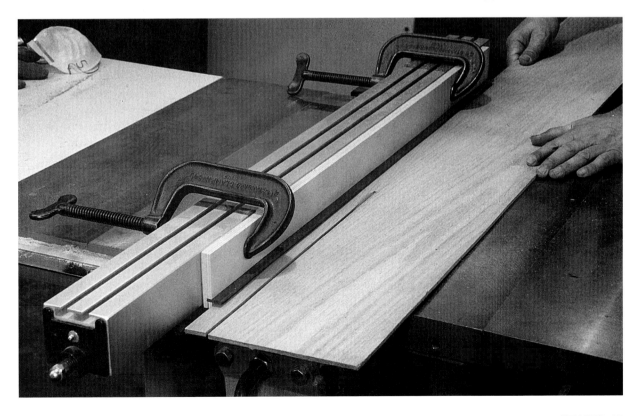

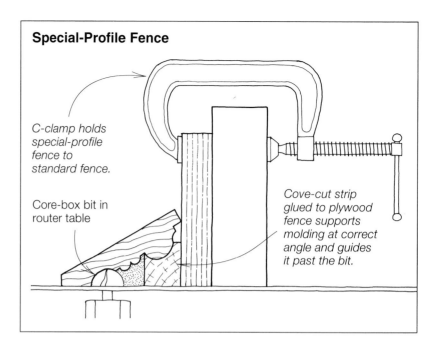

Special-Profile Fence

C-clamp holds special-profile fence to standard fence.

Core-box bit in router table

Cove-cut strip glued to plywood fence supports molding at correct angle and guides it past the bit.

drill-press table or with a mortising machine, to position the work at the correct angle and support it during boring or mortising operations (see the discussion of V-blocks on p. 153).

Another way to handle cuts on dowels or on irregular moldings that have small or no flat surfaces is to create a guide block that supports and orients the workpiece (see the top drawing on the facing page). You can make this type of guide by creating a cutout that matches the molding's cross section in a thick block of wood using a drill press, scrollsaw or bandsaw. The guide can be clamped down to the machine table or even screwed to the machine's throat plate. Once secured, the machine's blade or bit can be raised up to intersect the cutout. If the guide must align the molding to cutter or blade at a special angle, say for slotting mitered frame members for angled splines, you can cut the angle on the bottom of the block before mounting it, which will change the workpiece's angle relative to the cutter.

Mounting a kerf splitter at the near end of the jig just behind the sawblade or bit helps to stabilize the work and keep it from rotating and binding (see the bottom drawing on the facing page). A kerf splitter also provides enough stability to cut lengthwise grooves in dowels or rip them in half safely. The splitter need be nothing more than a thin piece of wood mounted into the guide block at a slight angle raked back away from the blade as shown. I prefer to use a piece of teak for the splitter, taking advantage of that wood's natural lubricity to prevent it from sticking in the newly cut kerf.

Guide Block for Grooving Dowels on the Table Saw

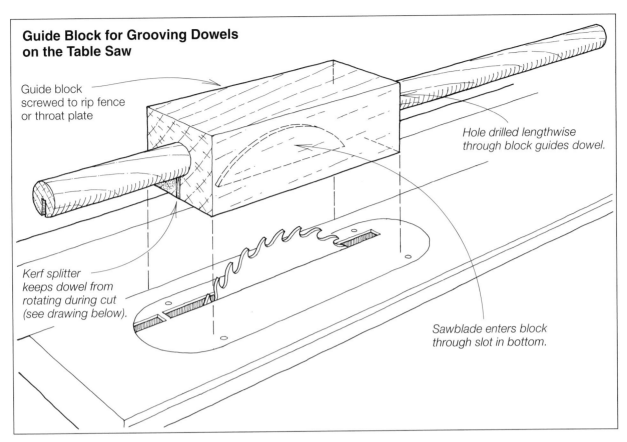

Guide block screwed to rip fence or throat plate

Hole drilled lengthwise through block guides dowel.

Kerf splitter keeps dowel from rotating during cut (see drawing below).

Sawblade enters block through slot in bottom.

Guide-Block Kerf Splitter

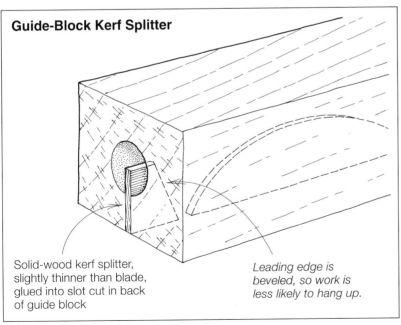

Solid-wood kerf splitter, slightly thinner than blade, glued into slot cut in back of guide block

Leading edge is beveled, so work is less likely to hang up.

Angled fence

Adding an angled auxiliary fence that tilts the workpiece relative to the cutter can provide a useful way to cut, shape or sand angled edges instead of using a tilting-arbor or tilting-table machine. Adding an angled fence to a table saw permits panel-raising cuts with a perpendicular blade, saving the time it takes to set the tilt angle. Fitted to a router table or shaper fence, an angled auxiliary fence allows different profiles to be shaped using standard bits, as shown in the photo above. And, added to the fence on a sliding miter carriage, an angled fence makes compound-angle cuts possible, as when mitering crown molding (see pp. 43-45). At its simplest, an angled fence is just a rectangular piece of plywood, proportioned as needed and supported by two braces. A cross member glued and screwed between the vertical edges of the braces stabilizes them and provides a convenient way to clamp or screw the jig to a standard fence or to the machine table.

Mitering fence

Cutting miters with a radial-arm saw or compound-sliding miter saw can be a pain because of the time it takes to set them, then reset them back to square. The mitering fence shown in the drawing on the facing page can be used with a radial-arm saw (as shown), a sliding compound miter saw or a powered miter saw (chop box), or even a table

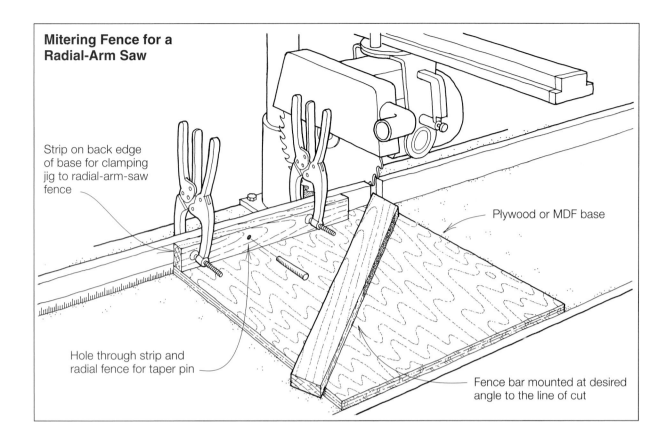

Mitering Fence for a Radial-Arm Saw

Strip on back edge of base for clamping jig to radial-arm-saw fence

Hole through strip and radial fence for taper pin

Plywood or MDF base

Fence bar mounted at desired angle to the line of cut

saw with a pull-style crosscut feature, such as the Mafell Erika. The mitering fence references and clamps to the saw's regular fence and changes the angle of the workpiece relative to the saw's standard 90° line of cut. This kind of jig is especially valuable for cutting miters at angles far greater than 45°, which most radial-arm saws and powered chop boxes are incapable of doing. The only thing to remember when using this jig is that workpieces must be trimmed close to final length before mitering.

To build the jig you'll need a square piece of plywood or MDF for a base, with a wood strip glued and screwed to the face flush with one edge for clamping the jig to the saw's fence. Make the strip a couple of inches shorter than the edge of the plywood base to leave room for the miter fence bar, and don't use screws or nails near the line of cut. Raise the saw's blade and clamp the jig to the machine's fence with the right edge of the base slightly overlapping the line of cut. Now, with the blade running, make a crosscut with the same blade you plan to use for mitering. Next, temporarily screw the fence bar down to the base at the desired angle relative to the line of cut (let the end of the bar overhang the line of cut). Cut two parts, butt them together and check with an accurate protractor or combination square; any inaccuracy in the angle will be doubled. Readjust the bar and repeat the check as necessary until the desired angle is achieved. Finally, mark the correct position of the bar and glue and screw it down. A piece of sandpaper or other high-friction material glued to the face of the fence (see p. 190) will help keep workpieces from slipping during mitering. Before unclamping the jig, you might want to drill a hole through the jig's lip and into the saw's fence for a taper pin (see p. 12). That will allow the jig to be accurately repositioned for future use.

Partial Fences

Sometimes it's better to use a short fence than a long one. Each of the shop-made partial fences discussed in this section provides a way of performing operations, such as ripping, resawing and shaping, that standard fences aren't ideally suited for.

Short rip fence

In Europe, it's common to see table saws fitted with short rip fences that extend from ahead of the front of the table to just beyond the leading edge of the sawblade (see the photo below). The reason is that boards sometimes distort during ripping due to reaction grain or other stresses in the wood. When this happens on a table saw fitted with a full-length fence, the board often binds between the fence and the blade and kicks back—not a happy situation for the wood or the woodworker. A short rip fence guides the board into the blade for a straight cut, yet allows the wood to distort on both sides of the newly cut kerf. This jig can be an auxiliary face that screws to a standard rip fence or a separate fence used solely for ripping.

A short fence bolted to a standard rip fence allows clearance between fence and blade past the cut, averting a possible kickback.

Resawing fences

Because of the bandsaw's relatively narrow blade and low kickback potential, short or partial fences are often adequate for guiding the workpiece through the cut. They also allow you to compensate for the bandsaw blade's tendency to drift (deviate) from parallel, which can cause problems when ripping with a standard long fence. For this reason, many woodworkers prefer to make a special resawing fence that keeps the work square and at a fixed distance to the blade, yet allows the user to change the angle of the work whenever necessary to compensate for blade drift. This kind of fence is most commonly used for resawing wide boards, but it's also great for making a cut parallel to a curved edge for parts like rocking-chair rockers.

The resawing fence shown in the drawing below and in the bottom photo on p. 200 consists of a half-dowel (¾ in. in diameter) glued to the edge of a plywood triangle that's mounted at the center of a base. Braces on either side of the triangle reinforce it and help keep it square to the base. A slot cut out of the base provides clearance for the

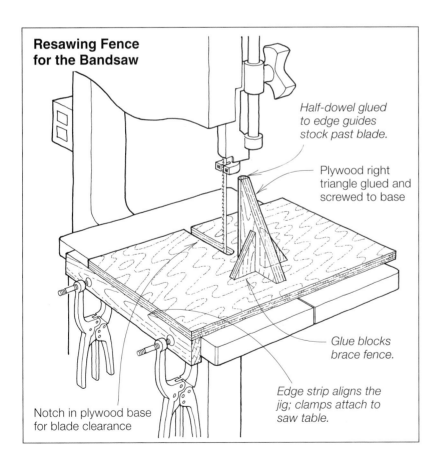

Resawing Fence for the Bandsaw

Half-dowel glued to edge guides stock past blade.

Plywood right triangle glued and screwed to base

Glue blocks brace fence.

Edge strip aligns the jig; clamps attach to saw table.

Notch in plywood base for blade clearance

Roller Fence for Bandsaw

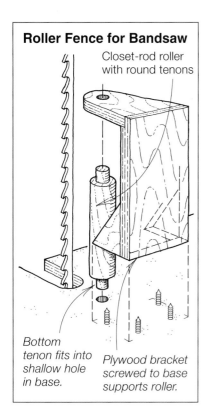

Closet-rod roller with round tenons

Bottom tenon fits into shallow hole in base.

Plywood bracket screwed to base supports roller.

bandsaw blade. A wood strip glued and screwed to the front edge of the base keeps the fence aligned with the blade (the teeth should be just tangent to the centerline of the dowel) and allows the jig to be clamped to the edge of bandsaw's table with C-clamps or plier-type quick-release toggle clamps (see the photo at left on p. 49).

If you have a really big bandsaw (don't brag now) or resaw a lot of heavy stock, you might want to make a roller fence, as shown in the drawing at left, which reduces the friction of the work pressed against it. The roller is made from a length of 1-in. dia. to 1½-in. dia. dowel with round tenons shaped on the ends (tenoning can be done using the V-block carriage shown in the photo on p. 50). The top tenon rides in a plywood bracket attached to the base; the bottom tenon sits in a shallow hole in the base. The hole is not as deep as the length of the tenon, so the roller can move freely without binding on the base.

Split fence

Shapers and router tables often are used with cutters or bits that can vary tremendously in diameter, from ¼-in. dia. veining bits to 3½-in. dia. raised-panel cutters. If the opening in the fence is big enough for the largest cutters, it will be too large when smaller cutters are used, and the stock won't be supported close to the bit. A traditional solu-

Split Fence on a Router Table

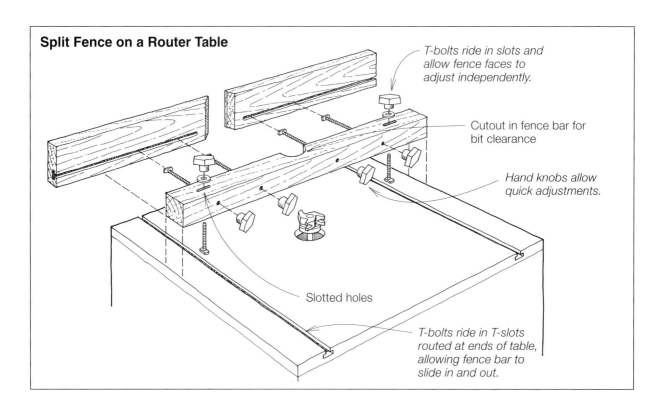

T-bolts ride in slots and allow fence faces to adjust independently.

Cutout in fence bar for bit clearance

Hand knobs allow quick adjustments.

Slotted holes

T-bolts ride in T-slots routed at ends of table, allowing fence bar to slide in and out.

tion to this problem is a split fence with two independently sliding faces that can be adjusted to suit the bit diameter, as shown in the bottom drawing on the facing page.

Construction of the split fence starts with a fence bar, made from 8/4 material—thicker if you plan to use really large bits. The bar is notched in the center for bit clearance and drilled with holes for mounting the fence faces. The system of mounting I used for the split fence on my router table relies on a pair of parallel T-slots routed at both ends of the table; it can be adapted to mount many other kinds of fences as well (see the simple fence I use on my drill-press tilting table, shown in the drawing on p. 79). T-bolts in slotted holes at both ends of the fence bar ride in the T-slots, allowing the fence in-and-out adjustment, and two hand knobs lock it in position. The two fence faces are cut to length and beveled on one end, and a T-slot is routed along each, as described on pp. 195-197. This slot holds two T-bolts for each face; hand knobs lock these in place, once the faces are set. The removable fence faces allow you to insert shims behind one face, as shown in the photo below. This is a useful feature for jointing with a straight bit. The outfeed fence face is shimmed up as much as the desired depth of cut, then positioned so it is tangent to the cutting circle of the bit.

By shimming one side of a split fence flush with the cutting circle of a straight bit, you can joint a board on the router table. Stock is fed into the bit from the un-raised side of the fence; the difference in fence settings equals the depth of cut.

Fences for Curved Parts

Just as a straight-edged workpiece is guided smoothly by a straight fence, a disc, ring or curved part with a fixed radius can be guided smoothly by a fence designed for curved work. Curve fences can be used to guide parts with either convex or concave radiuses for operations on a wide variety of machines. On a router table or shaper, you can shape the face and outside edge of a disc, as well as the inside edge of a ring, using non-piloted bits and cutters. On the scrollsaw you can cut clean rings; on the drill press you can drill holes a set distance from the edge of a curved part. Although I won't go into it here, it is also possible to create elaborate fence setups for shaping parts with compound curves, such as spiral stairway railings.

Basic disc-shaping fence

The simplest fence I know for shaping the edge of a disc with a non-piloted cutter requires only two dowel guide pins set into a base (see the drawing below). The dowel guide pins are set into holes drilled halfway through the base and screwed on from underneath. The disc bears against both pins, which regulate the cut as the disc is rotated by hand. A strip on the lower edge of the base rides against the edge of the router table, centering the pins relative to the bit. The distance between the pins depends on the radius of the disc you're working

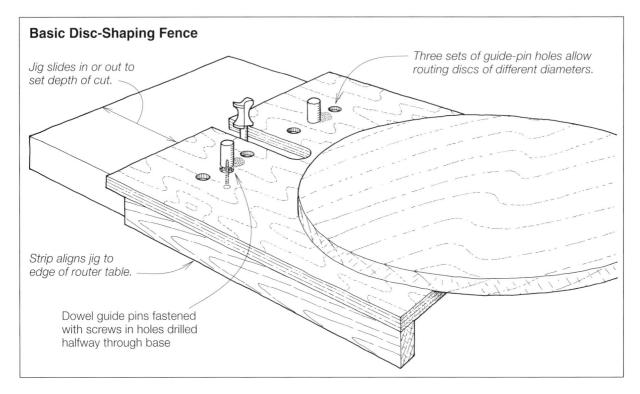

Basic Disc-Shaping Fence

Jig slides in or out to set depth of cut.

Three sets of guide-pin holes allow routing discs of different diameters.

Strip aligns jig to edge of router table.

Dowel guide pins fastened with screws in holes drilled halfway through base with; this distance should be roughly equal to the radius of the disc. Three sets of holes with different spacing allow the jig to handle a variety of different-diameter workpieces. The only thing that you can't do with this jig is to trim the entire edge of the disc, say with a straight bit—this would cause a spiralling cut, with the disc getting smaller with every rotation.

Vertical disc fence

Most curved parts to be shaped can be handled flat on the jig base or the machine table. But what if you want to resaw a disc or put a groove on the edge of a rim for a spinning wheel using a veining bit on the router table? One solution is to saw a concave fence that matches the radius of the part and mount it vertically, as in the jig shown in the drawing below. The fence stock should be slightly thicker than the round parts you'll work with. Pieces of plywood are tacked over each side of the fence to capture the workpiece and prevent it from skating out during cutting.

To use this jig, clamp it to the rip fence and set the fence so that the jig is directly over the bit or blade. Raise the bit or blade until it projects through the jig as far as needed. (Since the jig surrounds the cutter, it provides protection as well.) The workpiece is slowly lowered into the spinning cutter and rotated to complete the job. You could also

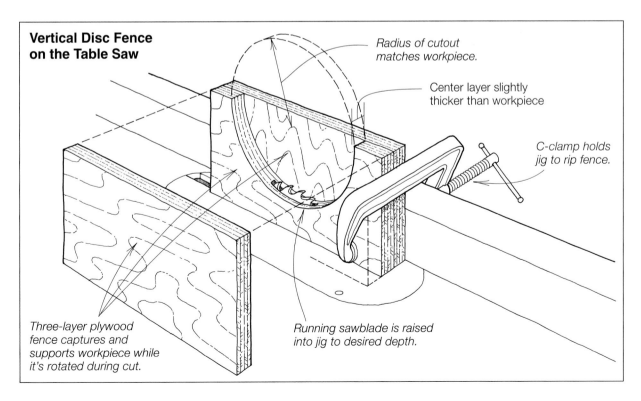

Vertical Disc Fence on the Table Saw

Radius of cutout matches workpiece.

Center layer slightly thicker than workpiece

C-clamp holds jig to rip fence.

Three-layer plywood fence captures and supports workpiece while it's rotated during cut.

Running sawblade is raised into jig to desired depth.

use this fence on the table saw with a dado head or molding head to make a variety of decorative edge cuts; just cut the concave fence from thicker stock to accommodate a thicker blade. Another variation would be to bevel the bottom of the jig's base, for angled cuts.

Fences that Attach to the Workpiece

Often, the best strategy for handling large or unwieldy panels or planks is to clamp a fence directly to the workpiece and use a portable power tool or hand tool to make the cut. Clamp-on fences can also provide a straight edge to guide an irregular workpiece along a standard fence.

Quick clamp panel-cutting fence

Using a fence clamped to a large panel to guide a portable tool is an easy way to machine panels too cumbersome to lift onto a stationary tool. While just about any straight stick or yardstick will serve as a fence in a pinch (for many years I used an aluminum carpenter's level as a clamp-on fence), a dedicated clamp-on fence will make your chores a lot easier. My version, as shown in the drawing on the facing page, features two sliding quick-release toggle-clamp assemblies that ride in a T-slot machined on the entire length of the underside of the fence. The fence can be set square or at an angle across the panel; the clamps slide in to accommodate different distances. Having built-in clamps saves the tedium of handling loose C-clamps befoer setting each cut. The slot for the toggle-clamp assemblies is routed with a straight bit, then a special T-slotting bit, as described on pp. 195-197. I made two short sliders from Corian scraps (maple would also work) to fit the slots, using a kerf-cutting bit in the router table to machine their I-beam-like profiles (see the detail drawing on the facing page). I attached a small quick-release toggle clamp to each of these sliders, using short wood screws. The clamps I used are De-Sta-Co model #217, but many other brands and models could work equally well.

If you wish to use a clamp-on panel cutting fence for square cuts alone, adding a 90° crossbar to a clamp-on fence, as shown in the detail drawing on the facing page, makes it work like a draftsman's T-square, allowing perpendicular cutting or routing jobs without painstaking alignment. This is great for situations where many grooves must be made at 90°, such as for shelves in bookcase sides. Used with a portable circular saw, the perpendicular fence allows accurate crosscutting on wide panels without a radial-arm saw. Incidentally, it would also be possible to make both the fence and slider assemblies curved, for curved panel shaping with a round-based router. You could also use a curved fence with a saber saw for sawing large-radius arcs by attaching a shop-made sub-base that matched the fence's curve.

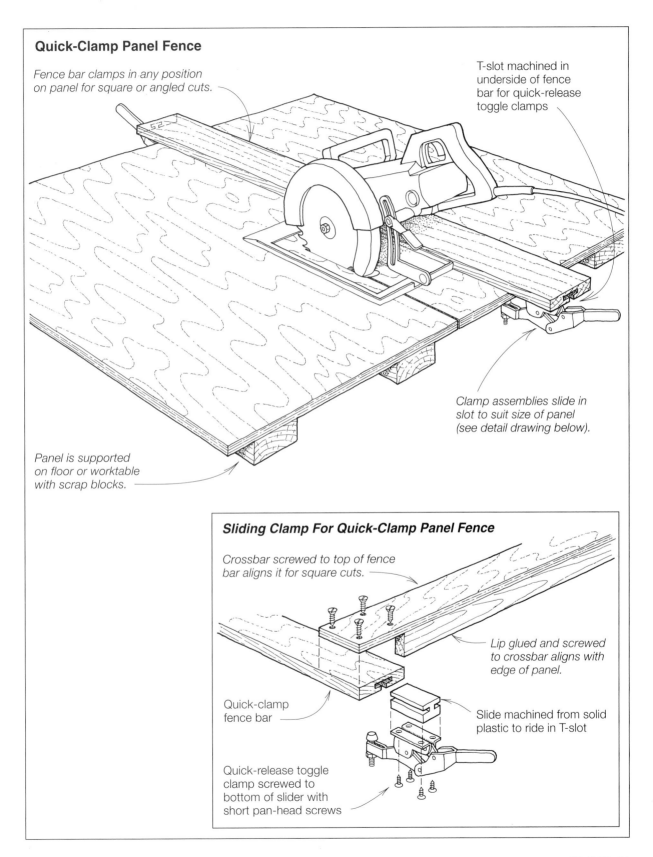

Quick-Clamp Panel Fence

Fence bar clamps in any position on panel for square or angled cuts.

T-slot machined in underside of fence bar for quick-release toggle clamps

Clamp assemblies slide in slot to suit size of panel (see detail drawing below).

Panel is supported on floor or worktable with scrap blocks.

Sliding Clamp For Quick-Clamp Panel Fence

Crossbar screwed to top of fence bar aligns it for square cuts.

Lip glued and screwed to crossbar aligns with edge of panel.

Quick-clamp fence bar

Slide machined from solid plastic to ride in T-slot

Quick-release toggle clamp screwed to bottom of slider with short pan-head screws

Quick-aligning fence

If you're willing to dedicate a quick-clamp fence to work exclusively with a particular tool, adding a thin guide plate to the bottom of the fence bar, as shown in the drawing below, speeds up aligning the fence to the desired line of cut. How does it work? The guide plate that the portable tool rides on is cut exactly as wide as the distance between the fence and the tool's blade or bit. You locate a cut simply by aligning the edge of the guide plate with the "good side" of the desired line of cut—there is no confusing measuring and accounting for the distance between the baseplate of the tool and the cutter. I make great use of this kind of fence when cutting 4x8 plywood sheets to size with a small panel saw.

To add the guide plate, first make a wide, ⅛-in. deep rabbet in one edge of the underside of the fence bar. Then cut a strip wider than necessary from ⅛-in. tempered Masonite or plywood and glue it into the rabbet. After fitting the portable power tool with the blade or bit that will be used, clamp the fence to a piece of scrap and take a cut. This trims the guide plate to exactly the right width. If the power tool has a thin baseplate, you might need to shim the side opposite the guide—a job well suited for adhesive transfer tape (see p. 140). If you're using a circular saw, be sure to check that the blade and base edge are parallel; if they are not, you might have to readjust the base or add a sub-base to the tool. This fence can also be used with a router, if you use only one bit diameter or add a sub-base that establishes the correct distance between the edge of the bit and the edge of the bottom fence.

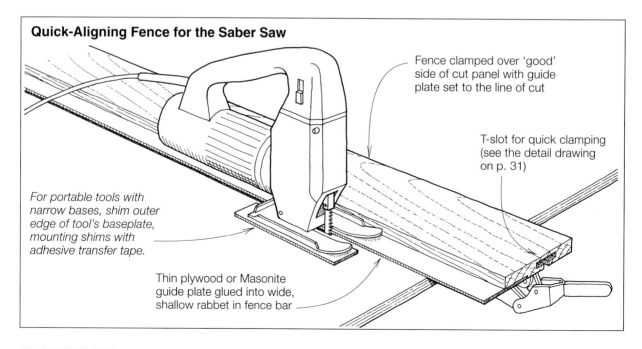

Quick-Aligning Fence for the Saber Saw

Fence clamped over 'good' side of cut panel with guide plate set to the line of cut

T-slot for quick clamping (see the detail drawing on p. 31)

For portable tools with narrow bases, shim outer edge of tool's baseplate, mounting shims with adhesive transfer tape.

Thin plywood or Masonite guide plate glued into wide, shallow rabbet in fence bar

Double fence

You can easily create a clamp-on fence jig that allows both faces or edges of a board to be machined without repositioning the jig. This is useful for shaping a perfectly centered tongue on the end of a panel, as shown in the photo below left, or for sawing dadoes for shelves at the same position on both sides of a bookcase divider. The double fence has two fence bars joined by a crosspiece at one end. The crosspiece not only keeps the fences aligned, but also references to the edge of the work to square the fences before the jig is clamped on the work.

Shooting boards

A shooting board is usually a straight fence that guides a hand plane square to or at a precise angle over a workpiece, to true an edge or bevel or chamfer it. A small shooting board can be used to guide a chisel to trim the inside corners of a frame or shaped panel. An angled shooting board used in conjunction with a rabbet plane can make a V-shaped groove, as shown in the photo below right. This shooting board is simply a straight-grained length of 2x4 beveled at 45° on the table saw. Notches sawn out of the board's top edge allow it to be clamped down without the heads of the C-clamps getting in the way of the plane.

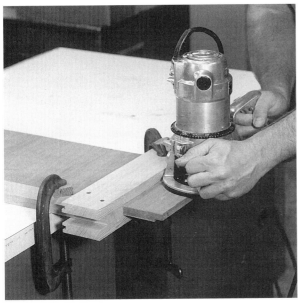

This double fence has two fence bars joined by a crosspiece at one end, which clamps to the work so cuts can be taken in the same position on opposite sides of a workpiece. Here, the fence is used to guide a router for shaping a tongue on the end of a carcase part.

A shooting board can be used to guide a hand plane at a precise angle. Here, a bull-nosed plane rides against a 45° shooting board to shape a V-groove for pigeonhole dividers. Notches in the fence allow C-clamps to stay clear of the fence's surface.

A two-part clamp-on handsaw guide acts as a miter box, controlling the cut of a dovetail saw as it rips a tenon diagonally. The saw kerfs will be wedged when the through-tenons are fitted in their mortises.

Clamp-on hand-tool guide

Sometimes, the simplest way to make a cut on the end of a long board that can't conveniently be cut with a power saw is to use a hand tool in conjunction with a clamp-on guide. For example, when sawing a kerf diagonally across through tenons (for wedges to expand and lock the tenons in their mortises), a pair of wooden guides, shown in the photo above, act as a tiny miter box, maintaining a correct sawing angle and keeping the blade plumb. Each guide consists of a notched block nailed to a clamping strip. The blocks are arranged at diagonal corners of the tenon, while the strip is use to align them square and clamp them to the stock. If the blocks are cut to the same length as the width of the sawblade (a backed sawblade, such as a dovetail saw), they act as depth stops as well.

Fences that Attach to Portable Tools

Often, it's more practical to mount a fence directly to a portable power tool than to haul the work to a stationary machine or attach a fence to the workpiece. Standard fences are made by manufacturers for many portables, including routers and saber saws. But a custom, shop-made fence can adapt ordinary tools to do jobs that are out of the ordinary. Many portable power tools have sub-bases that can be removed and refitted with a custom-made replacement. You can also drill and tap holes in the body or baseplate of a portable tool and bolt a sub-base on with machine screws, or temporarily attach a fence with C-clamps, hose clamps or adhesive transfer tape.

Two strips of wood beveled at a 45° angle act as fences when clamped to a low-angle block plane. The fence strips position the plane for a chamfer cut on the corner of a board, and at the same time limit the depth of cut.

Fences that attach to hand tools

While most baseplate-mounted fences I've made are for portable power tools, they can also be used on hand tools. For example, two 45° fence strips clamped to a low-angle block plane allow the plane to chamfer edges at a precise angle and to an exact depth (see the photo above). Other commonly used hand tools can benefit from the addition of a fence: Clamping a narrow strip of wood to a backsaw or dovetail saw parallel to the blade helps establish the correct sawing angle and limit the depth of cut, simplifying jobs like sawing complicated angled joinery.

Replacement sub-bases

If a fence can't conveniently be attached to the base of a tool, one solution that works with many portables is to remove the standard sub-base and fit a shop-made sub-base with a built-in fence or other guide strip. You can use the stock sub-base as a pattern for drilling the mounting holes in the replacement, using a Vix bit (see pp. 148-149). Routers are particularly good candidates for custom sub-bases, because they are exceptionally versatile tools and because their sub-bases are easily changed. You can fit a large sub-base with additional handles to add stability and control when edge routing, or you can create a sub-base that will make your router easier to mount quickly in a router table (see p. 98). Sub-bases can be designed to handle an infinite variety of woodworking jobs. On pp. 36-38 are four examples to get you started.

Making a series of equally spaced, parallel grooves in the side of a spice rack is easily accomplished with a router fitted with a custom sub-base. A fence strip on the sub-base rides in a previously cut groove while a straight bit plows the new groove.

Sub-base with fence strip   The router is often used for making evenly spaced grooves. To save the trouble of having to attach and reattach a fence to the work for each cut, you can make a replacement sub-base with a fence strip that rides on the edge of the stock, or in a previously routed groove. This sub-base, shown in the photo above, is useful for routing evenly spaced, parallel grooves across the grain, such as for the shelves in the sides of a spice rack or dividers in a jewelry case. The sub-base is made from thin stock (Masonite in this case) which extends well beyond the edge of the router's base on one side. A wooden strip that's just a hair thinner than the bit diameter is screwed to the underside of the new sub-base, positioned as far from the bit as the desired spacing of cuts. After the first groove is routed, the strip rides in it to guide the second cut, and so on until all the cuts are made.

Four-sided sub-base   When a router bit lacks a pilot bearing, another way to guide the cutter is to run the edge of the base, which acts as a guide, against a stationary fence clamped to the stock (see pp. 30-32). Carefully measuring the distance between the edge of the sub-base and the cutting circle of the bit allows you to set a fixed distance between bit and fence. For versatility, I often use a single sub-base that has four guide edges at different distances from the bit (see the drawing on the facing page). For example, by using a ¼-in. dia. straight bit and making the edges measure 3 in., 3½ in., 4 in., and 4½ in. from the

Four-Sided Router Sub-Base

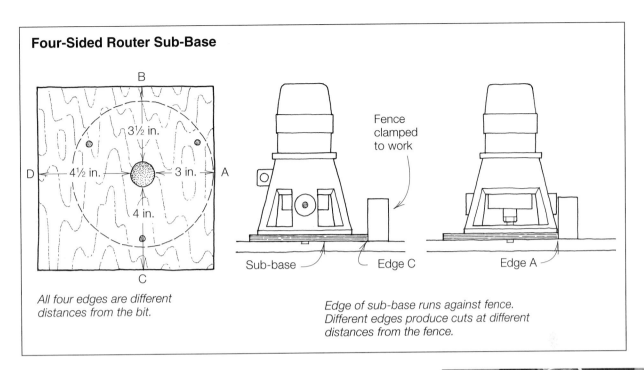

B

3½ in.

D — 4½ in. — 3 in. — A

4 in.

C

*All four edges are different
distances from the bit.*

Fence
clamped
to work

Sub-base — Edge C

Edge A

*Edge of sub-base runs against fence.
Different edges produce cuts at different
distances from the fence.*

bit on the four sides, I can cut grooves that are ¼ in. apart by simply rotating the router 90° between passes. You can also make a sub-base with edge-to-bit distances that change very slightly from side to side, a handy way to widen a dado without having to adjust the fence setting between passes. This also lets you tweak the degree of fit of joined parts such as mortises or sliding dovetails after the part is initially shaped using one or more of the guide edges.

Self-centering sub-base Another useful router jig, the self-centering sub-base, has guide pins that automatically center the bit on the workpiece for centered grooves and decorative shapes without the hassle of adjustment. Mounted on a plunge router, this sub-base can also be used for mortising, although it's limited in this application since it won't work near the end of the stock (both pins must bear on the stock). The jig has two guide pins that ride on either the face or the edge of a board. The jig (see the photo at right) consists of a flat disc with a center cutout for the bit and two guide pins, made from short lengths of ⅝-in. or ¾-in. dia. dowel, mounted on the underside with screws through the disc. For the jig to work correctly, the dowel pins must be placed equidistant from the center of the disc and set on a straight line with the center of the bit.

**Mortises or grooves are
automatically centered on the
edge of the stock using a router
fitted with a custom sub-base.
Two guide pins on the underside
of the sub-base straddle the
stock to center the bit.**

Sub-base for flush trimming By adding a combination of a fence strips and spacers to the bottom of a sub-base, you can easily change the attitude of the bit relative to the workpiece. For example, attaching a fence to a replacement sub-base as shown in the drawing below allows a regular straight bit to be used for trimming edges flush with a surface. The jig is made from a fence strip and semicircular spacer glued to a basic plywood or Masonite sub-base sized to fit the router. The fence overlaps the cutout in the sub-base for the bit; a notch in the fence provides clearance. The spacer is mounted on the opposite side of the baseplate, just clearing the bit cutout. Longer-than-standard screws fitted through holes in the glued-up fence assembly attach the jig to the router. In use, the bottom of the bit is adjusted flush with the spacer, which provides a gliding surface for the router. This jig is great for flush-trimming solid-wood edge banding applied to the edges of hardwood-plywood carcases and shelves.

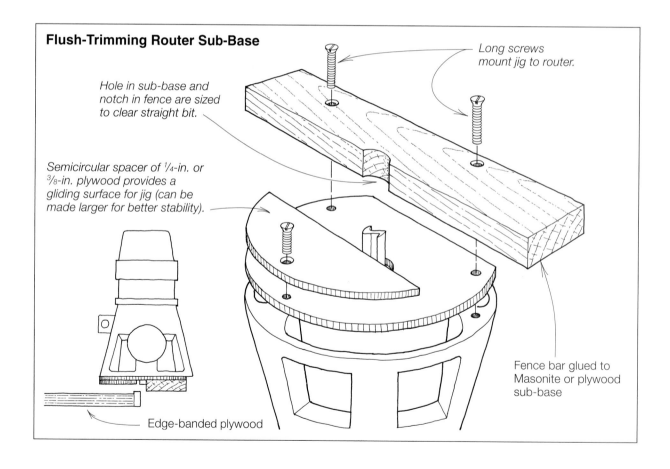

Flush-Trimming Router Sub-Base

Long screws mount jig to router.

Hole in sub-base and notch in fence are sized to clear straight bit.

Semicircular spacer of ¹/₄-in. or ³/₈-in. plywood provides a gliding surface for jig (can be made larger for better stability).

Fence bar glued to Masonite or plywood sub-base

Edge-banded plywood

Fences that Attach to Positioning Jigs and Fixtures

Thus far this chapter has focused on fairly simple fences and guides that are used in conjunction with stationary machines and portable tools. However, fences are also used in more elaborate woodworking jigs and fixtures. These devices are sometimes necessary for complicated cuts (often on round or irregularly shaped parts) where one part of the jig holds and positions the workpiece while another part guides the tool. Such fence jigs are especially useful for machining long or heavy workpieces that can't easily be moved past a stationary tool. A good example of this is the fluting jig shown in the drawing below. This box-style jig bolts to the lathe's ways over a bedpost chucked in the lathe. A fence added to the top of the jig guides a router that will cut straight flutes along the length of the bedpost. If you taper the top edges on the sides of the box, you can use this same setup to flute tapered cylinders. For non-regular cylinders, you could even make a router carriage with curved runners, as described in the section on simple curved profiles (see pp. 69-70) and make the top edges of the jig box curved guide rails. Jig boxes (see pp. 141-142) are also useful for many shaping and joinery cutting operations.

Jig for Fluting Turnings on the Lathe

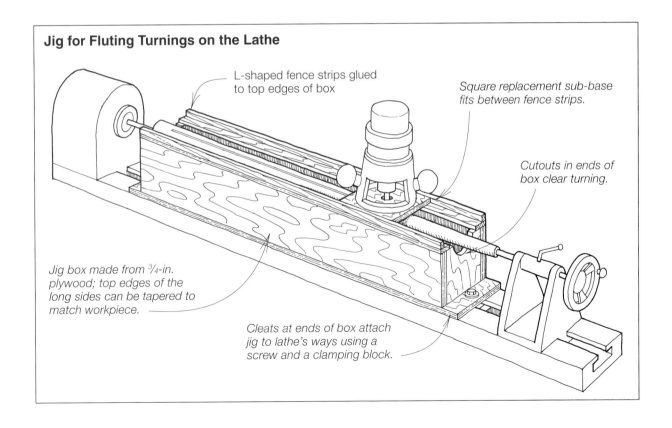

L-shaped fence strips glued to top edges of box

Square replacement sub-base fits between fence strips.

Cutouts in ends of box clear turning.

Jig box made from ¾-in. plywood; top edges of the long sides can be tapered to match workpiece.

Cleats at ends of box attach jig to lathe's ways using a screw and a clamping block.

CHAPTER 2
Carriages that Slide

As we have seen in the previous chapter, fences can serve a wide range of jigging duties to keep our workpieces and tools moving in a controlled fashion. But while fences can provide the necessary guidance to move a part or tool in a straight line or keep it at the correct angle while it's being cut or shaped, skill and attention are required to keep things from going off track. Why walk along a fence if you can ride in a carriage? Although they usually take more effort to build, carriages hold tools or workpieces square or at the proper angle and carry them past a blade, bit, cutter or abrasive with more control, accuracy and safety than a fence alone can offer.

Carriages excel at handling workpieces that are too small or too large to feed past tools by hand. And they provide superior control for moving power tools past work that is too cumbersome to machine on stationary tools. Carriages can be designed to travel in a straight line, guided by a miter-gauge slot, fence, table or shop-made guide rail, or they can be used freehand. Special carriages can be made to scribe a circle or arc, or move in three dimensions to create cylinders, spheres or more complicated forms. As with other jigs, safety guards should be built into all jigs shown, including exit guards and clear blade guards, which are described in detail on pp. 208-213.

Carriages like this sliding tapering jig (pp. 53-54) carry the work past the blade or cutter. Here a small toggle clamp fastened to the end of the jig locks the workpiece to the carriage during the cut.

Miter-Slot-Guided Carriages

The miter slot built into the tables of many stationary machines is an excellent way to guide a workpiece through a cut or for shaping, sanding, mortising and more. Most miter-slot guided carriages described in this section are fitted with standard-size guide bars (⅜ in. thick, ¾ in. wide). You can mill your own bars from a dense hardwood such as maple, but you can also buy ready-made metal bars, which are available from several sources (see pp. 197-198). Although they're more expensive, ready-made bars are straight, won't swell or shrink like wood, and are adjustable for a tight, accurate fit in your miter slots. For homemade machines and devices without miter slots, you can always add an auxiliary table top that has a slot cut into it (see p. 81).

Sliding crosscut box

I have rarely visited a shop that didn't have some version of a crosscut or cutoff box, used with the table saw for crosscutting lumber or sheet goods. A basic sliding crosscut box, such as the one shown in the photo below, consists of just five pieces: a base, a front crossmember, a fence (which doubles as a rear crossmember) and two guide bars. The crossmember and fence are glued and screwed to the top of the base at front and back edges, with the screws driven in from underneath. If you wish, you can add one or two quick-release toggle clamps to hold down the workpiece, and I highly recommend that you add a protective-enclosure style guard, as shown on p. 209.

A sliding crosscut box, guided by a pair of guide bars riding in the saw's miter-gauge slots, provides an accurate, safe way of crosscutting wide or long boards on the table saw. Note the block attached to the rear of the jig, which serves as an exit guard.

The dimensions of all basic parts of the cutoff box can be adjusted over a large range to suit your application. If you make models, a very small crosscut box that's 6 in. wide and just slightly longer than the distance between the slots in your saw table will comfortably handle diminutive parts. At the other extreme, if you do a lot of plywood carcase work, you can build a really large version of the cutoff box—I've seen boxes more than 5 ft. long and 2½ ft. wide. Boxes this large can be quite heavy, so they require some kind of low-friction strips on the bottom, such as nylon tape (see Sources of Supply on pp. 224-227), and a sturdy outfeed table behind the saw. You'll probably also need to add support rails and extension tables to support the cutoff box ahead of and after the cut.

Sliding miter carriage

For cutting accurate 45° miters on the table saw, woodworkers often use a dedicated sliding miter carriage and save the saw's stock miter gauge for the occasional odd-angle cut. This type of carriage can also be used on other machines, such as the shaper, to do angled cope-and-stick work or other shaping of mitered parts.

Like the cutoff box, the sliding miter carriage has a base, a front cross-member and guide bars that run in the saw table's twin slots. But this jig has two fences mounted to the base, at 90° to each other and at 45° to the line of cut. The arrangement ensures that all right- and left-hand cuts will form a 90° corner—essential for square frames. The V formed by the fences may point either forward or back. The more common design orients the V toward the blade, as shown in the photo below. The advantage to this arrangement is that stock of almost any width or length can be cut; the fences don't interfere with the stock running past. And since the tip of the miter is cut first, the blade has little tendency to tear out the fragile point of each frame member.

Accurate 45° miter cuts are a cinch using a basic sliding miter carriage on the table saw. Because the jig's fences are precisely 45° to the blade and at 90° to each other, square frame corners are ensured.

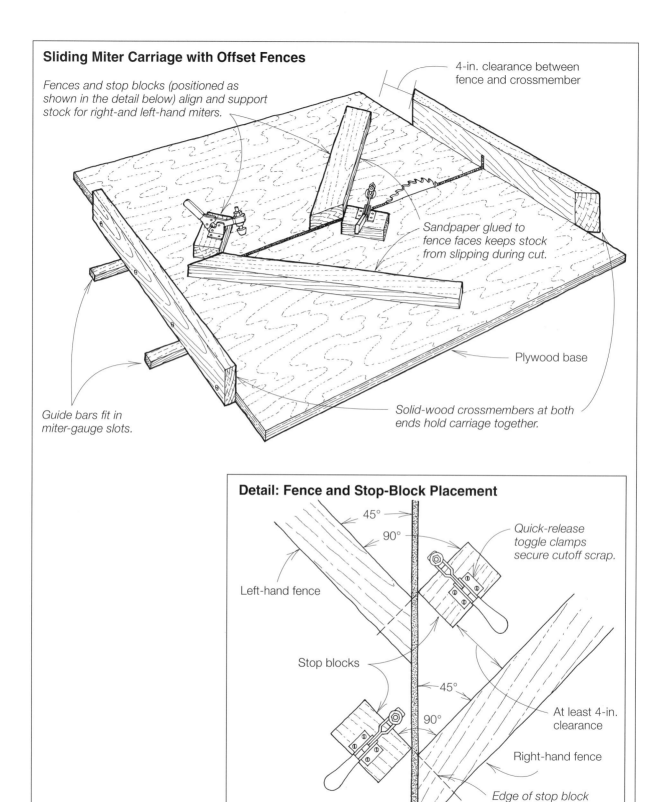

Sliding Miter Carriage with Offset Fences

Fences and stop blocks (positioned as shown in the detail below) align and support stock for right-and left-hand miters.

4-in. clearance between fence and crossmember

Sandpaper glued to fence faces keeps stock from slipping during cut.

Plywood base

Guide bars fit in miter-gauge slots.

Solid-wood crossmembers at both ends hold carriage together.

Detail: Fence and Stop-Block Placement

45°

90°

Quick-release toggle clamps secure cutoff scrap.

Left-hand fence

Stop blocks

45°

90°

At least 4-in. clearance

Right-hand fence

Edge of stop block aligns perfectly with inside edge of fence.

For mitering relatively narrow stock, such as picture-frame molding 4 in. wide and less, I prefer to use a different sliding miter jig, shown in the drawing on the facing page. While the fences on this jig are still 45° to the line of cut and square to each other, their positions are off-set. This arrangement and a stop block positioned just beyond the tip of each fence allow frame members already cut to final length to be precisely mitered without any need for additional measuring, marking, or adjusting of stops. Further, each fence supports the miter at the tip to minimize tearout.

To construct either of these sliding miter carriages, cut out a base from ¼-in., ⅜-in., ½-in. or ¾-in. plywood (thicker bases are sturdier, but they decrease the possible depth of cut). Crossmembers and guide bars are attached as described for crosscut boxes (see pp. 42-43). Before attaching the fences, "cut in" the jig on the saw. Now align one fence to the kerf in the base, using a large, accurate 45° triangle, then glue and tack it in place temporarily. Using a large try square or framing square, align the second fence at 90° to the first and attach it as well. After taking two trial cuts (quickly, before the glue dries), placing the mitered parts together and checking for square, reposition either fence as necessary, then add additional screws, driving the fasteners up through the base into the fences. For special mitering jobs, you can set the fences on either style of sliding miter jig to any other angles or add auxiliary faces to the fences. The addition of an angled fence (see p. 22) allows you to cut crown molding at a compound angle.

The stop blocks used in the offset-fence version are positioned as shown in the detail drawing on the facing page. I recommend that you screw small quick-release toggle clamps (I used De-Sta-Co #202) atop these stop blocks. The clamps not only hold the workpiece in place during cutting, but also keep cutoffs, which can become trapped against the stop, from being thrown by the blade.

Sliding bevel carriages

Like the miter carriage, the sliding bevel carriage shown in the drawing on p. 46 orients workpieces at a precise 45° angle to the surface of the saw table, ensuring accurately cut beveled edges for parts such as chest or box sides without having to set the tilt of the saw. The base, crossmembers and guide bars are arranged as for the sliding miter jigs described above, but with two fences mounted at a 45° angle relative to the base and 90° to the line of cut. Each fence is made up of a plywood or MDF strip that's 4 in. to 12 in. wide (or wider, if needed) and beveled at one end. A lip glued to each fence's back edge keeps workpieces square during cutting. The fences are supported by triangular plywood braces attached to the base. With this jig, workpieces must be cut to length and clamped down on before their ends are beveled.

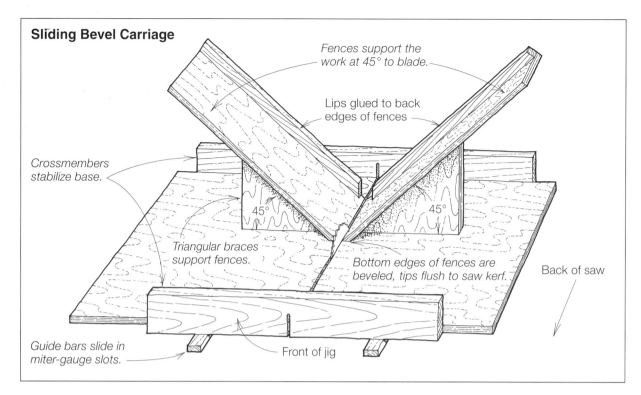

Sliding Bevel Carriage

Fences support the work at 45° to blade.

Lips glued to back edges of fences

Crossmembers stabilize base.

45°   45°

Triangular braces support fences.

Bottom edges of fences are beveled, tips flush to saw kerf.

Back of saw

Guide bars slide in miter-gauge slots.

Front of jig

An angled fence mounted to a standard miter gauge creates a sliding bevel carriage for the bandsaw. With this carriage you can make compound cuts on the ends of narrow moldings.

Another sliding bevel carriage is shown in the photo at left. This jig, designed for the bandsaw, is designed for sawing compound cuts on narrow or shaped workpieces, like moldings. The carriage mounts on the bandsaw's miter gauge and is simple to make. First, cut out a triangular piece of plywood to the desired bevel angle and add thin strips of wood adjacent to the hypotenuse, as lips to hold and align the workpiece. Bolt the triangle to a standard miter gauge, set to the desired miter angle, and you're ready to cut. A little trigonometry or a compound-miter chart will help you find the correct miter and bevel settings for the desired compound cut.

Bevel slotting jig

An adaptation of the table-saw sliding bevel carriage is the bevel slotting jig, which is shown in the drawing on the facing page. This cross-sliding carriage jig is used for cutting slots for plate-joinery biscuits or splines in the ends of beveled frame members, though it could also serve for shaping the beveled ends of members for angled cope-and-stick work. As on the sliding bevel carriage, a lipped fence is mounted atop a wedge-shape plywood box with 45° sides. A guide bar mounted on the bottom of this box rides in a slot routed in the top of the jig's base—a square of ½-in. plywood. A guide bar mounted on the bottom side of the base perpendicular to the top slot rides in the router table's

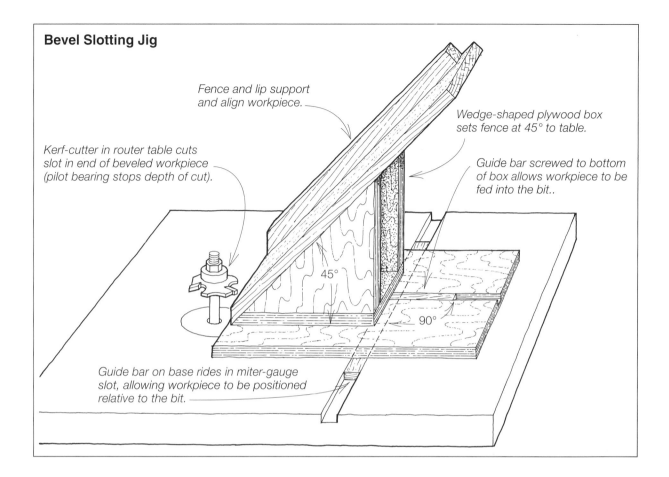

Bevel Slotting Jig

Fence and lip support and align workpiece.

Kerf-cutter in router table cuts slot in end of beveled workpiece (pilot bearing stops depth of cut).

Wedge-shaped plywood box sets fence at 45° to table.

Guide bar screwed to bottom of box allows workpiece to be fed into the bit..

45°

90°

Guide bar on base rides in miter-gauge slot, allowing workpiece to be positioned relative to the bit.

or shaper's miter slot. In use, the workpiece is held against the lip and clamped to the fence as the upper carriage slides the work into the spinning bit. The base is then moved forward and back, so the slot (or shape on the edge of the workpiece) can be lengthened.

Box-joint jig

The big trick to cutting joinery on a table saw or router table is getting the spacing of the cuts accurate, so that opposite halves of the joints fit together snugly. One popular jig for cutting box joints on the table saw (it could also be used with a router table) is easy to make and mounts to the saw's standard miter gauge. This jig, shown in the drawing on p. 48, has a face plate that keeps the workpiece perpendicular to the table as the gauge is slid forward and a dado blade cuts out the spaces between fingers one at a time. An index pin protruding from the face plate controls the spacing of the cuts, so the positive and negative halves of the joint mesh accurately. This rectangular index pin, made from hardwood or plastic, is the same width as the desired joint finger and equals the width of the dado blade. The pin is mounted to the face plate this same distance away from the edge of the blade. (If

Fixed-Pin Box-Joint Jig

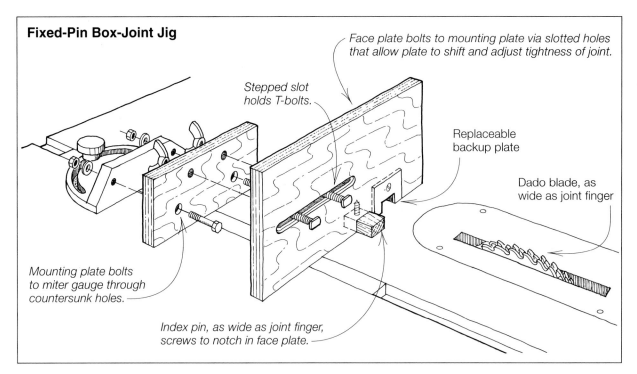

Face plate bolts to mounting plate via slotted holes that allow plate to shift and adjust tightness of joint.

Stepped slot holds T-bolts.

Replaceable backup plate

Dado blade, as wide as joint finger

Mounting plate bolts to miter gauge through countersunk holes.

Index pin, as wide as joint finger, screws to notch in face plate.

Detail: Side View

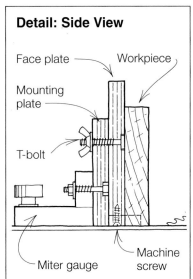

Face plate

Workpiece

Mounting plate

T-bolt

Miter gauge

Machine screw

the index pin is mounted with a screw, you can replace it with different-size pins for other box joints). The face plate attaches to a mounting plate with T-bolts (see p. 196), which ride in stepped, slotted holes in face plate, as shown in the detail drawing at left. This allows the face plate to be shifted slightly from side to side, to fine-tune the pin-to-blade distance and subsequently the fit of the joint. A backup plate, made from 1/8-in. thick Masonite and mortised in flush with the surface of the face plate where the blade cuts through it, reduces tearout as the blade exits the workpiece after each cut. Attached with a small brass screw (in case the blade hits it), the backup plate is replaced when worn or after setting changes. Machine screws through holes in the mounting plate attach the entire jig to the table saw's miter gauge, which is set square to the blade.

After setting the depth of cut to equal the stock thickness, the box side or drawer member is held against the face plate by hand and/or clamp and is butted up to the index pin for the first cut. The resulting notch is set over the pin for the next cut, then the operation is repeated all along the edge of the part (see the photo at left on the facing page). To cut the opposite, matching side of the joint, the first cut is spaced a pin-width away from the index pin (I use an extra pin as a spacer).

Accurate box joints can be cut on the table saw with a dado blade and the aid of a fixed-pin sliding jig. Here a plier-type quick-release toggle clamp helps to secure a drawer side while cuts are made.

Trimming or machining curved or irregular parts can be done with accuracy and safety using a sliding carriage in a table saw's miter slot. Here, a curved bench leg is positioned atop the base with stop blocks that match the contour of the part and held down with quick-release toggle clamps.

Carriages for machining parts

One very powerful use for miter-slot-guided carriages is to machine curved or irregular parts that are difficult to align to standard straight fences. This type of carriage, often dedicated to handling a particular part, can be used on the table saw to trim the ends of curved chair or table legs, on the router table to shape ends and edges or cut joints and mortises, or on the drill press to bore a straight row of holes.

The jig, shown in the photo above right, consists of a base that's large enough to hold the part or parts. A guide bar is screwed to the base so that one edge just barely overhangs the line of cut. Support members glued and screwed to the top of the base at front and rear keep the base flat. After the jig has been "cut in," the part, is aligned and fastened to the base with quick-release toggle clamps, as shown, or with hold-down cleats and screws (see pp. 160-162). If the carriage is dedicated to cutting a particular part, you can make positioning blocks that fit the contour of the part and automatically align it. Otherwise, draw the outline of the part on the base and align by hand. With a little planning, you can use the same carriage for operations on several different machines without removing or repositioning the part. In lieu of building a separate parts carriage, you can use a regular crosscut box (see pp. 42-43) if you have only a few small parts to cut. Just set the line of cut on the kerf in the base and fasten the part down with cleats.

A V-block mounted perpendicular to the travel of a miter-slot-guided carriage positions a dowel while a dado blade shapes a round tenon on the end. The dowel is rotated by hand; a stop collar maintains tenon length.

Parts carriages can also be built to handle round or other non-flat workpieces. For an example, a V-block mounted perpendicular to the line of cut allows you to shape a round tenon on the end of a round stool or table leg with a dado blade on the table saw, as shown in the photo above. With the leg held firmly in the V-block, the carriage is slid forward until the part is centered over the blade, then it is rotated by hand from the far end. A stop collar—a disc with a hole in it locked onto the part with a screw—bears against the V-block's right-hand end to set the length of the tenon (for more on stop collars, see p. 119). Square parts can also be tenoned by fitting temporary round collars over the part, cut out in the middle to fit over the part, so the part can rotate in the V-block.

Fence-Guided Carriages

Most modern stationary machines come with accurately made rip fences, many constructed with extruded aluminum fence bars. These serve as excellent guides for moving a carriage in a straight line past a blade, cutter or abrasive.

Sliding tenon carriage

For years I used a miter-slot-guided tenoning carriage jig with a fairly complicated adjustable base for setting the distance between the face of the jig and the sawblades (I mount two blades and cut both cheeks simultaneously, as many woodworkers do). However, I've switched to a new jig, shown in the drawing on the facing page and in the top left photo on p. 209, that has a channel that straddles my stock rip fence (for better stability) and uses the fence's quick-setting capabilities for adjustment. This jig, as well as the panel-raising jig and sliding tapering jig that follow, uses a three-sided channel made from 1/2-in. plywood sized to fit snugly over the rip-fence bar. Adding long strips of self-stick nylon tape (see p. 188) to the inside surfaces and bottom edges of the channel helps it glide smoothly over the fence bar. The jig's face plate and fence are glued and screwed to the channel at precisely 90° to the saw table. If you have a narrow rip fence, you can add a pair of plywood braces and a glide strip to stabilize the jig (something like an outrigger canoe), as shown in the drawing. I prefer to hold workpieces in the jig by hand, but you can add one or two quick-release toggle clamps to the face plate, which will clamp stock more securely and also keep your hands farther from the blade.

Sliding panel-raising carriage

When cutting or shaping panels vertically, many woodworkers find it more practical (and safer) to use a sliding carriage instead of a tall auxiliary fence. The sliding panel-raising carriage will handle panels of practically any size, including cabinet door panels, and is especially useful for raising the ends of long, narrow panels. To save the time it would take to adjust the tilt of the sawblade, the jig's face plate is

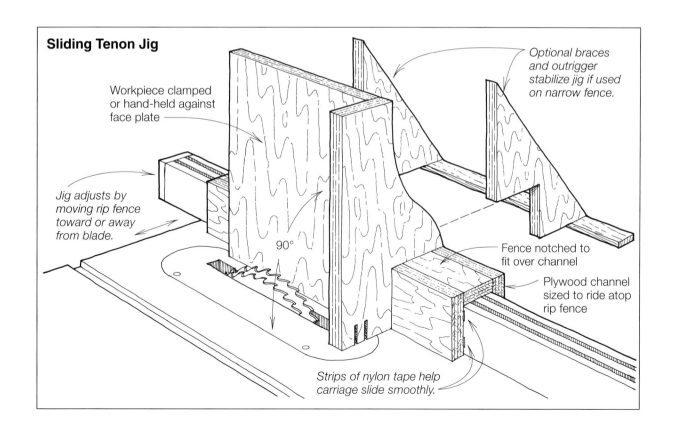

Sliding Tenon Jig

Workpiece clamped or hand-held against face plate

Jig adjusts by moving rip fence toward or away from blade.

90°

Optional braces and outrigger stabilize jig if used on narrow fence.

Fence notched to fit over channel

Plywood channel sized to ride atop rip fence

Strips of nylon tape help carriage slide smoothly.

mounted at the desired angle. This makes it convenient to raise panels on the table saw, whether your saw's arbor tilts left or right. The jig can also be used on a shaper or router table.

The sliding panel-raising carriage shown in the drawing below is based on the plywood sliding channel used for the tenon carriage, described on p. 51. However, the face plate on this jig is made larger—as large as need be to handle the panels you plan to cut. (If the panels are too long for your table and fence, you can add a box-beam-style length extension over your regular rip fence, as explained on p. 18 and shown in the photo on p. 5.) A beveled strip at the bottom and pair of triangular braces at the top secure the face plate to the channel at whatever angle off plumb produces the raising profile you desire (between 15° and 30° is typical). A narrow vertical strip screwed to the back edge of the face plate and a ledge at the bottom support the workpiece and prevent thin panel edges from getting hung up on the saw's throat plate. I designed my jig to raise panels on the table saw, but you could also mount the face plate at 90° and use the jig on a router table with a vertical panel-raising bit. Alternatively, tilting the workpiece relative to a vertical panel-raising bit will yield a new profile.

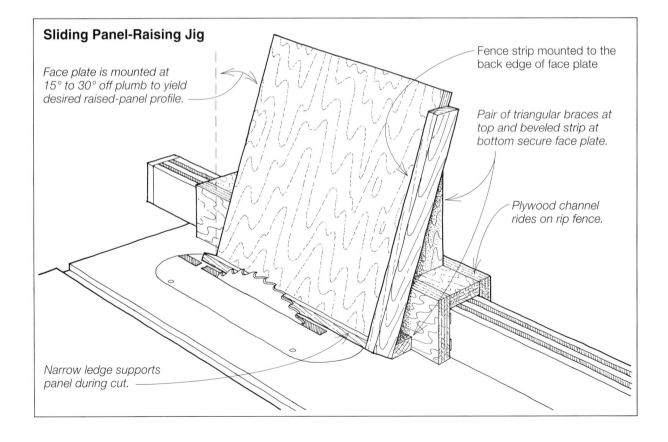

Sliding Panel-Raising Jig

Face plate is mounted at 15° to 30° off plumb to yield desired raised-panel profile.

Fence strip mounted to the back edge of face plate

Pair of triangular braces at top and beveled strip at bottom secure face plate.

Plywood channel rides on rip fence.

Narrow ledge supports panel during cut.

Sliding tapering jigs

A basic, dedicated tapering jig can be nothing more than a rectangular piece of wood with a notch cut in it to hold a workpiece at a slight angle. The jig's edge opposite the notch runs along a rip fence as the part is taper cut on the table saw or bandsaw. Many parts, such as table or chair legs, often require both edges (or all four faces) to be tapered. For these, a dual tapering jig, shown in the photo below, is made from a rectangular piece with notches in both long sides. The first edge of the workpiece is tapered in the first notch as before. Then the jig and work are flipped side-for-side, and the second notch is used to cut the remaining edge. Note that the second notch has twice the angle of the first, since it supports an already tapered edge. The jig's width and notch depth should be carefully porportioned so that you don't need to reset the rip fence between cuts.

If you do a lot of tapering, you'll probably want to take the time to build an adjustable tapering jig, such as the one shown in the drawing on p. 54. Like my tenon and panel-raising carriages, its channel fits over and slides on the rip fence. It also has a top-mounted handle, so you don't need to hold the jig tight against the fence or get your hands anywhere near the line of cut—a hazard with the simple tapering jigs described above. A small quick-release toggle clamp (I used a De-Sta-Co 205-UB) presses the stock lengthwise against the end stop (see the photo on p. 41). The position of the end stop is adjustable—it's mounted on a T-bolt that slides in a T-slot routed into the fence rail—and can handle workpieces between 8 in. and 24 in. long. Self-adhesive non-skid stair-tread tape (see p. 190) is stuck on the face of the stop and the plunger of the toggle clamp to keep the work from creeping during a

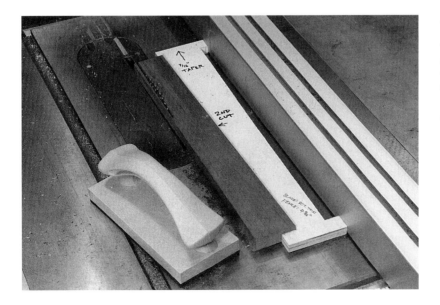

A dual tapering jig, made from a rectangular piece of plywood with two notches cut out, guides cuts for identical degrees of taper on both edge of the workpiece. The jig and work have been flipped over for the second cut, shown here.

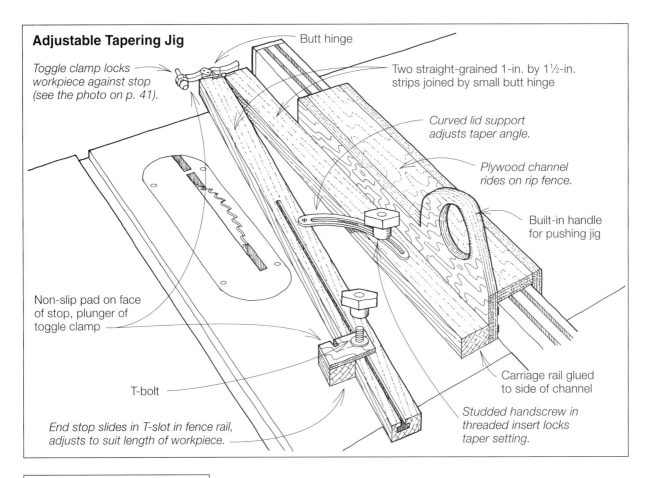

Adjustable Tapering Jig

Toggle clamp locks workpiece against stop (see the photo on p. 41).

Butt hinge

Two straight-grained 1-in. by 1½-in. strips joined by small butt hinge

Curved lid support adjusts taper angle.

Plywood channel rides on rip fence.

Built-in handle for pushing jig

Non-slip pad on face of stop, plunger of toggle clamp

T-bolt

Carriage rail glued to side of channel

Studded handscrew in threaded insert locks taper setting.

End stop slides in T-slot in fence rail, adjusts to suit length of workpiece.

Detail: Hole Positions for Mounting Compass (Top View)

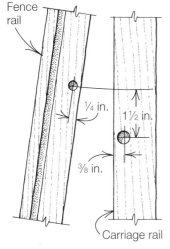

Fence rail

¼ in.

1½ in.

⅜ in.

Carriage rail

Holes for curved lid support can be placed anywhere along rails, but must be 1½ in. apart.

cut. The fence rail pivots on the carriage rail with a small butt hinge. The taper angle is set with a compass (made from a hardware-store curved lid support), which pivots on a screw in the fence rail, and locked with a studded handscrew set into a threaded insert in the carriage rail. Hole positions along the rails are shown in the detail at left.

Locating the front of the workpiece at the jig's hinge actually makes my adjustable tapering jig easier to set than other jigs I've used. After clamping the workpiece, you can set and lock the rip fence so that the work will be cut to the correct width at that end. Now slide the jig past the lowered sawblade and set and lock the angle of the tapering jig to yield the correct cut at that end. The front end of the work moves very little in or out, so only minor compensation is necessary in rip-fence position for great changes in taper angle.

Lumber-sawing carriage

If you're a wood scavenger who often needs to bandsaw logs or branches into dimensional lumber, a sliding lumber carriage makes the job safer and easier. As shown in the top photo on the facing page, the carriage is made up of a base and vertical support dadoed together and reinforced with triangular braces. Vertical slots routed through the support allow two L-shaped cleats to be mounted and adjusted up and down to accommodate logs of various diameters. Slots routed through the cleats provide horizontal adjustment, so stock of different lengths can be mounted on the jig. After cleat positions are set and fastened with machine screws, two 2½-in. long brass screws in each cleat are driven into the ends of the log to hold it in place (if the bandsaw blade contacts brass screws it will cut right through them, rather than creating a shower of sparks and broken saw teeth). The carriage can then be run along the rip fence to slice boards from the log. After half of the log has been sawn up, the workpiece is rotated 180° and sawing continues. If logs are heavier than 10 lb. or so, you'll need to add weight to counterbalance the jig: A bag of lead shot or a concrete brick on top of the base does the trick.

Small-parts carriages

Carriages that handle small parts may be run along a fence freehand. For example, small irregularly shaped parts that have very short straight edges—too short to run stably against a router-table fence—can be slotted for biscuit joints with a small carriage that holds the part firmly, yet creates a long guiding surface (see the photo below). Such a carriage need be nothing more than a plywood base with two spacer blocks, cut the same thickness as the part and glued at either end with a wood strip screwed on top to keep the part from lifting. The part bears against a stop block shaped with a negative profile of the part, and a quick-release toggle clamp holds it down.

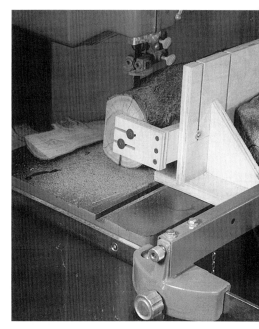

A plywood bandsaw carriage guided by the rip fence can be used to saw small logs into dimensional lumber. Two adjustable brackets screwed into the ends of the log attach it to the carriage. A concrete brick provides a counterweight to keep the carriage from tipping.

A sliding carriage guides a small, curved toy part along a fence to cut a slot in an edge for a plate-joinery biscuit. The part is held by a stop block and a quick-release toggle clamp; a post-style handle makes controlling the carriage easier.

Crosscutting tiny parts is safe and easy with a special small-parts carriage mounted to a miter gauge. Two clothespins hold the part flat on the base, supporting it near the line of cut so the operator's hands can be kept a safe distance away.

Although not fence guided, a very simple jig for crosscutting or shaping really tiny parts (for model building or perhaps for a dollhouse) attaches to a standard miter gauge and uses two regular clothespins to secure the part. The jig, shown in the photo above, has a base made from ⅛-in. Masonite with a wood mounting plate glued on that screws to the gauge head. The clothespins, each with the lower half of its head trimmed off, are epoxied to the base. A strip of sandpaper glued to the base and mounting plate further helps parts to stay put.

Table-Guided Carriages

Some carriages don't need to travel in a straight line. Their job is to support the workpiece—or portable power tool—in a flat plane during the machining operation, such as thickness planing, sawing or shaping. The flat surface is provided by the machine's table or by an auxiliary table constructed for the task (see p. 76).

Carriages for the thickness planer

A table-guided carriage is just the ticket for supporting warped stock as it is being flattened in the thickness planer. The simplest carriage consists of a flat, thick plywood or particleboard panel. The board can be temporarily secured to the top of this with cleats, hot-melt glue or adhesive transfer tape—a special kind of double-stick tape (see p. 140). Areas of the board that don't contact the carriage need to be shimmed up with small scraps or tapered wedges to prevent the planer's pressure rollers from flattening the board.

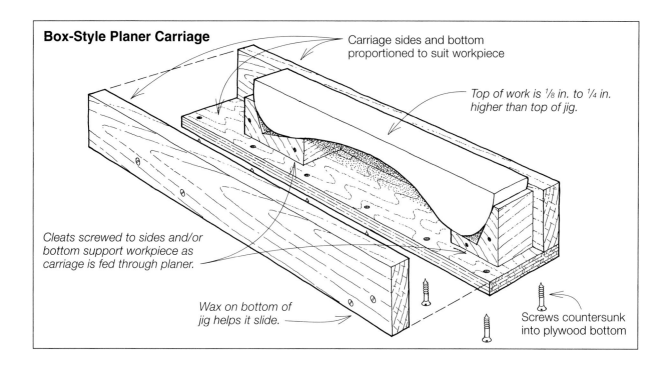

Box-Style Planer Carriage

Carriage sides and bottom proportioned to suit workpiece

Top of work is 1/8 in. to 1/4 in. higher than top of jig.

Cleats screwed to sides and/or bottom support workpiece as carriage is fed through planer.

Wax on bottom of jig helps it slide.

Screws countersunk into plywood bottom

A box-style planer carriage, such as the one shown in the drawing above, can be used to thickness-plane surfaces on odd-shaped, tapered or turned work. A box-style carriage can also provide the necessary length for thicknessing or edge trimming parts too short to pass through the planer unassisted. Make the carriage by screwing two straight side boards to a plywood or MDF bottom, proportioning it to handle the length, width and thickness of the workpiece. Support blocks or cleats screwed in from the bottom or sides hold the workpiece so that the edge or surface to be planed protrudes 1/8 in. to 1/4 in. above the top of the jig.

When planing long, shallow tapers, a precut tapered wedge screwed to the bottom of the jig will support the work. Another way to secure the work is to leave the ends long and screw into them through the sides of the jig, then trim them off after planing. By attaching a high block in the center and lower blocks at either end, a thin workpiece can be held in a bowed position during planing, resulting in a regular hollow on its face or edge when the piece straightens out. You can also use the jig to plane halved or quartered turnings flat on one or more sides. And by fitting a rotary indexing plate (similar to the one shown in the drawing on p. 115), you can plane evenly proportioned facets around the circumference of a turning, say for an octagonal-section newel post for a stair railing.

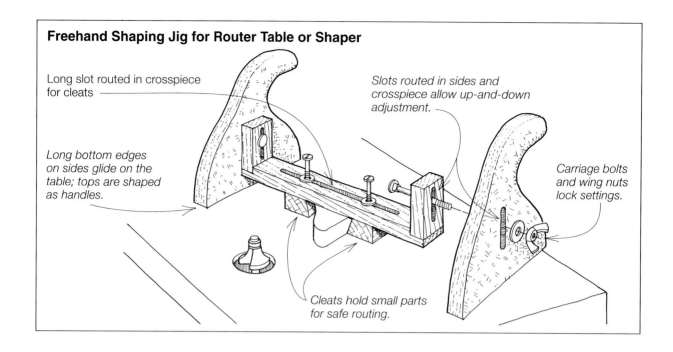

Freehand Shaping Jig for Router Table or Shaper

Long slot routed in crosspiece for cleats

Long bottom edges on sides glide on the table; tops are shaped as handles.

Slots routed in sides and crosspiece allow up-and-down adjustment.

Carriage bolts and wing nuts lock settings.

Cleats hold small parts for safe routing.

Carriage for freehand shaping

Sawing, shaping, drilling or sanding small parts can be a harrowing task, since a powered machine can easily grab the part and ruin it, or worse, pull your fingers into danger. One way to sidestep problems is to make a freehand carriage that holds the piece securely and provides hand grips located well away from the action. The basic jig, shown in the drawing above, has two sides (shaped like push sticks) that function as both handles and a gliding base. A crossmember connects the sides. Slotted holes in the upturned ends of the C-shaped crossmember allow its height to be set up or down to suit the thickness of the workpiece. A slot routed down the center of the crossmember allows the work to be mounted with a pair of cleats that grab the part from two sides. The faces of these cleats can be cut V-shaped, convex or concave—whatever arrangement best holds the part. You can also use the cleats to hold a part with an attached template for pattern routing, as described on pp. 126-129.

Portable-Tool Carriages

There are lots of instances when you want to make some sort of cut, machine a surface or shape a groove at a fixed distance from a surface or edge. As we saw in the section on router sub-bases (see pp. 35-38), adding a fence to the baseplate of a tool provides a way to do this. Expanding on this concept, you can create a wide variety of carriages that reorient the position of tool and guide it past the work.

Angled carriage

One jig I've used for angled work is basically a carriage that tilts a portable power tool and guides it over the workpiece. Used with a router, the jig, shown in the drawing below, makes it easier to create an angled groove or flute on a table leg or cabinet stile that is too long or too heavy to maneuver over the router table. The jig could also be used with a plate joiner for angled biscuit slotting, or for cove cuts using a small panel saw mounted skewed relative to carriage travel.

The angled carriage has two guide rails, one high and one low, that are held parallel by crosspieces at each end. A spacer strip screwed to one of the rails captures the edge of the workpiece and adapts the jig to stock of different widths. A square base, which provides a tool mount, attaches to the top of the guide rails with screws through slotted holes. The slots allow the tool position to be shifted to change the location of the cut on the workpiece, which is clamped down to the benchtop. By making the taller guide rail ride on top of a panel, the jig can be used for shaping raised panels with a large straight or core-box bit in a router. But the most exciting application for an angled carriage is creating new moldings and profiles using the same old router bits: A standard Roman ogee bit (with the pilot bearing removed) tilted 30°, 45° or more out of plumb produces a surprising array of profiles that are far different from those made using the bit in the regular way.

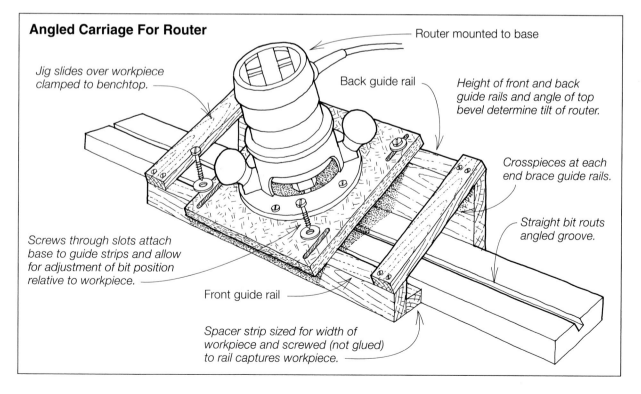

Angled Carriage For Router

Router mounted to base

Jig slides over workpiece clamped to benchtop.

Back guide rail

Height of front and back guide rails and angle of top bevel determine tilt of router.

Crosspieces at each end brace guide rails.

Straight bit routs angled groove.

Screws through slots attach base to guide strips and allow for adjustment of bit position relative to workpiece.

Front guide rail

Spacer strip sized for width of workpiece and screwed (not glued) to rail captures workpiece.

A custom carriage clamped to a belt sander supports the tool parallel and at a fixed distance from the work surface. This setup is used here for sanding decorative plugs that will remain 'proud' to the same height.

Carriages for portable tools without baseplates

If the portable tool you want to use doesn't have a removable baseplate to allow mounting a custom plate, you can still build a carriage jig that'll get the job done. Such a jig can be used to keep the tool square or at a steady angle relative to the workpiece or to allow the tool to pivot or slide to make the cut. A fence can also be added to ride against the edge of the work and guide the tool. Carriages can be created to work with all kinds of portable power tools, such as right-angle body grinders, electric drills, disc sanders and die grinders. For example, the carriage clamped to the body of a belt sander, as shown in the photo at left, has two guide strips that keep the belt at a fixed distance above a surface, allowing the tool to level the tops of dowel plugs, decorative pegs, or proud through-joinery members. This setup could also be used for thickness planing narrow strips, fed between a sander and a base.

Rail-Guided Carriages

If you often need to cut up full-size sheets of plywood but can't afford a panel saw, you'll benefit greatly if you build a rail-guided carriage jig. This kind of jig handles large panels with ease, since the workpiece stays put while the portable power tool travels over it in a straight line to do the cutting. It's also versatile enough to handle different sorts of operations; you can fit a router for rabbets, dadoes or decorative shaping across wide surfaces. Rail-guided carriages can also be adapted nicely for various mortising operations.

Basic rail-guided carriage

The simplest rail-guided setups I've seen consisted of nothing more than two solid wood rails, each with a lengthwise groove that accept the edges of a square Plexiglas baseplate for the power tool. More complicated jigs employ machined or extruded rails and linear-motion bearings—expensive items. A happy medium between these extremes is the carriage shown in the drawing on the facing page. It features a carriage that mounts the power tool with flange-mounted bronze bearings that glide on a pair of drill-rod guide rails. To construct the jig, first cut out a plywood platform large enough to hold the tool (or tools) you plan to use. You may be able to make the same platform accept two different tools, say a router and a circular saw, by drilling two sets of mounting holes and cutting out a bit hole and a blade slot. Just make sure the platform is wide enough so that the guide rods will clear the tool. To get the maximum depth of cut from the tool, you may wish to mortise the platform and remove the tool's baseplate. Next, cut two carriage sides and carefully drill the holes for the guide rods. Glue and screw the sides to the platform.

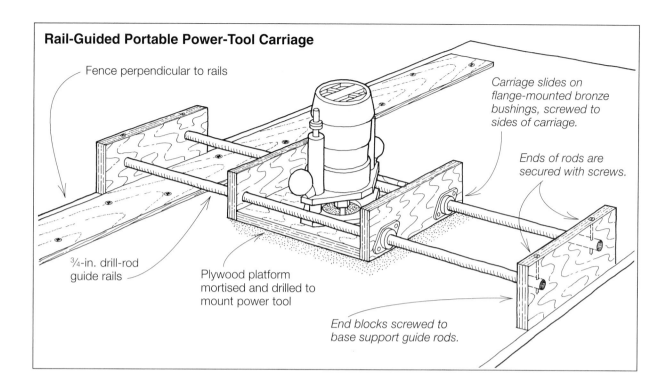

Rail-Guided Portable Power-Tool Carriage

Fence perpendicular to rails

Carriage slides on flange-mounted bronze bushings, screwed to sides of carriage.

Ends of rods are secured with screws.

¾-in. drill-rod guide rails

Plywood platform mortised and drilled to mount power tool

End blocks screwed to base support guide rods.

For the bearings in my medium-size jig (the rails are ¾ in. dia., 60 in. long), I bought four inexpensive ¾-in. I.D. (inside diameter) flange-mounted pillow blocks with bronze, self aligning bushings from my local bearing supplier (they're also available from W.W. Grainger; see Sources of Supply on pp. 224-227). The drill-rod guide rails are available at industrial-supply stores and steel-supply houses. If the rods fit too tightly in the bushings, lap the inside by twirling a short length of dowel with a piece of fine emery paper wrapped around it in an electric drill. Coating the rods with a dry lubricant, such as Sandaro Top-Cote, will also help keep the bushings gliding smoothly. The rods are set into end blocks that align and support them above the work surface. The end blocks are screwed down to a plywood base. A fence attached to the base next to one end block and perpendicular to the rails lets you quickly square up sheet goods to the travel of the carriage.

The variations to the basic rail-guided carriage jig are virtually limitless. If you need a larger-capacity carriage, you could use larger-diameter rails and special roller-bearing hardware, as described for the construction of a sliding table on pp. 88-90. If you need to perform angled panel cuts or router work, you can mount one end block on a pivot, swing the rails to the desired angle relative to the panel and clamp the outboard block to the base. For beveled work, you can make the carriage tilt to change the angle of the tool. For stopped cuts or dadoes, add stop collars to the guide rails (see p. 119). Used with a plunge router and a large straight bit, a basic rail-guided carriage could even be used to surface lumber—a tedious way to accomplish this job, but serviceable in a pinch.

Rail-guided mortising carriage

A basic rail-guided carriage as described in the last section can easily be adapted for mortising by fitting a control arm, which moves the carriage back and forth as far as the length of the mortise. This is great for production mortising, since the stock remains clamped while it is shifted sideways for repeated cuts to lengthen the mortise to full dimension. The jig, shown in the drawing on the facing page, has a plywood table with the bushing blocks and guide rails running underneath. A fence is glued and screwed to top of the table, which extends over the rails to keep chips from fouling the rails. Two plunger-type quick-release toggle clamps (I use De-Sta-Co #605) hold the workpiece firmly against the fence and perpendicular to the mortising bit.

To keep the stock from lifting as the mortising chisel is extracted, a pair of hold-down blocks bolt to the fence; three pairs of holes allow adjustment to suit the width of the stock. A 12-in. long rub block glued and screwed to the underside of the table beneath the mortising area prevents deflection due to the considerable downward pressure of the mortising chisel (see the detail drawing). A UHMW polyethylene strip (see p. 188) on the underside of the block helps it glide easily against the base. The end blocks that hold the rails are mounted to a base made from two thicknesses of plywood or MDF for rigidity; the base can be clamped or screwed to the machine's table. Mounted on the base (beneath the rails) is a motion control arm that attaches to the end of the carriage with a connecting link. The arm works with a compound action that moves the carriage and workpiece less than half as far as the handle travels, allowing fine adjustments in the position of the workpiece. To set the length of mortises, stops are added to the base or fitted on the guide rails (see pp. 118-119).

Carriage guided by lathe bed

The twin, parallel rails—flat cast iron or tubular steel—that make up the beds on most wood lathes are excellent for guiding a carriage that holds a router (or other portable power tool) for jobs like fluting and veining. You can also use such a setup for machining flat surfaces on a round turning for joinery, such as mounting legs on a Shaker-style pedestal table. The carriage shown in the top photo on p. 64 is a simple four-sided plywood box that's drilled on top to accept a plunge router. A hard maple (or teak) guide bar screwed to the bottom of the box is sized to ride between the bed rails. The box allows the router to

Sliding Mortising Carriage

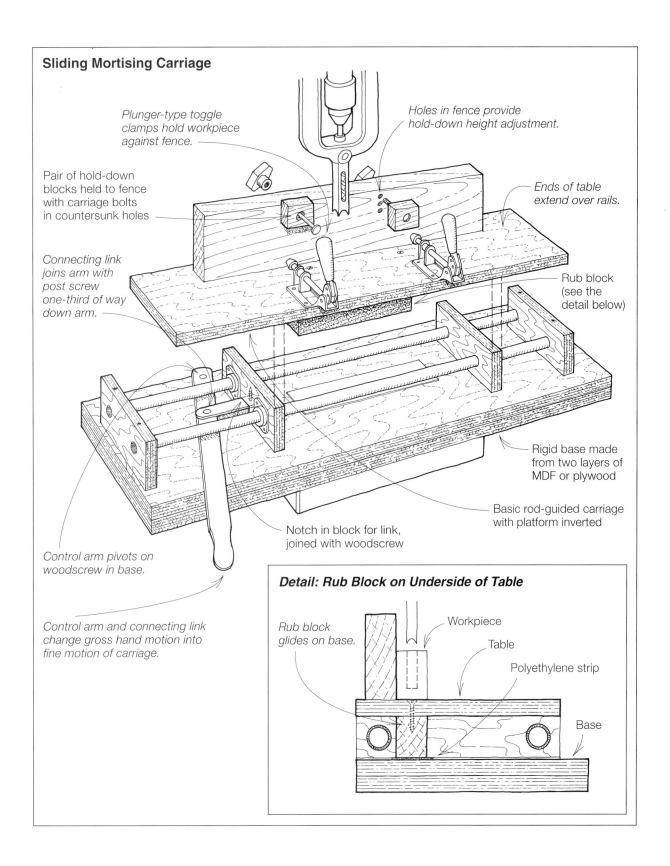

Plunger-type toggle clamps hold workpiece against fence.

Holes in fence provide hold-down height adjustment.

Pair of hold-down blocks held to fence with carriage bolts in countersunk holes

Ends of table extend over rails.

Connecting link joins arm with post screw one-third of way down arm.

Rub block (see the detail below)

Control arm pivots on woodscrew in base.

Control arm and connecting link change gross hand motion into fine motion of carriage.

Notch in block for link, joined with woodscrew

Rigid base made from two layers of MDF or plywood

Basic rod-guided carriage with platform inverted

Detail: Rub Block on Underside of Table

Rub block glides on base.

Workpiece

Table

Polyethylene strip

Base

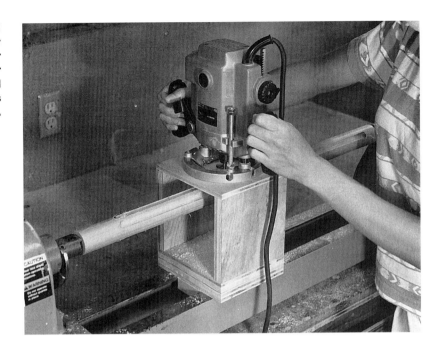

The twin bed rails of the wood lathe provide the necessary track for guiding a router carriage in a straight line over a turning. A plunge router fitted with a corebox bit shapes flutes in this turned table leg.

Press-fit into the bandsaw's miter slot, this pivoting circle jig makes accurately sized wooden wheels and discs in a wide range of sizes. The jig's pivot arm is swung into the blade as the workpiece is rotated. An adjustable stop limits arm travel and determines disc size.

pass over the turning, which is locked in position with a rotary indexing plate (see p. 115). If the carriage seems top-heavy and unstable, add weight, such as lead bars or a bag of lead shot, to the inside or bottom of the carriage.

Curved-Motion Carriages

Moving something at a fixed distance from a point will create a circle or an arc of constant radius. You can take advantage of this fact to make a curved-motion carriage that will work with many portable power tools, including the router, laminate trimmer and saber saw. These carriages are excellent for moving a tool—or a workpiece—in an arc, for shaping, cutting and sanding simple discs or curved parts.

Pivoting circle jig

Mounting a workpiece on end of a pivot arm is good way to introduce a round part to a running bandsaw blade, stationary disc sander or vertical belt sander. For example, the pivot jig shown in the photo at left was designed for bandsawing wooden wheels for toy cars. A pivot arm attached to a plywood base with a post screw holds the square wheel blank, which is mounted by being pressed down onto a small nail protruding from the arm. An arc-shaped plywood strip provides a positive stop for the pivot arm; its setting determines the diameter of the part. A carriage bolt countersunk up through the base and a slot routed in the stop allows adjustment; a T-knob locks in settings. The jig, which can be proportioned to handle circles of many sizes, mounts to the saw with a wooden guide bar pressed into the miter-gauge slot. The jig should be positioned in the slot so that the point of blade contact of the disc will be in line with the pivot pin. The arm is then swung into the blade as the disc is rotated by hand to make the cut.

Circle jig

The jig shown in the photo and drawing below allows you to cut or shape large discs—from 24 in. to 60 in. in diameter (the jig can be made smaller or larger as need be), and it's fully adjustable to any fractional measurement in between. Used with a router, the jig lets you rout decorative arcs or semicircles into panels. The jig's extension arm and compass bar are sawn from 1/2-in. plywood. A sub-base-like platform on the end of the extension is shaped and drilled to suit the power tool: I drilled the base on my jig to mount both my router and my saber saw.

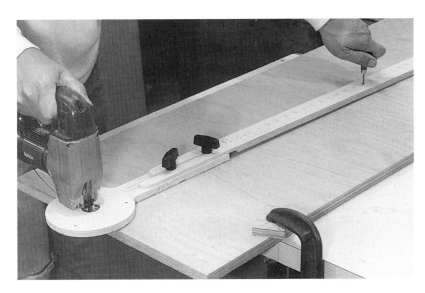

Large discs and arcs can be cut using this circle jig and a saber saw. Holes along the jig's compass bar are for the pivot pin—a scratch awl is used here. A sliding joint between the bar and extension arm on the tool sub-base allow fine adjustment of the circle radius.

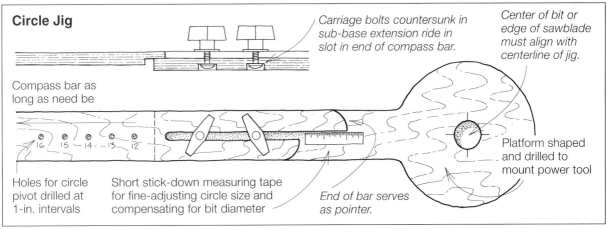

Circle Jig

Carriage bolts countersunk in sub-base extension ride in slot in end of compass bar.

Center of bit or edge of sawblade must align with centerline of jig.

Compass bar as long as need be

16 15 14 13 12

Holes for circle pivot drilled at 1-in. intervals

Short stick-down measuring tape for fine-adjusting circle size and compensating for bit diameter

End of bar serves as pointer.

Platform shaped and drilled to mount power tool

As shown in the drawing, an extension arm extends from the tool platform to attach it to the compass bar. The compass bar can be made as long as need be, with holes drilled at 1-in. intervals for a small nail or awl that acts as a pivot for the jig, allowing the tool to swing around for the cut. The extension arm and compass bar are joined with carriage bolts and hand knobs that ride in a slot routed in the end of the compass bar. The slot allows the distance from a pivot point to the cutter or blade to be adjusted for fractions of an inch or to account for the diameter of different router bits. A short length of stick-on measuring tape on the extension arm aids in establishing the setting.

Arc jig

By combining a circle jig with a base that limits tool travel and aligns the jig to the workpiece, you can cut or shape accurately sized arcs and semicircles. This jig is very useful for making top cuts on rails for arch-top cabinet door panels or lozenge-shaped tabletops with semicircular ends. The jig, shown in the drawing below, uses a circle jig, as described above, with a saber saw or router mounted on it. The circle jig is screwed through a pivot hole to a plywood or MDF base, end cut in an arc. Strips screwed to the underside of the base position the jig atop the workpiece. Two stop blocks are screwed on the base to limit the swing of the circle jig. If you're using a portable tool that overhangs the base of the circle jig, be sure to position the stops so they won't hang up the tool. By enlarging the base and reorienting the position of the circle jig relative to the workpiece, you can adapt the jig to cut or shape concave edges instead of convex ones.

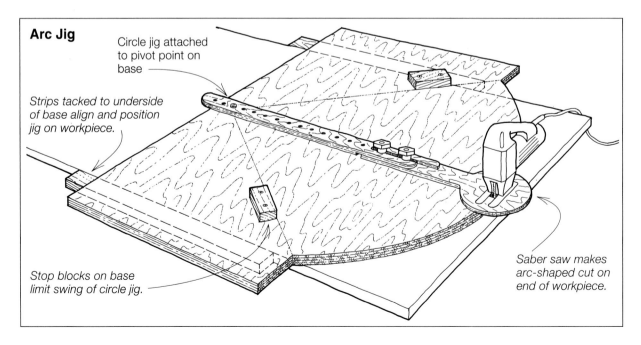

Arc Jig

Circle jig attached to pivot point on base

Strips tacked to underside of base align and position jig on workpiece.

Stop blocks on base limit swing of circle jig.

Saber saw makes arc-shaped cut on end of workpiece.

Router pantograph

A convenient way to create an incised design or inlay from a drawing is to use a pantograph jig, like the one in the drawing below. Based on an old draftsman's pantograph, this router jig can enlarge small originals at ratios from 3:4 (which means that a 3-in. high drawing yields a 4-in. high routed design) up to 1:5. The jig is made up of four struts joined at four pivot points to form a flexible parallelogram. The struts can be made from ¼-in. Baltic birch plywood, clear plastic or aluminum. Accurately placed sets of holes drilled in all four struts and located as shown in the drawing on p. 68, allow you to choose different enlarging ratios.

Plastic post screws act as pivots to join struts 1 and 2 and struts 3 and 4. Struts 1 and 4 and struts 2 and 3 are joined with hanger bolts (see p. 193). The hanger bolts have machine-screw ends that fit through holes in the ends of the struts and are secured loosely with nuts. Their wood-screw ends are driven into pilot holes in the ends of ¾-in. long, ⅜-in. dia. dowels. The end of the dowel at struts 2 and 3 is tapered to a slightly blunted point to act as a tracer stylus; the end of the other dowel is rounded over, to serve as a support post. The jig is mounted to the worktable on a pivot post, made from a 1-in. dia. dowel screwed to a wood disc with a hanger bolt fitted through a hole in the end of Strut 1. A custom sub-base is attached to the end of Strut 4 for a laminate trimmer, which is essentially a very small, light router.

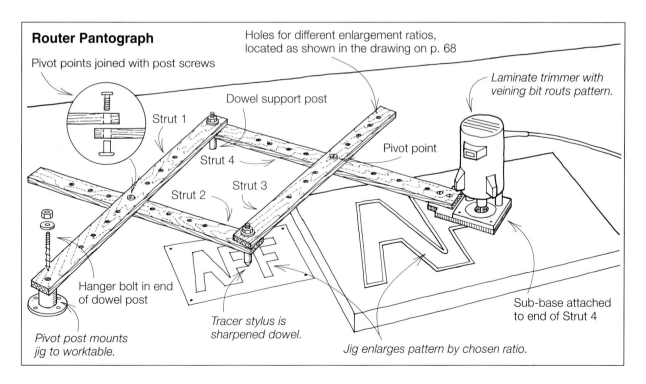

Router Pantograph

Holes for different enlargement ratios, located as shown in the drawing on p. 68

Pivot points joined with post screws

Laminate trimmer with veining bit routs pattern.

Strut 1

Dowel support post

Strut 4

Pivot point

Strut 3

Strut 2

Hanger bolt in end of dowel post

Pivot post mounts jig to worktable.

Tracer stylus is sharpened dowel.

Sub-base attached to end of Strut 4

Jig enlarges pattern by chosen ratio.

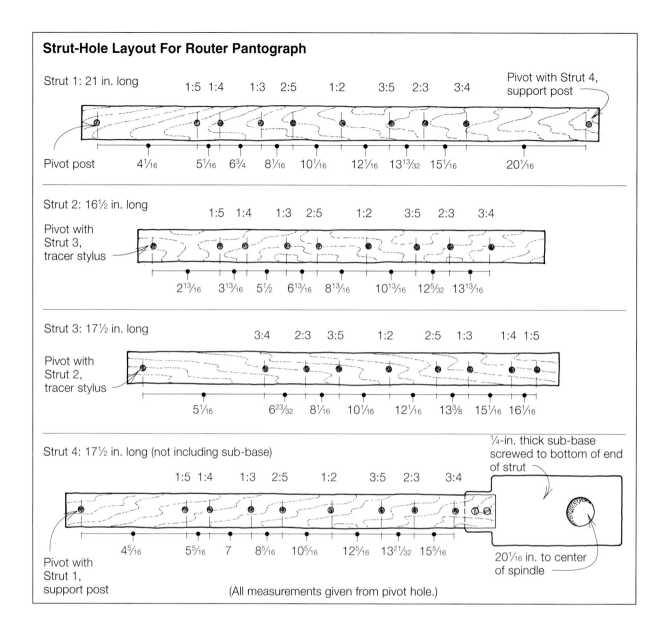

Strut-Hole Layout For Router Pantograph

Strut 1: 21 in. long

1:5 1:4   1:3   2:5   1:2   3:5   2:3   3:4

Pivot with Strut 4, support post

Pivot post

$4\frac{1}{16}$ $5\frac{1}{16}$ $6\frac{3}{4}$ $8\frac{1}{16}$ $10\frac{1}{16}$ $12\frac{1}{16}$ $13\frac{13}{32}$ $15\frac{1}{16}$ $20\frac{1}{16}$

Strut 2: $16\frac{1}{2}$ in. long

Pivot with Strut 3, tracer stylus

1:5   1:4   1:3   2:5   1:2   3:5   2:3   3:4

$2\frac{13}{16}$ $3\frac{13}{16}$ $5\frac{1}{2}$ $6\frac{13}{16}$ $8\frac{13}{16}$ $10\frac{13}{16}$ $12\frac{5}{32}$ $13\frac{13}{16}$

Strut 3: $17\frac{1}{2}$ in. long

3:4   2:3   3:5   1:2   2:5   1:3   1:4 1:5

Pivot with Strut 2, tracer stylus

$5\frac{1}{16}$ $6\frac{23}{32}$ $8\frac{1}{16}$ $10\frac{1}{16}$ $12\frac{1}{16}$ $13\frac{3}{8}$ $15\frac{1}{16}$ $16\frac{1}{16}$

Strut 4: $17\frac{1}{2}$ in. long (not including sub-base)

$\frac{1}{4}$-in. thick sub-base screwed to bottom of end of strut

1:5 1:4   1:3   2:5   1:2   3:5   2:3   3:4

Pivot with Strut 1, support post

$4\frac{5}{16}$ $5\frac{5}{16}$ 7 $8\frac{5}{16}$ $10\frac{5}{16}$ $12\frac{5}{16}$ $13\frac{21}{32}$ $15\frac{5}{16}$

$20\frac{1}{16}$ in. to center of spindle

(All measurements given from pivot hole.)

To use the router pantograph, choose holes in all four struts that correspond to the desired enlargement ratio and join them with the post screws/hanger screws. After the drawing is taped down and the workpiece is tacked down to the worktable, routing can begin. It's essential to hand guide both the router and the tracer stylus—a technique that takes some getting used to, especially at higher ratios (e.g., 1:5), but very good results can be achieved. If a larger drawing is used at a small enlargement ratio (e.g. 3:4), it's possible that the drawing and workpiece may overlap, in which case you should rout the sections of the work farthest from the drawing first, then fold back the overlapping section of the drawing when need be.

Carriages for Shaping Three-Dimensional Forms

As you've no doubt already discovered, the router is an extremely versatile tool for creating all sorts of edge profiles and two-dimensional shapes. Yet that is only the "carbide tip" of the iceberg. With the right carriage, routers can also be used to create a great variety of three-dimensional forms, such as cylinders and spheres, or even to shape compound-curved parts. With the right carriage, even the bandsaw is capable of producing some pretty complex 3-D parts.

Carriage for shaping simple curves

The basic carriage jig, shown in the drawing below, can be adapted for shaping practically any simple convex or concave form on a wide leg, frame member or panel surface. The jig shown in the drawing was used to create a very slight hollow profile on a wide panel (too wide to be cove cut on the table saw). The jig's router carriage consists of a square, thin plywood base with two curved runners glued on the sides. (It's important to make the base from thin plywood—⅜ in. to ½ in.—and to keep the runners narrow; otherwise, very long bits are required for shaping the workpiece.) The runners ride on guide rails cut concave to match their curve. Each curved rail is glued to a straight rail to keep the sliding carriage from slipping off. The rail assemblies are

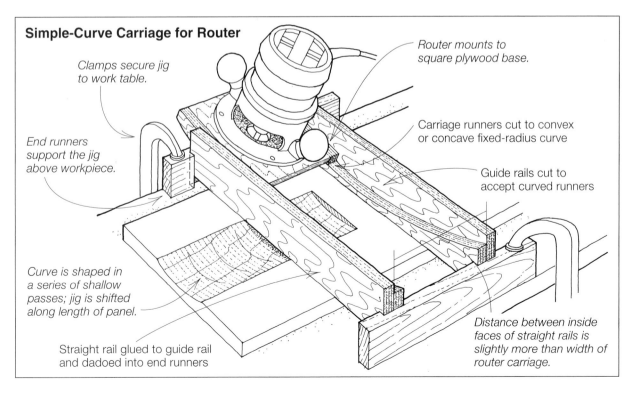

Simple-Curve Carriage for Router

Clamps secure jig to work table.

Router mounts to square plywood base.

End runners support the jig above workpiece.

Carriage runners cut to convex or concave fixed-radius curve

Guide rails cut to accept curved runners

Curve is shaped in a series of shallow passes; jig is shifted along length of panel.

Straight rail glued to guide rail and dadoed into end runners

Distance between inside faces of straight rails is slightly more than width of router carriage.

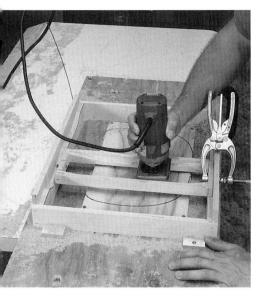

The poplar seat of a child's rocking chair is roughed out with a laminate trimmer guided by a special compound-curve jig. Shaping is done in multiple passes, with the curved rail assembly shifted and temporarily clamped to the jig's frame before each pass. A bent coat hanger keeps the tool's cord clear.

set parallel and spaced far enough apart to accept the carriage and are dadoed to end runners at both ends. The end runners (which get clamped to the benchtop) support the jig above the workpiece. A length of coat hanger wire, looped on one end and screwed to an end runner, a helix bent on the other, will keep the tool's cord clear (see the photo at left). Incidentally, this simple cord holder can be employed effectively on any jig that uses a portable power tool.

In use, the panel is shaped in a series of shallow passes, starting at one end and working toward the other. After each pass with a long, round-nose bit, the jig is unclamped, shifted slightly and reclamped for the next cut. After the entire panel has been routed once, the process is repeated with the router's depth of cut set slightly deeper. This is done until the final depth has been reached.

Carriage for shaping compound curves

Starting with the simple-curve-shaping carriage described in the previous section, you can create a jig that will shape a wide array of compound curvatures, such as for making a serpentine drawer front or Bombay chest. This setup, shown in the drawing on the facing page, uses the simple-curve carriage described above with its end runners sawn curved, to ride on a secondary set of guide rails cut to match the runners. These secondary guide rails are positioned parallel and far enough apart so the end runners are on top of them. They are then glued and nailed to a pair of end rails to form a box-like frame. Wood strips glued to the outside faces of the secondary rails keep the secondary runners from slipping off. Cleats on the end rails allow the jig to be screwed to a plywood base, which the workpiece is also screwed down to before routing begins. In use, the secondary runners are positioned and clamped before each pass with the router carriage.

The compound-curve jig just described is capable of regular compound curves. When I needed a more versatile jig for rough-shaping a dozen chair seats for children's rockers. I adapted the compound jig by substituting a horizontally mounted dowel pin for the curved secondary runner on one side. This pin follows the secondary guide rail, shaped with an undulating curve, allowing the jig to shape the two hollows for the sitter's legs near the front of the seat (see the photo above left). The other secondary runner and rail are cut to a shallow concave curve (as are the primary runners/rails), so the rear portion of the seat is shaped hollow for the sitter's rear. A laminate trimmer was hefty enough for routing the child-size softwood seats I made, but the jig could be expanded for full-size seats or larger work.

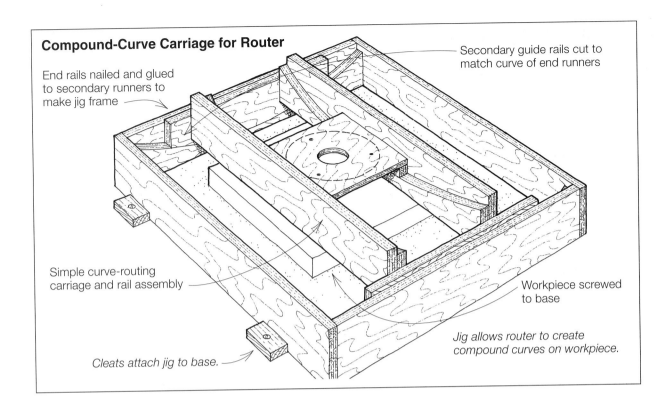

Compound-Curve Carriage for Router

End rails nailed and glued to secondary runners to make jig frame

Secondary guide rails cut to match curve of end runners

Simple curve-routing carriage and rail assembly

Workpiece screwed to base

Jig allows router to create compound curves on workpiece.

Cleats attach jig to base.

Carriages for cylindrical shapes

A basic box-style jig, such as the one shown on p. 39, can be used in conjunction with a plunge router for shaping large-diameter dowels or cylindrical forms, such as legs or lamp bases. With the lathe rotated slowly by hand, a round-nosed straight bit is plunged down and shallow cuts are taken as the carriage is slid along the length of the work (stops screwed to the lathe bed keep the bit clear of the head and tailstock). The bit is lowered slightly for subsequent passes until the cylinder is correctly sized.

A more novel, but effective, way to create regular (or irregular) cylindrical forms is to create a carriage of sorts by screwing a pair of round, oval or elliptical discs to the ends of a workpiece. The discs, cut from plywood, MDF or plastic, ride against a fence (at least as high as the center or foci of the disc) on a router table, keeping the work at a fixed distance from a spinning straight bit (see the drawing at right). For this setup, I've found it best to use a solid-carbide "up-cut" spiral bit, such as the CMT #880-515 or the Woodhaven #12408 (see Sources of Supply on pp. 224-227) for two reasons: Solid carbide bits don't deflect as easily as standard carbide-tipped bits, and the up-cut design used in a router table tends to pull the workpiece down toward the table, adding stability to the operation.

Shaping Cylindrical Forms

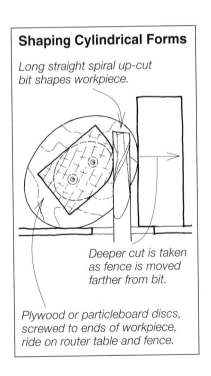

Long straight spiral up-cut bit shapes workpiece.

Deeper cut is taken as fence is moved farther from bit.

Plywood or particleboard discs, screwed to ends of workpiece, ride on router table and fence.

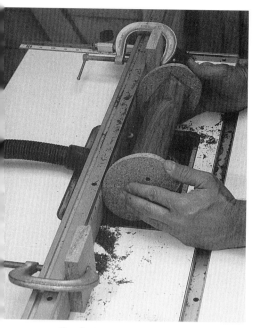

The long bit shapes the workpiece while it is slowly rotated by hand and moved along the length of the fence, as shown in the photo at left. Stops clamped to the fence keep the bit from cutting into the discs, as well as keeping hands a safe distance away. A light pass is first taken, then the fence is moved farther away from the bit, thus increasing cutting depth. Repeated passes are taken until the workpiece is entirely shaped; then it is trimmed to final length. To create a tapered form, discs with the same curvature can be made different sizes.

Carriage for sawing complex forms with the bandsaw

I once had to make about a dozen decorative stands for small pots containing bonsai. To get the desired shape, the curvaceous stands needed to be sawn in all three axes, which proved to be a tough proposition. I came up with the carriage jig shown in the drawing below to make it easier for me to saw such a complex shape. The carriage is a four-sided plywood box that slides on the bandsaw's table. The rough workpiece (which in the case of my stands, was sawn cylindrical) screws to the front side of this box and the pattern for the desired cut, drawn on a thin plywood scrap, is held on top of the jig by a small toggle clamp. (The pattern can also be screwed on, if your clamp won't clear the bandsaw body). As you saw along the flat pattern, the workpiece positioned below is cut accordingly (see the photo below). To saw the second axis, the workpiece is rotated and realigned at 90° to the previous cut with the help of alignment marks drawn on the front

Oval-shaped discs screwed to the ends of a piece of claro walnut ride against a router table fence, controlling the cut of a long straight bit that shapes the blank as it is rotated. Stops clamped to the fence prevent the bit from contacting the discs — or the hands that are rotating them.

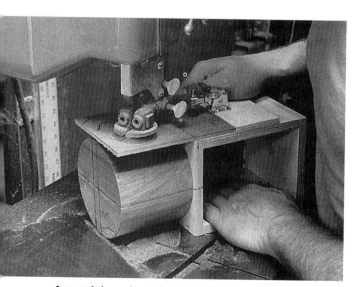

A special carriage jig is used for bandsawing a complicated part in all three dimensions. The pattern mounted on top shows where to cut; index marks on the carriage allow the part to be rotated between cuts.

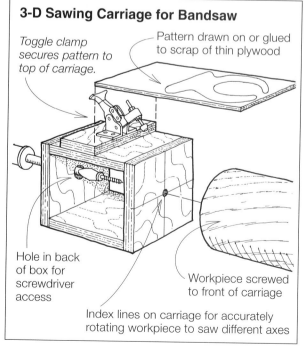

3-D Sawing Carriage for Bandsaw

Toggle clamp secures pattern to top of carriage.

Pattern drawn on or glued to scrap of thin plywood

Hole in back of box for screwdriver access

Workpiece screwed to front of carriage

Index lines on carriage for accurately rotating workpiece to saw different axes of the jig. A new pattern must be used for each cut, but if you have a lot of identical parts to saw, paper patterns can be photocopied and glued atop plywood scraps. This bandsaw carriage can be used to cut out small cabriole legs, sculptural drawer pulls, geometrical puzzle pieces, and more.

Carriage for shaping a sphere

The cradle-type carriage shown in the drawing below works in conjunction with the router table to shape nearly perfect spheres. The jig has two frames: The three-sided outer frame is screwed or clamped down on the router table through mounting blocks at the bottom of the sides. Post screws fitted through holes centered on the sides provide pivots for the four-sided inner frame, sized to fit within the outer frame. The workpiece—a sphere blank that's been roughed out on the lathe or bandsaw—is mounted to the inner frame with screws through the sides opposite the pivots. The screws act as axles to allow the workpiece to rotate. When everything's ready, the workpiece is rotated carefully by hand over a spinning round-nose bit. The inner frame is pivoted as well, and a series of passes is taken, with the bit raised slightly each time, until the sphere's surface is smooth. Notches cut out of the inner frame adjacent to the sphere's axles allow the corebox bit to cut close to the sphere's axes (a small area next to the top and bottom must be cleaned up by hand). The bit is raised on subsequent passes, until the sphere's surface is reasonably smooth.

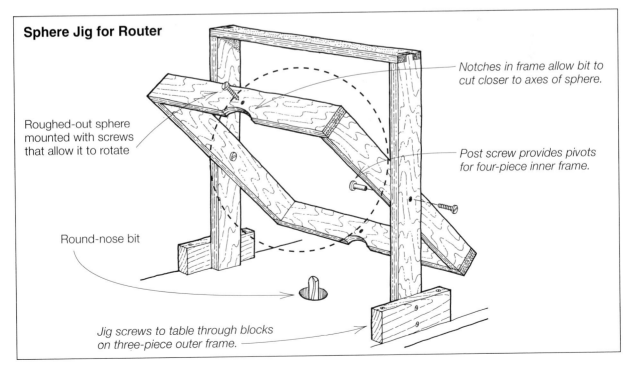

Sphere Jig for Router

Roughed-out sphere mounted with screws that allow it to rotate

Round-nose bit

Jig screws to table through blocks on three-piece outer frame.

Notches in frame allow bit to cut closer to axes of sphere.

Post screw provides pivots for four-piece inner frame.

CHAPTER 3
Tables that Support

If you didn't have a dining table, you'd have to eat your dinner out of your lap. Without a table to support a board or a plywood part, most stationary machines wouldn't be much different from portable power tools used freehand. Fortunately, practically all stationary machines have some sort of table to keep the work level and in a flat plane. But what if you want to bevel the edge of a large panel on a tool that doesn't have a tilting arbor? Or if the plank you're straightening the edges of is too long to run over your jointer's tables without wobbling? Or if you need to bore many holes on a drill press, all at different angles? The best way to surmount the shortcomings of stock machine tables is to build your own table jigs that extend the capabilities of your machines. Conversely, table jigs can enable portable power tools to do much of the work of their stationary brethren.

Like other jigs discussed in this book, shop-built tables are important devices that adapt and customize both stationary and portable power tools in your shop to suit your woodworking needs. In this chapter, we'll explore three basic kinds of tables. Auxiliary tables mount atop stationary machines to change the angle of the work surface, hold down workpieces or add amenities, such as miter slots, that a machine table might lack. Accessory tables work in conjunction with stationary machines to extend working surfaces and aid the support and movement of large or long workpieces; they can also funtion as stand-alone

Adding an adjustable tilting top to the drill-press table allows you to bore angled holes or chop angled mortises. This jig (pp. 79-80) features a replaceable backing board to reduce tearout and an adjustable T-slot fence that keeps the workpiece from slipping out of position.

units that serve as versatile hold-downs or control sanding dust. Special tables can transform portable tools into stationary ones and expand their capacities in the bargain. In addition to building some of these tables as presented, you may glean features that can be adapted and incorporated into other types of jigs you build.

Auxiliary Tables

It's often to a woodworker's advantage to fasten an auxiliary table over the top of a machine's table. Auxiliary tables can be built to compensate for shortcomings of the machine. Fixtures, fences and carriages can also be mounted directly to auxiliary tables, allowing complicated jigs to be set up in moments, or the same table can be designed to work with more than one machine. If made large enough, auxiliary tables can also serve to increase the surface area of a machine's table, which yields more stablity when handling large workpieces. And if you make your own shop machines using ready-made arbors or spindles, or build portable power tools into stationary devices such as router tables, you can incorporate many of the ideas described in this section directly into them.

There are dozens of ways to attach auxiliary tables to stationary machinery, from simple C-clamps, screws and bolts to taper pins, latches and toggle clamps. For tops that must be fitted and removed in a hurry, you can easily use a pair of studded hand knobs fitted through holes in the auxiliary table into tapped holes in the machine's cast-iron or aluminum top. If the machine is shop made with a wood or composite-material top, the knobs can lock into threaded inserts. One versatile attachment system employs sliding cleats that lock the table onto the machine with T-bolts riding in T-slots routed into the underside of the auxiliary table; I often incorporate this arrangement into the auxiliary tables I build. For an example, see the cleats used on the miter-slot auxiliary table, shown in the photo on p. 81. For a more detailed account of making these cleats, see pp. 160-162.

Tilting tables

Many stationary machines, such as shapers, drill presses, bandsaws and spindle sanders, don't have tilting arbors or tables to allow you to perform angled work. One solution is to add an auxiliary table to the machine and change the angle of the work relative to the blade, abrasive or bit. Even if your machine tilts, it can be a lot faster to add a tilting table than to readjust the angle of the table to machine one or two parts, then square it back up again.

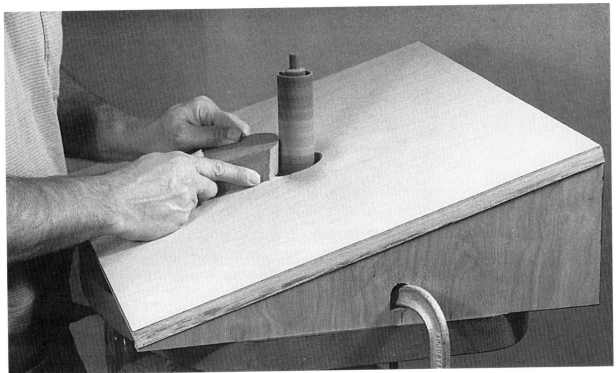

An easy way to add angled working capabilities to a non-tilting-arbor machine is to attach a fixed-angle top to the machine table. Clamped to an oscillating spindle sander, the angled top allows the curved edges of beveled parts to be sanded accurately.

Fixed-angle table   The simplest version of a tilt table, shown in the photo above, is a plywood or MDF top with wedge-shaped sides that rest on the machine table to keep the work at a fixed angle. A cutout can be made in the top to provide clearance for a shaper or router cutter, sanding spindle or blade, as necessary. Notches in the sides allow the top to be clamped to the machine table so it can be quickly fitted and removed as needed.

In situations where the fixed-angle table is clamped with the low end adjacent to a bit or blade, the front edge of the top can be beveled on the underside and fitted to the sides so the surface is closer to the level of the machine table. This is especially important with router tables, since bit length is limited and you don't want to lose too much depth of cut.

Adjustable tilting table   If your angled drilling, sanding or milling jobs are more varied than a fixed-angle table will serve, you may opt for a fully adjustable tilting table, such as the one shown in the drawing on p. 78. This tilting table is capable of angles between 0° (level) and 45° (it could be built to tilt to steeper angles, if you find it necessary). The table can be mounted to a machine of any size, and it's only ¾ in. thick when folded flat. A table like this has many applications. It could be mounted atop the table saw and set to a low angle (about 6° to 10°) for

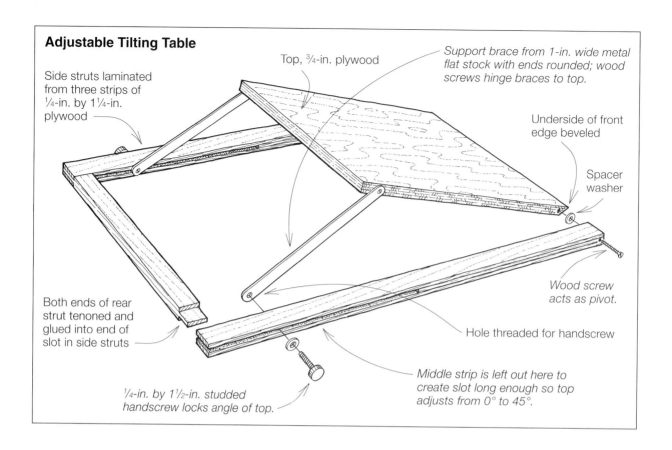

Adjustable Tilting Table

Side struts laminated from three strips of ¼-in. by 1¼-in. plywood

Top, ¾-in. plywood

Support brace from 1-in. wide metal flat stock with ends rounded; wood screws hinge braces to top.

Underside of front edge beveled

Spacer washer

Wood screw acts as pivot.

Both ends of rear strut tenoned and glued into end of slot in side struts

Hole threaded for handscrew

Middle strip is left out here to create slot long enough so top adjusts from 0° to 45°.

¼-in. by 1½-in. studded handscrew locks angle of top.

panel raising with a molding cutter. The tilt table could also be mounted on a stationary disc or belt sander for angled sanding or to a multipurpose joinery machine for routing angled mortises or tenons.

The major components of the adjustable tilting table are the top, two side struts, two braces and a rear strut. The ¾-in. top pivots near the front edge on two long wood screws, which also join the top to the side struts. The underside of the top's front edge is beveled, for clearance when the top is angled. The ¾-in. thick, 1¼-in. wide side struts are laminated from three layers of good quality ¼-in. plywood, such as Baltic birch. The center lamination is shorter than the full length of the strut, to create a slot for the jig's adjustment mechanism. This mechanism sets by means of two 1-in. wide flat iron (steel) or aluminum braces. One end of each brace is screwed to the top through a slightly oversize hole, so it can pivot. The other end has a threaded hole that takes a ¼-in. by 1½-in. long studded handscrew. This handscrew rides in the slot in the side struts. Both ends of the ¾-in. by 1¼-in. rear strut have ¼-in. thick tenons, and the ends of the side-strut laminations are glued to the tenon cheeks, connecting side and rear struts.

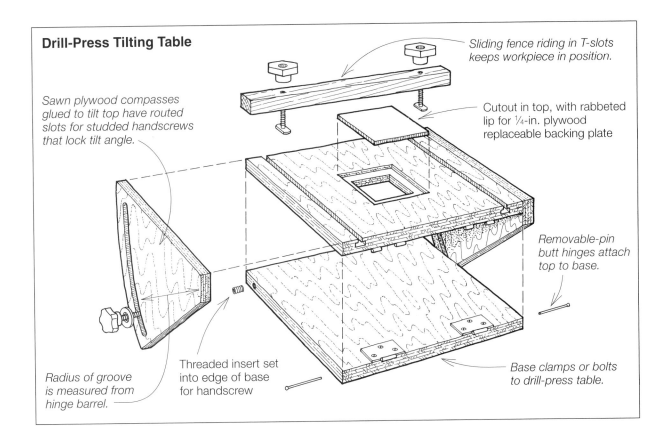

Drill-Press Tilting Table

Sliding fence riding in T-slots keeps workpiece in position.

Sawn plywood compasses glued to tilt top have routed slots for studded handscrews that lock tilt angle.

Cutout in top, with rabbeted lip for ¼-in. plywood replaceable backing plate

Removable-pin butt hinges attach top to base.

Radius of groove is measured from hinge barrel.

Threaded insert set into edge of base for handscrew

Base clamps or bolts to drill-press table.

Drill-press tilting table   Another tilting table I use often, shown in the photo on p. 75, is designed to work on the relatively small table of a drill press for boring angled holes. This sturdy and compact jig could also be used with a vertical mill/drill (a light-duty milling machine) for small-scale shaping jobs. The drill-press tilting table features a replaceable backing plate, which reduces tearout, and an adjustable fence, which keeps parts from slipping out of position during angled drilling.

The jig's components are shown in the drawing above. The top is attached to the base with a pair of removable-pin butt hinges. The base must be large enough to extend beyond the edges of the drill-press table to clear the two quarter-round plywood compasses that are glued and screwed to the edges of the top. Curved slots are routed in the compasses with a radius measured from the barrels of the hinges. Studded handscrews go through the curved slots and into threaded inserts in the edges of the base. The base is clamped or bolted to the machine table. The tilt top is fitted with a backing plate: a square cutout in the center with a rabbeted lip deep enough for a piece of ¼-in. plywood or hardboard. This plate keeps the workpiece from tearing out on the exit side of the hole. The backing plate can be replaced after it has been torn up. At edges of the top are routed a pair of T-slots (see pp. 195-197) that mount a wood fence. This fence has oversize holes for T-bolts and washers, which lock down the fence with hand knobs.

Compound-angle tables   Whenever you have to drill holes or machine joints that are angled along two axes, a compound-angle table is called for. This kind of table has a surface that can be tilted both front to back and side to side. The simplest way to achieve a compound angle is to shim under one of the wedges on a fixed-angle top. If you have a standard compound angle you often work at, you can build a fixed-angle top with one wedge higher than the other to get the desired compound angle. Another possibility is to stack two fixed-angle tables, orienting their slopes perpendicular to one another. The lower top is fastened to the machine in the usual way; the upper is screwed or clamped to the lower.

If you often need to drill holes at odd compound angles, you can build a fully adjustable compound angle table, which is very much like two adjustable tilting tables stacked, as shown in the drawing below. The lower table is built just like the basic adjustable tilting table, except that the ends of the lower top extend ½ in. or so beyond the base to

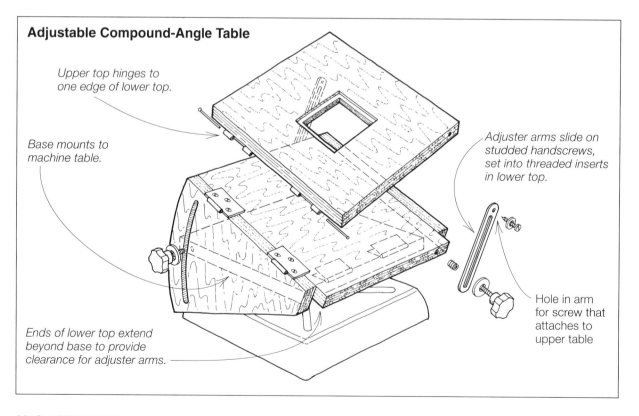

Adjustable Compound-Angle Table

Upper top hinges to one edge of lower top.

Base mounts to machine table.

Adjuster arms slide on studded handscrews, set into threaded inserts in lower top.

Hole in arm for screw that attaches to upper table

Ends of lower top extend beyond base to provide clearance for adjuster arms.

clear the adjuster arms. The jig's base is screwed or clamped to the drill-press table. The top serves as the base for the upper tilting top, whose hinges are mounted on one of the compass edges of the lower top. The tilt of the upper table is set and locked with two sliding adjuster arms, made from a pair of sliding lid supports (available at a hardware store) or machined from $\frac{1}{4}$-in. tempered Masonite. A screw through the hole in the top end of the arm attaches it to the edge of the upper table. A studded handscrew, set into a threaded insert in the lower top, rides in a long slot in the arm, letting you adjust the tilt.

Miter-slot and T-slot tables

To use a miter gauge or other miter-slot-guided carriage or jig on a machine that lacks a slot, such as a drill press or scrollsaw, you can fit an auxiliary table top. The top shown in the photo below is made from $\frac{3}{4}$-in. veneered MDF, with a standard-size $\frac{3}{8}$-in. deep by $\frac{3}{4}$-in. wide slot cut into the top with a dado blade on the table saw. If the slot is accurately machined and well lubricated (with wax or a dry lubricant, such as Sandaro TopCote), the slot will be good enough for occasional use. However, changes in humidity may cause a slot to swell, making the guide bar fit too tightly. Also, composite-wood materials tend to wear quickly, which result in miter-gauge inaccuracy. If the jig will receive a lot of use, I'd recommend routing an oversize slot and inlaying an extruded aluminum miter-gauge track, such as FastTTrack (see Sources of Supply on pp. 224-227), which screws in place and accepts a standard miter-gauge bar. I like this track because it adjusts to the fit of the bar: Screwing it down tighter makes for a tighter bar fit.

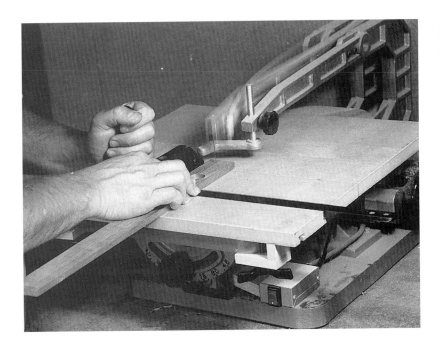

A miter slot can be a useful addition to a scrollsaw or other machine that lacks one, allowing the use of a miter gauge for right-angle crosscuts. The add-on table is mounted with cleats held by T-bolts that slide in a T-slot routed on the underside.

A T-slotted auxiliary table bolted atop a drill-press table provides a convenient means of firmly holding down workpieces during boring. Machinist-style universal clamps that slide in the T-slots are applied where needed.

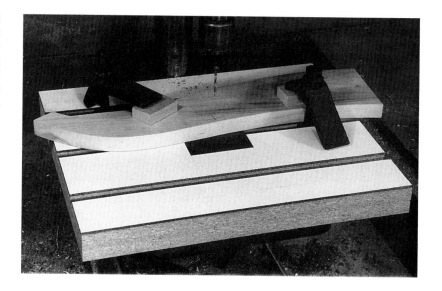

Another kind of slotted table provides a very useful auxiliary top for holding parts down securely on a drill press, horizontal borer or milling machine. The table, shown in the photo above, is made from two layers of ¾-in. MDF with a series of parallel T-slots routed in the top (slots can be perpendicular or arranged as needed). Each slot is routed first with a ⅝-in. dia. straight bit, then with a special wall-groover bit (Eagle America #143-1705) and is sized to accept the base of a machinist's universal adjustable clamp (see Sources of Supply on pp. 224-227). Clamps slide in the slots and are tightened with a wrench wherever needed. The replaceable backing plate—a piece of thin Masonite set into a lipped cutout in the middle of the table—can be changed when it's torn up from drilling or milling operations.

Dedicated jig tables

If there is a particular operation that you often perform on a stationary machine that requires a lengthy setup, you can save time by permanently mounting the jig on an auxiliary table top. Dedicated jig tables can be outfitted with all manner of different components, such as fences, positioning blocks, hold-down clamps, pivoting arms, dust collection and more. For example, if you have 100 chair parts and each needs an angled hole drilled in exactly the same spot, a simple fixture that accurately positions the part and clamps it down mounted to an auxiliary table attached to the drill-press table allows the operation to be done accurately now and repeated if you need 100 more parts a month from now.

I often mount a dedicated jig table to my router table that's set up with a pair of pivoting arms that provide a means to cut the slots for plate-joinery biscuits. I've used this system for slotting members joined with

Setting up a complicated jig on a machine table can be time-consuming. An alternative is mount the jig on a dedicated auxiliary table, then just screw or clamp it to the machine when needed. This biscuit-joinery jig table, complete with built-in dust collection, easily mounts to a small router table with four screws.

Auxiliary Table for Biscuit Joinery

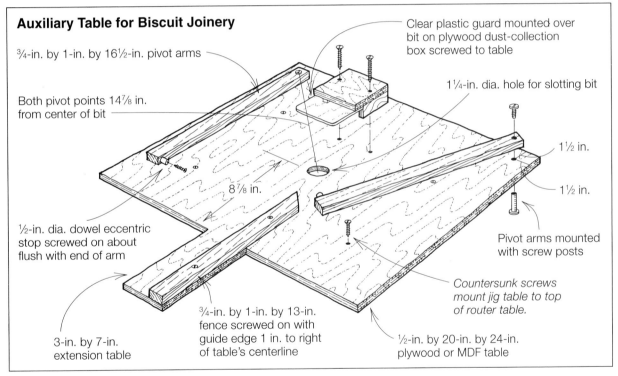

¾-in. by 1-in. by 16½-in. pivot arms

Both pivot points 14⅞ in. from center of bit

½-in. dia. dowel eccentric stop screwed on about flush with end of arm

3-in. by 7-in. extension table

¾-in. by 1-in. by 13-in. fence screwed on with guide edge 1 in. to right of table's centerline

Clear plastic guard mounted over bit on plywood dust-collection box screwed to table

1¼-in. dia. hole for slotting bit

1½ in.

1½ in.

Pivot arms mounted with screw posts

Countersunk screws mount jig table to top of router table.

½-in. by 20-in. by 24-in. plywood or MDF table

8⅞ in.

biscuits and assembled into face frames for cabinets and furniture. The jig table, shown in the photo and drawing above, is dimensioned to work for slotting 2-in. wide frame members to accept Lamello's #11 round biscuits, but dimensions can easily be adapted to work with other stock sizes or biscuit systems, such as Woodhaven's standard compressed composite-material biscuits or Itty Bitty biscuits (special bits are required for each type; see Sources of Supply on pp. 224-227).

The jig consists of a plywood table, which serves as a base for the jig, on top of which are mounted two arms that pivot on screw posts. Each is designed to align and guide a frame stile as it is swung into the bit for slotting the edge near the end; two arms are needed for right-hand and left-hand cuts. An eccentric-cam end stop made from a dowel (see p. 109) provides for positive, yet adjustable positioning for the end of the stile. A small extension table attached to the front of the jig serves as a support for a fence that guides rails into the cutter for slotting their ends. The fence is located so that clockwise-spinning cutter will force the member tighter to the fence. To rout slots in the middle of frame members, the fence and eccentric end stops are removed and pivot arms are used. A clear plastic guard mounted on a plywood dust-collection box (see the photo on p. 221) prevents the fingers from getting nipped as work is pivoted into the bit. The jig table is fixed to the top of the router table with with four countersunk screws.

Vacuum hold-down tables

One of the problems with holding workpieces down during machining is that the clamps take time to attach, and they can get in the way. Clamps have other drawbacks as well: They can mar the surface of the work, and they are difficult to apply to rounded or irregularly shaped workpieces. Auxiliary vacuum air tables secure the work by pulling it down to the table with suction created by either a vacuum pump or a venturi vacuum device powered by compressed air (vacuum hold-down system design and hardware are discussed more fully on pp. 167-169). The table top, made from plastic-laminate-covered MDF, is drilled and threaded to accept a pipe fitting that mates to a vacuum hose connected to the suction device. A special seal tape (available from Woodhaven or Vacuum Pressing Systems) or closed-cell foam weatherstripping is applied in a continous ribbon around the opening slightly smaller than the workpiece. The workpiece is placed on the table and the vacuum is turned on to secure it. After machining, closing the valve cuts off the vacuum and air seeps in, releasing the part.

Vacuum hold-down tables can be made any size and mount easily atop stationary tools. They come in handy for holding parts while performing light machining or boring on the drill press, as shown in the photo at left on the facing page (for drill-press jigs, seal tape must be applied so that holes bored through the part won't release the vacuum prematurely). Vacuum tables also make terrific freestanding tables to secure workpieces for handwork, such as scooping out a seat with a scorp or inshave, routing an edge, sanding and so on. I keep a general-purpose vacuum table on a portable stand in my shop, as shown in the photo at right on the facing page. I set the stand up whenever I have to trim, chamfer or round over the edges of carcase parts, door panels or shelves.

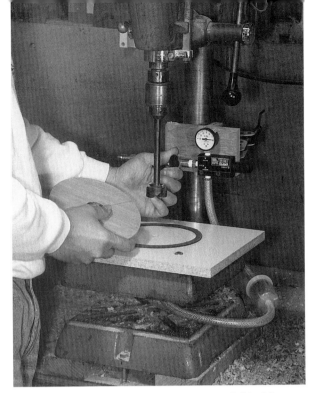

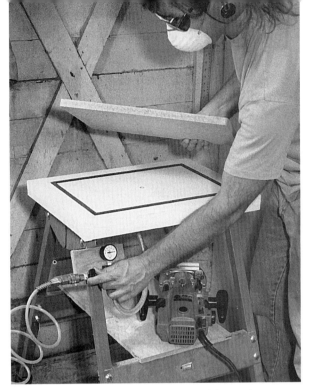

A vacuum valve device creates a powerful hold-down force with compressed air. This vacuum hold-down jig mounts on the drill-press table and secures round clock backs for boring. The Forstner bit doesn't bore all the way through, which would release the vacuum.

A freestanding vacuum table can hold panels or carcase parts during machining and is a versatile addition to any shop. The plastic-laminate covered table and vacuum-valve device have been mounted to a powered-miter-saw stand.

Glue-up tables

Regardless of whether you build cabinets, furniture or musical instruments, clamping up and gluing parts can be an odious task. Clamps take time and bother to position, and excess glue seems to get all over everything. But an auxiliary table top designed specifically for handling glue-ups can make the job neater and more efficient. First, the auxiliary top can be made to fit over your regular workbench. Make the top slightly larger than your bench and add cleats to the bottom near the edge to keep it in place during glue-up. Covering the top with plastic laminate makes it easier to clean off glue drips. To make clamping easier, the top can be fitted with all manner of devices and fixtures: mounting brackets for attaching bar or pipe clamps, holes for fitting bench dogs, Veritas Wonder Dogs or Vise Grip hold-downs, T-slots for cleats, quick-release toggle clamps, and so on (for more on clamping fixtures, see pp. 173-175). In a large production shop, you may wish to build a freestanding accessory table for glue-up. For face-frame glue-up, attach the table to a stand that allows the top to tilt up, like a drafting table. Set near a wall, a tilted table will take up less room and be easier to reach across to clamp parts in place.

Accessory Tables

Accessory tables work in conjunction with machine tools to perform a wide range of necessary duties, such as supporting workpieces ahead of and after machining, making the handling of large workpieces easier, removing chips and more. Other accessory tables, such as the rotary turntable, can be used as freestanding devices. These don't work directly with a machine but they do serve to speed up production efficiency and generally make life easier around the shop.

Extension tables

As certain jigs and devices are built and added to machine tools to extend their abilities, so extension tables must occasionally be added to enhance those capacities. Such tables are most often necessary when machining long stock, which involves attaching support tables on the outfeed and/or infeed sides of a machine or jig setup or when supporting large workpieces, which involves adding support tables alongside the machine. Many outfeed and infeed tables are little more than plywood or particleboard tops with legs or support brackets. Large-surface extensions, however, will benefit from torsion-box type construction, which is described in detail on pp. 202-203. In addition to lending rigidity and keeping critical support surfaces flat, the hollowness of a torsion box could lend itself quite nicely to incorporating air-gliding or vacuum hold-down features (see pp. 90-93).

Sometimes an extension table needn't be a real table at all: Rollers mouted to brackets hung off the machine or mounted to independent floor stands are often employed to support long boards on a planer, jointer or radial-arm saw. Such devices take up less room than an actual table does. When I crosscut full sheets of plywood on the table saw, I often use a support beam mounted to the left of the saw table, as shown in the photo on the facing page. Besides supporting heavy sheet goods, the beam keeps the overhanging end of the sheet from deflecting and ruining the accuracy of the cut. I mounted two pairs of captured-ball style glides called Handy Rollers (some woodworkers prefer ball-bearing work rollers; see Sources of Supply on pp. 224-227) atop the beam to reduce friction and keep the workpiece gliding smoothly and with less effort. By supporting the beam with a pair of removable plywood sawhorses, the setup could be made both free-standing and easily collapsable for storage when it's not needed.

The difficult task of cutting large panels into manageable sizes on a table saw can be made easier with a roller beam: a long 4x4 post supported at saw-table level with legs. The top is fitted with commercially available roller-ball devices.

In small shops where space is at a premium, a basic extension table can do double duty as a router table. Woodworkers often mount their routers in the extension table to the right of the blade on a table saw. A cutout and rabbeted ledge in the extension provide a mount for the router, which bolts to a removable insert plate that replaces its sub-base. Besides saving the space a separate router table would occupy, a saw-extension router table can take advantage of the saw's adjustable rip fence. Also, sliding carriages made to work with the table saw can be designed to function with the extension router table as well.

Fence-hung extensions Sometimes it's practical to add extensions directly to a fence, instead of a machine table. For example, adding a longer fence to a powered miter box (chop box) provides a good opportunity to fit rudimentary extension tables as well, as shown in the photo on p. 88. The extensions are simply ½-in. plywood strips screwed to the bottom of a plywood fence bar, which is bolted to the tool's built-in fence. While the setup shown has only narrow support surfaces designed for small stock and moldings, a heftier version could

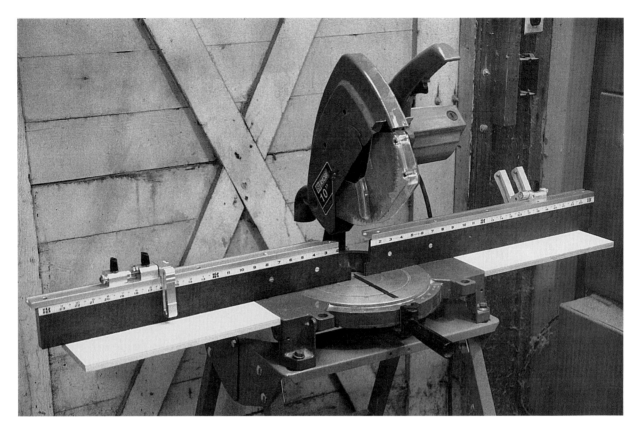

Extension tables can sometimes be attached directly to the fence of a portable power tool, such as this power miter box. The tool shown here has simple plywood tables, each screwed directly to the underside of a 24-in. long fence bar. A FasTTrack stop system mounted on the fences makes it easier to cut short parts to precise lengths.

be fabricated to handle beefier lumber. Another example of extensions attached directly to a jig is the rip-fence extension with built-in infeed and outfeed tables shown on p. 17. Similarly, a pair of narrow tables or rollers held by brackets (see Sources of Supply on pp. 224-227) on either side of the base of a mortising jig, radial-arm saw or drill-press boring jig helps keep long workpieces level and eases the process of sliding a workpiece side to side.

Sliding tables

Looking like an upside-down version of a rail-guided sliding carriage, a sliding table can make it a lot easier to move a large plank or panel in a straight line past a cutter or blade. Sliding tables can be used as extension or support tables in conjunction with table saws, shapers, router tables, stationary sanders, horizontal borers and bandsaws. Most commercially made sliding tables work with guide rails and bearings of some kind for smooth, low-friction operation. This arrangement not only ensures a straighter cut on a large panels, but also requires less muscle power to propel heavy workpieces through a cut.

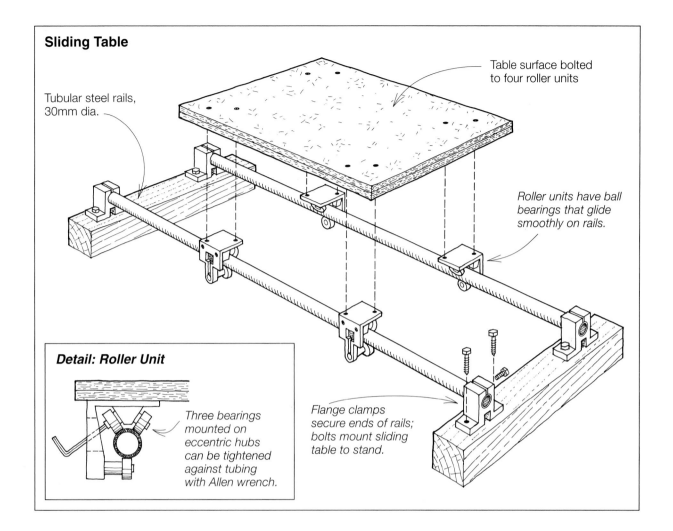

Sliding Table

Table surface bolted to four roller units

Tubular steel rails, 30mm dia.

Roller units have ball bearings that glide smoothly on rails.

Detail: Roller Unit

Three bearings mounted on eccentric hubs can be tightened against tubing with Allen wrench.

Flange clamps secure ends of rails; bolts mount sliding table to stand.

An alternative to buying an expensive sliding table is to build your own, but this can become a very complicated and ambitious project. Fortunately, while I was writing this book, I discovered some stock hardware available from RK Industries (see Sources of Supply on pp. 224-227) that simplifies the process somewhat. While a sliding table is still an involved project to build, you can tailor its size and design to suit your own needs. You could even mount two sliding tables, one atop the other, for an X/Y style table for horizontal mortising. The table shown in the drawing above is built with two tubular steel rails on which ride four ball-bearing roller units, two on each rail. Each roller unit has three ball bearings that capture the rail (see the detail drawing above) on three sides. To ensure accuracy and smoothness in sliding, each bearing is mounted on an eccentric hub. All it takes to adjust the tightness of bearings against the tubing is a few minutes and an Allen wrench. A table top, made of wood or metal, bolts atop the roller units. Special bases, called flange clamps, capture the ends of the rails, securing them and providing mounting holes to bolt down the sliding-table assembly. You'll probably want to add an adjustable fence to your sliding table; many commercial tables use a pivoting fence similar to the one described on pp. 15-16.

To mount the sliding table next to a stationary machine, you might need to cobble up a separate stand from plywood and lumber. Adding leveling feet (see Sources of Supply on pp. 224-227) to the bottom of this stand is a must, since for best operation, the surface of the sliding table must be brought into plane with the machine table (ideally, both should be level as well). To bolster stability, you'll also want to add weight to the stand—concrete blocks or bricks are good—as close to the bottom as possible to keep the center of gravity low. If your machine bolts to its own stand, it might be possible to add an extension to it, and bolt the sliding table to that. In this case, shims inserted beneath the mounting flanges will level the rails and sliding table.

Air tables

An elegant way of getting a flat workpiece to move across a table with very little effort is to have it glide on a cushion of air. An air table uses pressurized air blown through a series of holes drilled through the tabletop to create a cushion of air between the top and the workpiece. This thin layer of air allows even large panels to glide with very little effort as they are pushed against a fence and by a cutter or bit.

Air tables can be mounted next to any large machine, and they work well as infeed and outfeed tables. You can also build an air table as an auxiliary top or as a stand-alone unit to ease the task of moving panels around between work stations. A stand-alone unit is a great help in a large shop that uses the European system of flat panel processing for building 32mm cabinets. I call the air table used in my shop an "air beam." It's a narrow table 1 ft. wide by 5 ft. long that I can use next to my table saw or jointer in lieu of a sliding table or support rail. Next to the jointer, as shown in the photo on the facing page, the air beam allows large, unwieldy panels to be rabbeted with added stability and with less call for sheer muscle power.

Like most jigs, air tables can be built in a variety of ways to suit your needs. The air table shown in the top drawing on p. 93 is basically a hollow box with a laminate-covered top, built similar to a torsion box, with an inlet port for attaching a hose connected to a shop vacuum's blower outlet. The air holes drilled through this top are evenly spaced on a 2-in. grid, but holes can be spaced anywhere from $1\frac{1}{2}$ in. to $2\frac{1}{2}$ in. apart (the smaller the table, the closer the spacing). The diameter of the holes depends on many factors—size of the table, number of holes,

You don't have to be Arnold Schwartzenegger to manage wide, cumbersome panels or boards, if you have an air table. Here, as woodworker Ann Gibb rabbets the edge of a carcase on the jointer, the air table both supports the work and reduces the effort needed to feed the panel.

available air pressure and surface area and weight of the stock—but fortunately, hole diameter doesn't seem too critical to the serviceable operation of the table. I suggest first drilling holes that are $3/32$ in. or $1/8$ in. in diameter and trying the table; you might need to enlarge some or all of the holes, especially those that are farthest from the air inlet. Internal crossmembers to support the top in the center of the box should be located so they won't block any holes; they should also be notched or drilled out to allow air to pass from one chamber to another.

The sides and ends of the air table should be carefully fitted and glued to the top and bottom to ensure tight-fitting seams and prevent air leaks, which reduce efficiency. The port for the air inlet is bored in the bottom or side of the box in as central a location as possible. The end connector on a typical $2\frac{1}{2}$-in. flexible shop-vacuum hose requires a $2\frac{1}{4}$-in. to $2\frac{5}{16}$-in. dia. hole to attach snugly. For an air source, I use a Sears 16-gal. shop vacuum that claims 2.75 peak horsepower. I've actually used this vacuum to pressurize the air table and collect dust from the table saw at the same time. But the double duty puts quite a strain on the motor. You could also plumb in compressed air if you have a shop compressor with high enough cfm (cubic feet per minute) air output.

Shop-vacuum hold-down table

With a couple of simple adaptations, a similar version of the air table described above can be used as a hold-down table. The table is connected to the suction port on a shop vacuum or to the shop's dust-collection system. The part or panel is then set on top of the box, and the air drawn through small holes in the top holds it with surprising force. A sliding valve on the side of the box allows you to control the amount of suction. This is necessary because too much suction will cause the shop vacuum to strain and possibly overheat. (Sears now makes a variable-speed shop vacuum, which perhaps can be used without a suction valve.)

Start with a hollow box constructed just like the air table shown in the top drawing on the facing page, but sized to suit your needs. Add the air valve, shown in the bottom drawing on the facing page, by cutting a $\frac{3}{4}$-in. wide, 2-in. long slot through the side of the box. Two rabbeted strips, sized and positioned to hold a strip of hardboard that acts as the valve's sliding door, are screwed above and below this slot. A small knob screwed to the door acts as a handle.

Clamped to a work table or mounted on its own stand, the shop-vacuum hold-down table is great for temporarily securing parts for edge routing, planing or sanding. Depending on the shape and size of the part, applying seal tape to the top around the perimeter of the part as well as covering unsealed holes helps improve the hold. After each part is done, sliding the valve open releases the suction and frees the part. As handy as this is, don't expect this hold-down table to perform as well as the vacuum hold-down table described on p. 84. Parts smaller than about 10 sq. in. probably won't be held at all.

Air Table

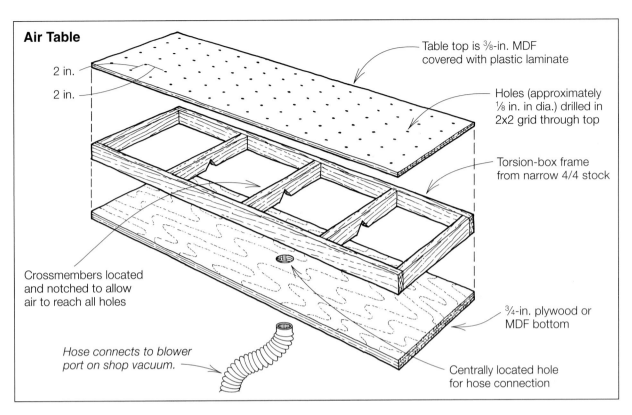

2 in.

2 in.

Table top is ³⁄₈-in. MDF covered with plastic laminate

Holes (approximately ¹⁄₈ in. in dia.) drilled in 2x2 grid through top

Torsion-box frame from narrow 4/4 stock

Crossmembers located and notched to allow air to reach all holes

¾-in. plywood or MDF bottom

Hose connects to blower port on shop vacuum.

Centrally located hole for hose connection

Shop-Vacuum Hold-Down Table

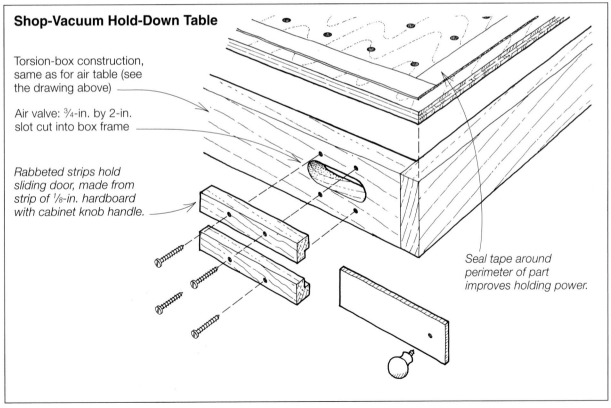

Torsion-box construction, same as for air table (see the drawing above)

Air valve: ¾-in. by 2-in. slot cut into box frame

Rabbeted strips hold sliding door, made from strip of ¹⁄₈-in. hardboard with cabinet knob handle.

Seal tape around perimeter of part improves holding power.

Dust-collecting tables

One of the bugaboos of woodworking is dealing with the mounds of chips and sawdust most machine tools generate. But you can build an accessory table that, with the help of a shop vacuum, will help keep things cleaner around the shop. A dust-collecting table is a thin, hollow box that connects to the vacuum (or dust-collection system) and draws dust through slits or holes in the top. Used as a stand-alone device, as shown in the drawing below, a dust-collecting table can become a sanding work station. In this case, the top of the table consists of close-spaced, narrow wood slats covered with strips of scrap carpet. As the part sitting on the table is sanded with a portable electric sander, the vacuum sucks dust down through the slits and away from your lungs.

I saw another variation on this theme in the Salem, Oregon, workshop of Paul Silke, who cleverly turned the extension tables on his radial-arm saw into dust-collecting devices. These were constructed similarly to the dust collection table described above, only with strips of straight, solid wood instead of slats and with no carpeting, so stock can glide back and forth as it is positioned for crosscutting. I've also seen router-table tops that were slatted for dust collection.

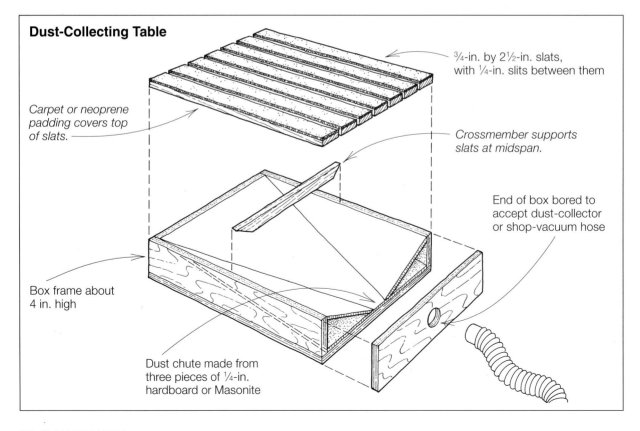

Dust-Collecting Table

¾-in. by 2½-in. slats, with ¼-in. slits between them

Carpet or neoprene padding covers top of slats.

Crossmember supports slats at midspan.

End of box bored to accept dust-collector or shop-vacuum hose

Box frame about 4 in. high

Dust chute made from three pieces of ¼-in. hardboard or Masonite

Rotary turntables

A carver who is sculpting a large block of wood and needs to rotate the model to view it from different angles can benefit from having the model on a turntable. A large turntable can also help a cabinetmaker who is installing hardware or spraying finish on a completed piece of furniture. Further, a production shop can profit from using a rotating worktable to transfer parts between two work stations. Lazy Susan bearings, which are available in many hardware stores and through mail order (see Sources of Supply on pp. 224-227), are good for small turntables up to 2 ft. in diameter. But these bearings are expensive in larger sizes.

Vermont woodworking teacher Richie Starr once showed me how he constructs large turntables, such as the one shown in the drawing below, by using plain glass marbles you can buy at a toy store and three plywood or MDF discs. The top and bottom discs are made from thick material, say ⅝ in. or ¾ in. The bottom sits flat on the floor or bench to support the turntable evenly. The marbles travel around in a sort of bearing cage made by one or several sets of holes arrayed in a circular pattern in a third disc, which is cut slightly smaller in diameter than the other two discs. This cage keeps the marbles from falling out and

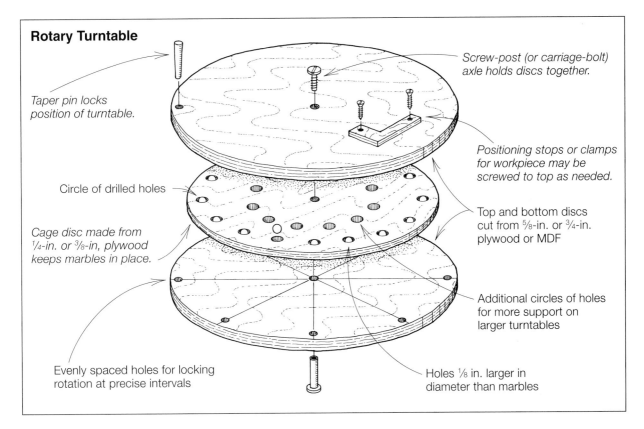

Rotary Turntable

Taper pin locks position of turntable.

Circle of drilled holes

Cage disc made from ¼-in. or ⅜-in. plywood keeps marbles in place.

Evenly spaced holes for locking rotation at precise intervals

Screw-post (or carriage-bolt) axle holds discs together.

Positioning stops or clamps for workpiece may be screwed to top as needed.

Top and bottom discs cut from ⅝-in. or ¾-in. plywood or MDF

Additional circles of holes for more support on larger turntables

Holes ⅛ in. larger in diameter than marbles

One of the biggest problems with portable power tools in general is the amount of noise they generate. Mounting them to a top that's part of a wood cabinet makes things even worse: The vibrating cabinet amplifies the sound of the tool's whirring motor, bearings and power train just as a guitar body acoustically amplifies plucked strings. An easy way to attenuate at least part of the noise is to fasten panels of sound board to the underside of the top and inside surfaces of the cabinet. This light, inexpensive product, made from loosely compressed fibers, is sold in 1/2-in. thick 4x8 sheets at lumberyards and home supply stores. Tacked on with nails or screws, sound board deadens vibrations and reduces reflected sounds remarkably well — a treat for your shopmates and neighbors.

rotates independently of the top disc. The cage disc can be cut from ¼-in. or ⅜-in. plywood—as long as it's thinner than the diameter of the marbles. (For the marbles you can substitute steel ball bearings, which are sometimes available cheap from industrial surplus stores.) The holes for the marbles are drilled anywhere from 3 in. to 8 in. apart, farther if the turntable is very large. These holes should be about ⅛ in. larger in diameter than the marbles to allow them to roll freely. A long screw post or carriage bolt is the axle that keeps the three discs together and rotating smoothly.

For really large platforms (I made one that's 6 ft. in diameter, but there's no reason you couldn't build a turntable that would span the floor of a small shop) you can drill holes for several rows of marbles to support the top in between the outer row and the center. Fixtures and other jig devices can be mounted to the top of the turntable to hold workpieces in place. If you need a lock to keep the turntable from rotating, drill a hole through the top near the edge. A taper pin or spring-loaded stop through this hole can lock into one or more holes drilled in the bottom disc. If you drill the bottom holes at regular intervals, you can accurately index the rotation of the top; for example, you can make it stop at 90° intervals (see the discussion of rotary indexing plates on p. 115).

Tables for Portable Tools

Shop-built tables can transform portable tools into stationary ones, which is both useful and economical if cost or space precludes your having a stationary tool for every purpose. While portable tools don't have the capacity, power or durability of stationary machines, for small tasks or light duties they sometimes fit the bill better than full-size machines. Portable tool tables need not be fancy to be effective, and simple versions can be made by mounting the tool beneath a simple plywood or MDF top. Practically any freestanding cabinet can be converted into a serviceable tool table (my first router table was made from an old mahogany-console television set) that also provides storage for accessories such as miter gauges, bits, stop devices and jigs. Four leveling feet fastened to the bottom of the cabinet will make it stable on uneven floors; adding a switch box, as described in the sidebar on the facing page, makes operation of the power tool easier and safer. Also, if lined with panels of sound board, the cabinet can be useful in reducing the noise from a screaming power tool (see the sidebar at left).

Some portable electric tools, like routers and saber saws, are usually easy to build into tables because they have threaded mounting holes and removable sub-bases, allowing them to be easily mounted on removable insert plates (see the sidebar on p. 98). Routers have built-in mechanisms for adjusting depth of cut as well. These qualities make the router table the most commonly used portable-tool table around— I've rarely walked into a shop that didn't have one. But even if your shop is very well equipped, you should consider constructing tables that outfit other portables, such as circular saws, belt sanders, plate joiners and electric drills for stationary operation. It's not as simple to mount these tools in stationary setups, but it's still possible and worthwhile to do so, especially if you are a woodworker on a budget and want to get the most out of every machine you own.

Router tables

Ideas for constructing a router table are as diverse as woodworking styles, and there seems to be no shortage of designs. There are router tables that are hinged to walls and supported by locking brackets that swing out of the way when not needed; there are tables that double as extension tables for stationary tools; there are tables that hold three routers at once, creating work stations for three separate production operations, such as coping, sticking and raising parts for panel doors. (There's probably a router table out there mounted through the trunk of a '57 Chevy—I just haven't seen it yet.) Despite the proliferation of concepts, I'd like to add my two bits by offering up a couple of table designs I've found particularly useful in my shop.

Tool-table insert plates perform two important functions. First, they allow you to mount a tool under a top without having to reach or crawl underneath. Second, because they are thinner than the table top itself, you don't lose cutting depth from the bit or blade. But one problem with insert plates that rest on lipped cutouts in a table top is that their edges often aren't perfectly flush with the surrounding top. Hence, the workpiece catches as it's run past the bit or blade, resulting in an uneven cut and/or scorch marks on the wood. One solution is to install screws through holes in the rabbeted lip of the table to level each corner of the plate separately. The screws can be wood screws or machine screws set through threaded inserts and locked with nylon lock nuts. Woodhaven makes a very nice insert-plate leveling kit that includes four plastic adjuster devices and thumbscrews (see Sources of Supply on pp. 224-227).

Another problem with router tables in particular is the size of the bit opening in the insert plate. If it's too small, you can't use large-diameter bits; if it's too big, the workpiece won't be supported close to small-diameter bits. Many manufacturers of router tables offer plates with different-size holes, but it's awfully time-consuming to remount the router whenever you change to significantly larger or smaller bits. An alternative is to make or buy an insert plate that has one or two removable collar-type rings — these are standard items on a shaper. These concentric rings fit into stepped lips, so their surfaces are flush with the plate. Remove one or more when using larger bits; leave them all in place for good support of the workpiece when using smaller bits. You can also machine your own rings or buy a ready-made router insert plate with collars (available from CMT; see Sources of Supply on pp. 224-227).

Quick router table   Many hobbyist woodworkers have only one router in their shops. Most router tables I've seen require that the tool's sub-base be removed so the tool can be mounted to the insert plate that fits into the table top, which is time-consuming. A handy small table that allows a single router to be used freehand, yet then be rapidly fastened to a small top for table-routing duties is shown in the photo at left. My "quick router table" is made from a plywood square with its bottom mortised to accept a rectangular Lexan replacement sub-base on my router. Four studded handscrews set into threaded inserts along two edges of the mortised area allow the sub-base to slide in and then lock in place. I can quickly pop the router in, then clamp this small table to a worktable, take a cut or two, then pop the router out again for freehand duties.

A quick router table can be set up to accept any router fitted with a square or rectangular replacement sub-base (the one shown is made from ¼-in. clear Lexan). The slightly oversize base is attached to the quick table with four studded handscrews and washers, and is left on the router all the time.

Horizontal Router Table with Tilting Top

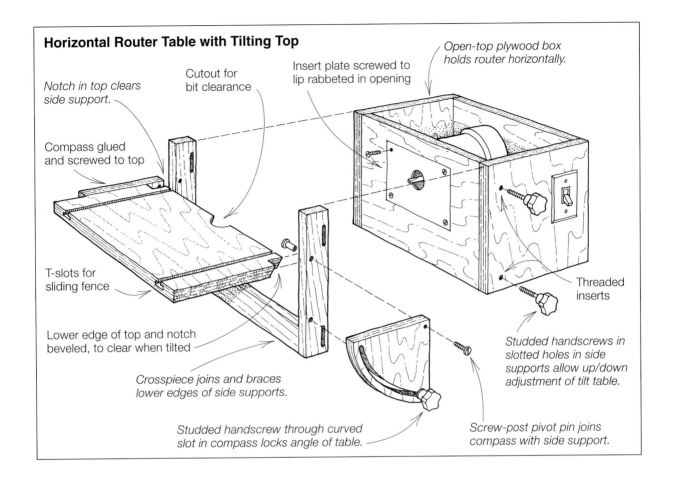

Notch in top clears side support.

Cutout for bit clearance

Insert plate screwed to lip rabbeted in opening

Open-top plywood box holds router horizontally.

Compass glued and screwed to top

T-slots for sliding fence

Lower edge of top and notch beveled, to clear when tilted

Crosspiece joins and braces lower edges of side supports.

Threaded inserts

Studded handscrews in slotted holes in side supports allow up/down adjustment of tilt table.

Studded handscrew through curved slot in compass locks angle of table.

Screw-post pivot pin joins compass with side support.

Horizontal router table Probably the most versatile router table I've ever used is one that mounts the router horizontally instead of vertically and has a tilting top. Besides being useful for router mortising and cutting sliding dovetail joints, a tilting table's great value is that it allows the work to be fed past the bit at an angle other than 90°, so the same bit can be used to create different shapes and profiles. For example, a Roman ogee, usually used to create a decorative shape on the edge of a board, can also be used at an angle (after removing the pilot bearing) to create a decorative profile on a flat surface. And a standard roundover bit can be used at a 45° angle to create an edge with a fingernail profile.

The horizontal router table, shown in the drawing above, mounts a standard router to an insert plate which is screwed to a lipped cutout in a simple open-top plywood box. The tilting top is mounted to the side of the box via two slotted side supports and studded handscrews driven into threaded inserts (T-nuts will also work here). The slots allow the entire table assembly to be raised and lowered to change the relationship of bit to table surface as needed.

The tilting table itself is similar to the drill-press tilting table described on pp. 79-80, with some important differences. First, it has no base or butt hinges; the plywood compasses attached to the table top pivot off of the side supports, using screw posts as hinge pins. The hinge point is directly in line with the edge of the top, so there's very little gap between the top and insert plate regardless of the angle of the table. The top is notched to clear the side supports, and the notches and front edge of the top are beveled to clear the supports and the front of the box when the top tilts. A crosspiece connects the side supports, so they move up and down as a unit. Curved slots in the compass accept studded handscrews that go into threaded inserts in the side supports to lock the table angle. Finally, the top has T-slots routed in it for a sliding fence like the one on the drill-press tilting table.

Belt-sander table

Another very useful portable power-tool table in my shop is the stationary belt-sander table, shown in the drawing on the facing page. The table's top can be adjusted to three different height settings on one side; the other side has a sliding compass and locking-knob assembly, which allows you to make fine adjustments in table height and also lets the table be tilted, as shown in the front elevation. Tipping the table up toward the back end of the sander causes the belt to press the workpiece down during sanding (see the front elevation in the drawing). It also increases the surface area used on the belt when sanding narrow workpieces, which distributes belt wear more evenly.

Built from mostly plywood parts glued and screwed together as shown in the drawing, the moving parts of the belt-sander table are fastened with studded handscrews fitted into threaded inserts. The compasses are made from curved brass lid supports (these are standard hardware-store items). Mounting the tool is one of the fussier parts of the whole setup: To mount my 4x24 Bosch belt sander, I had to cobble up and carefully position several wood blocks that support the sander's heavy frame. The tool is secured by a pair of plywood plates that lock over the hand grips; holes in the plates fit over threaded rods that are pinned into holes in the support blocks. Hand knobs lock the plates down. If you build more than one set of support blocks and lock-down plates, you can use this table with two or more portable power tools, perhaps with a horizontally mounted electric drill, for edge or end drilling for dowel joinery. You could also adapt the table to work with a portable circular saw, transforming it into a small table saw (if you do this, it's essential to add a blade guard). There are a lot of ways to teach an old tool new tricks.

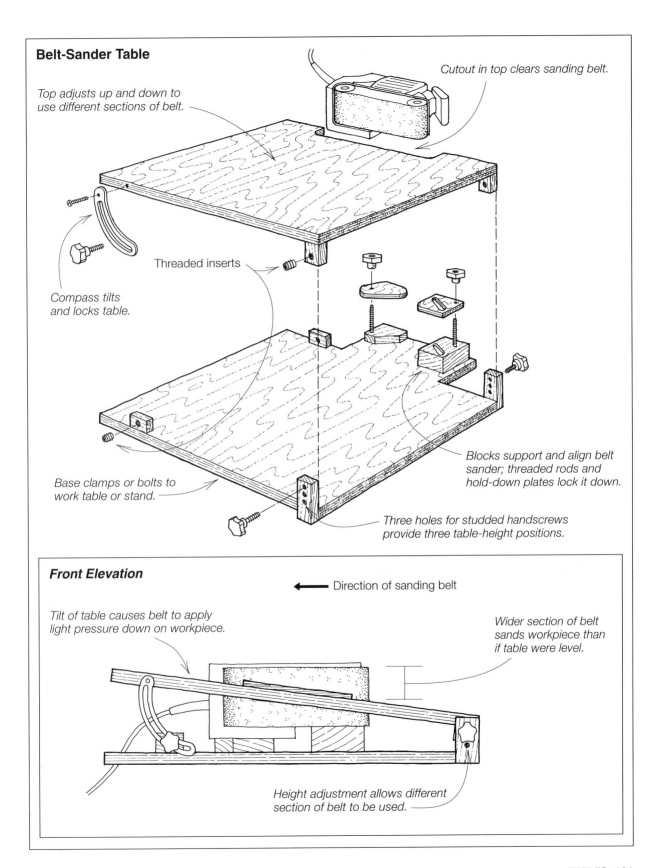

Belt-Sander Table

Top adjusts up and down to use different sections of belt.

Cutout in top clears sanding belt.

Threaded inserts

Compass tilts and locks table.

Base clamps or bolts to work table or stand.

Blocks support and align belt sander; threaded rods and hold-down plates lock it down.

Three holes for studded handscrews provide three table-height positions.

Front Elevation

← Direction of sanding belt

Tilt of table causes belt to apply light pressure down on workpiece.

Wider section of belt sands workpiece than if table were level.

Height adjustment allows different section of belt to be used.

CHAPTER 4
Stops that Set Limits

Most things that we do in our everyday lives have limits imposed on them: the maximum speed you are supposed to travel on the highway; the minimum age you must be in order to buy a bottle of liquor; the most books you can check out of a library at one time. The world of woodworking is no different, except that we call the limits measurements. We strive to maintain the exactness of measurements to make parts fit more precisely together, so the joinery will be strong and look clean. Some measurements are set on our machines and tools, such as the depth of cut of a table saw or hand plane, and some must be regulated by eye, as when chiseling down to a pencil line. But we regulate a great many limits—measurements for the length or width of parts, depth of grooves and holes, etc.—by using stops on our jigs and in conjunction with our tools.

As with other types of jigs and shop-made setups, there are many different kinds of stops to choose from, each appropriate for a particular range of tools and applications. The simplest stops are merely wood blocks, clamped or screwed to the machine, jig or the work itself. More ingenious stops rotate to adjust or incorporate micro-adjusters to fine-tune precise settings. The right stop can increase the accuracy of an operation, as well as save time when making repeat cuts, since parts need not be marked individually. This is why production shops couldn't do without the use of stops.

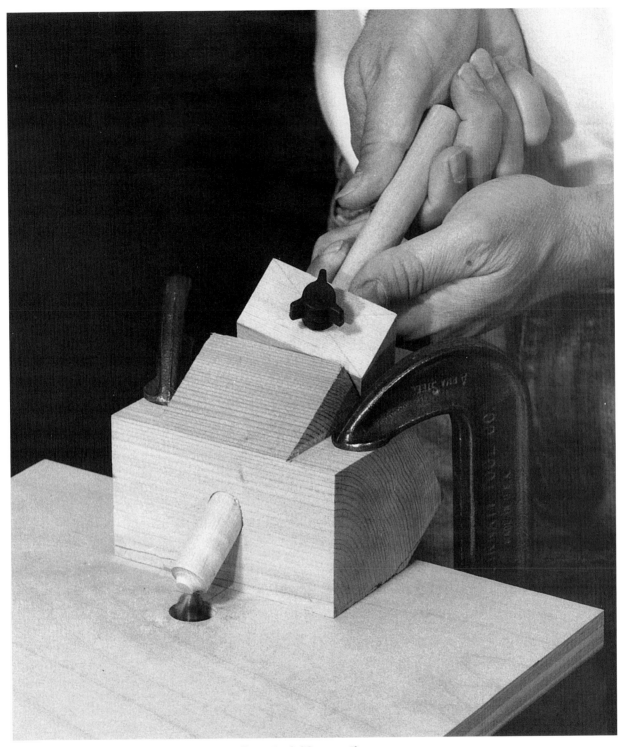

Although stops are usually mounted on a jig or tool, it's sometimes more convenient to attach them directly to the workpiece. The stop collar shown here locks on the shank of a dowel and controls the depth of cut as the end is routed. The collar rubs against a guide block, which aligns the dowel relative to the bit (p. 119).

Length Stops

Regulating the distance between the end of a part and the point where it's cut to length or machined is a basic function of stop devices. The stops discussed in this section are commonly used on radial-arm saws, sliding compound miter saws and both powered miter saws and non-powered (handsaw) miter boxes for crosscutting or dadoing or shaping across the width of stock. But they are easily adapted to work with other machines in a variety of applications. Length stops are welcome additions to fences used with miter gauges, drill presses, mortising machines, sliding crosscut boxes and other sliding carriage jigs.

While the stops described in this section are shop-built, there are several high-quality, commercially produced stop devices on the market, such as the FasTTrack stop system and the micro-adjusting Fastop. Also, the ProScale digital readout can be added to many of the shop-made stops described below. These products are described on pp. 197-201 and cited in Sources of Supply on pp. 224-227.

Adjustable flip-down stops

Probably the most useful kinds of stops for basic crosscutting applications are adjustable flip-down stops. A flip-down stop is more useful than a simple stop block clamped to the fence because it quickly flips out of the way when it's not needed. This allows one end of the workpiece (a frame member, molding, and so on) to be squared up with the stop flipped up. The part is then rotated end for end, and the stop (set and locked in the desired location) is flipped down to cut the part to final length. The two basic types of flip-down stops presented below are illustrated as applied to a radial-arm saw or other crosscuting saw; however, they can be used as adjustable length stops on many other machines as well.

Basic flip-down stop   The flip-down stop shown in the drawing on the facing page will work with just about any wood or metal crosscutting fence and can be set to any measurement, limited only by the length of the fence itself. The channel-shaped body of the stop should be about 6 in to 8 in. long and sized to fit not too snugly over the fence. A threaded insert driven into the back of the channel takes a studded handscrew, which locks the stop to the fence. The flip stop itself attaches to the channel with a wraparound-style cabinet hinge, located so the hinge barrel is behind the front face of the channel (see the end view in the drawing). This keeps the flip stop completely out of the way when it's up. The edge of the channel face and corner of the stop are chamfered to keep sawdust from misaligning the workpiece.

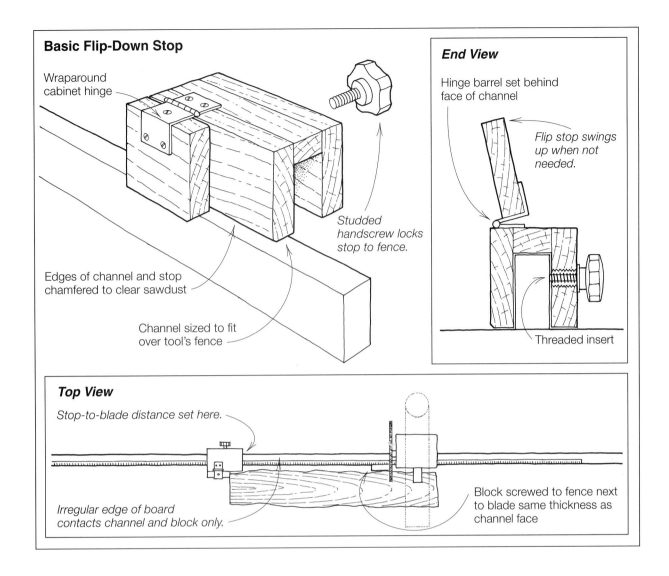

Basic Flip-Down Stop

Wraparound cabinet hinge

Edges of channel and stop chamfered to clear sawdust

Channel sized to fit over tool's fence

Studded handscrew locks stop to fence.

End View

Hinge barrel set behind face of channel

Flip stop swings up when not needed.

Threaded insert

Top View

Stop-to-blade distance set here.

Irregular edge of board contacts channel and block only.

Block screwed to fence next to blade same thickness as channel face

In use, the stock to be cut doesn't actually contact the machine's fence; one end bears against the face of the channel, while the other bears on a short block the same thickness as the channel that is screwed to the fence next to the blade (see the top view in the drawing). This arrangement allows you to cut stock that's bowed and wouldn't set stably against the straight fence. The block near the blade also supports the workpiece next to the kerf to prevent tearout. To use this stop with a stick-on measuring tape, offset the tape's position so that the blade-to-stop distance can be set by aligning the end of the channel with the desired measurement.

Setting a crosscut is a breeze with a flip-down stop. The cursor's crosshair of the T-track-mounted flip stop lines up with the desired measurement on a self-adhesive measuring tape stuck on the fence. The stop flips out of the way when not needed.

Track-mounted flip-down stop Another flip-down stop, shown in the photo above, rides on and locks to a T-slotted track strip. As shown in the drawing on the facing page, this adjustable stop setup has four basic pieces: a track strip with measuring tape, a sliding block, an L-shaped stop, and a cursor with a crosshair that allows very accurate settings. The solid-wood track strip has a T-slot routed in the top side and a stick-on measuring tape pressed on (see pp. 199-200). Flat-head screws through slotted holes routed in the center of the slot mount the track to the top of the tool's fence. These slots allow side-to-side adjustment for calibrating the strip's measuring tape to the blade.

The sliding block has a short tongue that loosely fits the T-slot. A vertical hole through the center of the block mounts the T-bolt and hand knob that lock the stop assembly to the track strip. Another hole drilled lengthwise through the upper rear corner of the block mounts the flip stop via a carriage bolt with a nylon lock nut (a steel nut with a nylon insert that prevents the nut from turning). A fender washer is fitted on the bolt between the sliding block and the flip stop.

The stop itself is made from ¾-in. good-quality plywood, such as Baltic or Finnish birch, cut into an L shape. A notch on the underside of the stop holds a clear plastic cursor, mounted with a small flat-head screw through a countersunk hole (for instructions on making a cursor, see

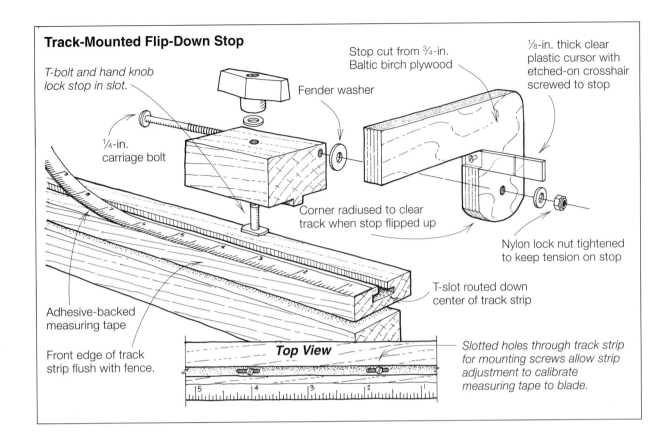

Track-Mounted Flip-Down Stop

T-bolt and hand knob lock stop in slot.

Stop cut from ¾-in. Baltic birch plywood

⅛-in. thick clear plastic cursor with etched-on crosshair screwed to stop

¼-in. carriage bolt

Fender washer

Corner radiused to clear track when stop flipped up

Nylon lock nut tightened to keep tension on stop

T-slot routed down center of track strip

Adhesive-backed measuring tape

Front edge of track strip flush with fence.

Top View

Slotted holes through track strip for mounting screws allow strip adjustment to calibrate measuring tape to blade.

p. 200). Mark and etch the crosshair after the track strip has been installed and calibrated. If you do a lot of dado work or change blades often, additional crosshairs can be added to the cursor to be used with those blades. To adjust the stop for different-thickness sawblades, you can reposition the track strip, or remove the flip stop from the carriage and add shims (I make these from aluminum beer cans with a leather punch) as necessary. You can also make up different stop assemblies, each with a cursor marked to work with different sawblades, molding heads or dado-blade thicknesses.

Multiple flip stops   Because unused flip stops can be set to desired measurements and then flipped out of the way, several flip stops can be set up along the length of the fence. This would be an advantage if, say, you had to cut all the face-frame components for an entire kitchen to length; stops could be set at all the standard measurements and flipped down whenever needed during the course of construction. Because flip stops are fairly easy to make, you may wish to make a half-dozen or more at one time. Cut stock for the channels (simple version) or sliding blocks (T-track version) as you would a length of molding, then slice off individual blocks.

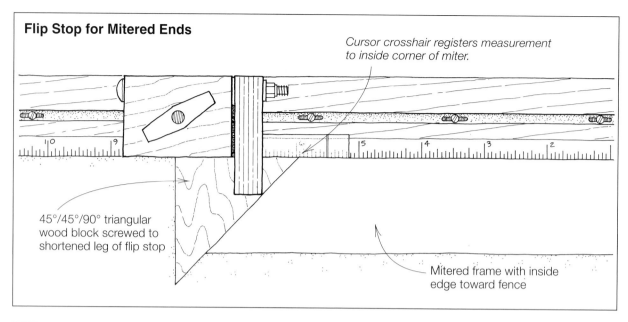

Flip Stop for Mitered Ends

Cursor crosshair registers measurement to inside corner of miter.

45°/45°/90° triangular wood block screwed to shortened leg of flip stop

Mitered frame with inside edge toward fence

This flip stop has been fitted with a 45° block that matches the cut ends of mitered frames and moldings. The stop's cursor is set to show the distance between the inside corner of the miter butted up to the stop and the miter created when the member is cut to final length.

Flip stop for mitered ends Both the basic and the track-mounted flip stop can be modified to handle boards with mitered ends. If wide picture-frame molding is mitered and the width of a standard stop doesn't catch the tip of the miter, simply make the face of the stop wider. Alternatively, when making picture frames, it's sometimes desirable to measure distances relative to the inside edge of the frame molding or rabbet in the back of the molding. As shown in the drawing above, a shortened flip stop with a 45° triangular block screwed on handles this situation. A longer cursor must be fitted and etched to register the position the inside edge of the molding butts up to, relative to the blade.

Eccentric end stop

Sometimes you need to position a workpiece along a fence in a fixed position, but in a way that allows some fine tuning. A simple device that provides a firm stop, yet allows for a limited amount of adjustment, is the eccentric end stop, shown in the photo at right. I use these on the ends of the pivot arms on my dedicated plate-joinery slotting table (see pp. 82-84) and they are extremely quick to make. First, cut a short length of dowel with a diameter that suits the application. For a small jig, a ½-in. dia. dowel is about right; for larger jigs—or to yield a greater amount of adjustability—use a 1-in., 1½-in. or larger diameter dowel. Now drill a hole through the dowel lengthwise that's equidistant between the center and edge. A round-head wood screw through this offset hole mounts the stop to the jig. To make fine adjustments to the stop's position, loosen the screw and rotate the dowel, then lock it in place. You can employ this same principle with even larger stops: Drill an off-center hole in a sawn-out plywood disc and screw it down where an adjustable stop is needed. Eccentric motion can also be put to good use for adjusting stops and other jig parts with micro-adjusters, discussed in the sidebar on p. 111.

Rotating stop

There are cases when you need to cut, rout or drill two, three or four grooves, shapes or holes that are closely spaced, but at a fixed distance from the end of a workpiece. A handy device for this is the rotating end stop, such as the one shown in the photo below. This stop mounts easily to any fence, carriage, or table and can be rotated and locked in any of four positions. Each position provides a different spacing between the end of the workpiece and the cutter or bit.

An eccentric end stop provides a positive stop along a fence on the end of a pivoting arm or on any type of jig. Fine adjustments can be made by rotating the stop; the off-center hole makes the position of the stop shift slightly. The screw locks it down.

A rotating stop allows you to choose one of four stop positions at a time. When used on a drill-press fence, as shown here, it can set distances between closely spaced holes.

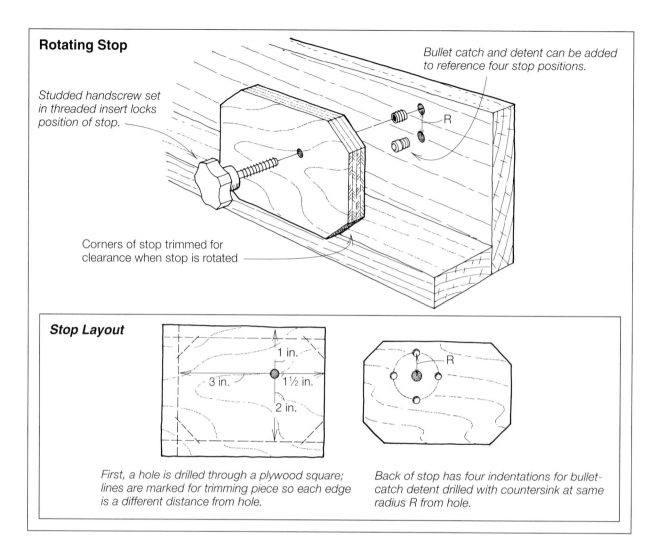

Rotating Stop

Studded handscrew set in threaded insert locks position of stop.

Bullet catch and detent can be added to reference four stop positions.

R

Corners of stop trimmed for clearance when stop is rotated

Stop Layout

1 in.

3 in.

1½ in.

2 in.

R

First, a hole is drilled through a plywood square; lines are marked for trimming piece so each edge is a different distance from hole.

Back of stop has four indentations for bullet-catch detent drilled with countersink at same radius R from hole.

Make the stop by laying out a piece of plywood so that its four sides are each a different distance from a single hole. Start with an oversize piece with a hole marked somewhere in the middle, then use a ruler and a square to mark how the piece must be trimmed (an example is shown in the drawing above). A studded handscrew fits through the hole and into a threaded insert driven into the fence. To allow the fence-mounted stop to clear the jig's base when it is rotated (it's usually too big diagonally to clear) the corners can be cut off, as on the stop in the drawing above and the photo on p. 109. The position of the rotating stop can be set manually, or a bullet-catch detent can be fitted to reference each position (see the explanation of detents on pp. 120-121).

Micro-adjusters

A micro-adjuster provides a highly controllable means for tweaking the position of an adjustable jig part before it is locked in place. Micro-adjusters are great because adjusting components that lock down with hand knobs or nuts and bolts is often an onerous task: After carefully prodding and nudging parts into correct alignment, the act of tightening throws off the setting. Micro-adjusters provide a means of moving the adjustable part in wee increments, then let you physically hold the setting in place while it is locked down.

One simple micro-adjuster, shown in the photo at right, can be used with practically any adjustable fence or jig component that requires fine adjustment over a very limited range. To suit the adjustable veneer-trimming fence shown in the photo, I mounted a 5-in. long adjustment lever at the movable end of the fence. (I made the lever shown from ¼-in. Masonite, but plywood or plastic would also do.) A round-head screw through a pivot hole 1 in. from the tapered end of the lever mounts it to the base of the jig. The tapered end engages a notched ½-in. hole in the fence. The notch is flared slightly, to match the taper in the lever. With the bolt that tightens the fence down loosened, the lever is moved back and forth for fine

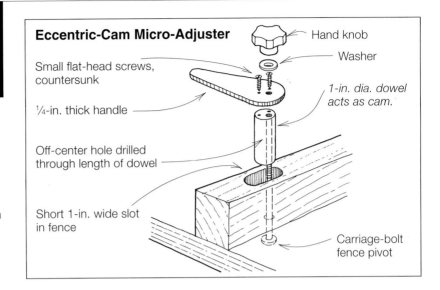

Eccentric-Cam Micro-Adjuster

Hand knob

Washer

Small flat-head screws, countersunk

1-in. dia. dowel acts as cam.

¼-in. thick handle

Off-center hole drilled through length of dowel

Short 1-in. wide slot in fence

Carriage-bolt fence pivot

adjustment. For adjustable fences that must keep parallel to a blade or other part, adjustment levers can be fitted at both ends.

Another versatile micro-adjuster is the eccentric cam adjuster, shown in the drawing above. This device works with the fence's pivot bolt and provides fine adjustment after coarser adjustment has been set at the fence's movable end (see the pivoting fence on pp. 15-16). The adjuster has a small lever handle, made from Masonite or thin plywood, glued and screwed on the end of a 1-in. dia. dowel as long as the fence is tall. An off-center hole drilled through the length of the dowel is sized to accept a carriage bolt, which is the pivot bolt for the fence. The dowel-and-lever assembly sits inside a short slot bored through the fence bar or jig part (the slot allows the dowel some lateral motion as it rotates eccentrically). With the movable end of the fence set and locked,

the lever is turned, rotating the dowel, which acts like a cam to move the fence slightly. A hand knob screwed onto the end of the pivot bolt locks the fine adjustment in place.

A simple micro-adjuster: A lever handle attached to the base of the jig on a pivot screw near its pointed end engages a notch in the end of the fence. With the fence's lock-down bolts loosened, the handle is moved back and forth for fine adjustment.

Adjustable extension stop

Another type of stop that is extremely versatile and can expand the usefulness of a short fence is the adjustable extension stop. It can be used with power miter boxes, handsaw miter boxes, miter gauges, fence jigs and sliding carriages of all kinds. Adding an extension stop lets you accurately cut multiple parts that exceed the length of a jig's or tool's fence, such as the fence on the sliding miter jig shown in the photo below. This extremely simple stop can be made from a length of dowel or steel rod (available at many hardware stores) with a square plywood stop attached perpendicular to it at one end with epoxy and/or screws. The dowel/rod slides in and out of a hole bored into the machine's fence, table, or any suitable part of the jig so long as it is "in line" with the length of the workpiece. A smaller hole intersecting the rod hole is fitted with a threaded insert and studded handscrew to lock in length settings. A simple rotation of the rod moves the plywood stop out of the way when not needed. The length of cut is limited by the rod's length; obviously, longer rods need to be thicker to prevent excessive deflection. For commonly used settings, make a pencil mark where the rod goes into its hole, or add a stop collar, as described on p. 119.

An extension stop provides a positive stop past the end of a fence or table surface, allowing you to cut longer pieces to exact lengths. Here, a hole in the end of the fence on a sliding miter jig accepts a ⅜-in. dia. dowel with a plywood stop plate. A studded handscrew in a threaded insert on the back of the fence locks the stop in position.

Indexing Stops

Indexing devices are ideal for regulating the spacing or centering of holes, cuts, or shapes machined along the surface of a part or around the circumference of a turning. They eliminate the need for tediously marking many evenly spaced positions along the length of a part. For example, one common use for indexing stops is setting the locations of holes for shelf pins on the sides of a bookcase.

Linear indexing stop

If you needed to crosscut a series of dadoes at fixed intervals along the length of a carcase part and the position of the cuts wasn't absolutely critical, the simplest way to get even spacing would be to add an index pin to your fence or table that is the same distance from the blade or bit as the spacing you desire. For an illustration of how this works, see the box-joint jig on pp. 47-48. After each cut, the stock is shifted over and the kerf is fitted over the reference pin. The biggest problem with this setup is that the slightest inaccuracy accumulates with each successive cut.

A more involved, but accurate indexing stop system is shown in the photo below. It works in conjunction with a flip stop to regulate the location of cuts or holes along the length of the work. A spring-loaded catch made from a clothespin mounted to the top of the stop block

To cut or drill at regular intervals, a linear indexing stop is used along with a flip-type stop. The sawtooth-like index strip is mounted behind the flip stop's track. A clothespin locks into the notches on the strip, regulating the distance between cuts or holes.

engages a series of notches in an index strip fastened behind the fence and spaces the holes or cuts as desired. The saw-tooth shape of the notches allow the catch and stop block to slide in one direction and lock in the other. The workpiece is drilled or cut in one spot, then the stop is advanced to the next notch. The entire sequence is repeated until all the holes or cuts are complete.

The index strip is made by carefully laying out a series of shallow (¼-in. to ⅜-in. deep) crosscuts in a 1x2 strip of straight-grained solid wood. Crosscuts are spaced exactly as you wish the indexed holes or cuts to be: They can be equidistant or at whatever intervals you like, say at 1 in., 4 in. and 6½ in. Next, a bandsaw or saber saw is used to cut slanted notches from one crosscut to the next, resulting in a sawtooth pattern. The index strip is then mounted behind the fence, as shown in the drawing below. The spring catch is made from a standard wooden clothespin, with one leg trimmed short. The clothespin is glued and nailed to the top of the sliding stop, positioned as shown. An area underneath the long leg of the catch is routed out to clear the clothespin's spring and allow the catch to work freely.

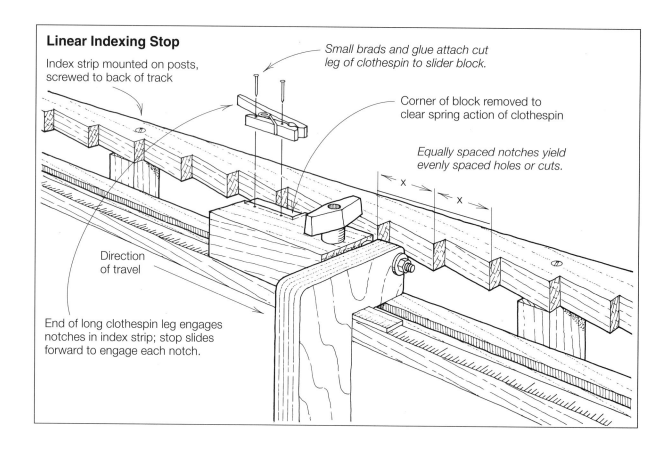

Linear Indexing Stop

Index strip mounted on posts, screwed to back of track

Small brads and glue attach cut leg of clothespin to slider block.

Corner of block removed to clear spring action of clothespin

Equally spaced notches yield evenly spaced holes or cuts.

Direction of travel

End of long clothespin leg engages notches in index strip; stop slides forward to engage each notch.

Rotary indexing plate

While normally a lathe device, index plates can be used with all manner of carriages and jigs for cutting, drilling or shaping parts. With the part mounted between centers in the jig, the index plate keeps the part from rotating, positioning it for operations such as routing evenly spaced flutes or facets. An index plate, such as the one shown in the drawing below, is fundamentally a disc, sawn from plywood or MDF, with a series of evenly spaced holes drilled near its circumference. These can be located at any chosen interval. For example, dividing the disc into eight even segments yields holes placed 45° apart. The disc's diameter can be made to suit the jig, but the larger the diameter of disc, the more precise the intervals will be, since errors in hole location will amount to a smaller percentage of the overall circumference.

The index plate is attached directly to the end of the part or locked on the shaft that holds the workpiece in the jig. A spring-loaded taper pin set through a matching tapered hole in the body of the jig slips into any of the holes in the index plate to lock the position of the workpiece (see the section view in the drawing). The spring is made by tacking one end of a thin strip of oak or ash to a small block. The block is glued to the body of the jig so that the free end of the strip contacts the fat end of the pin. The strip keeps the pin tightly engaged with the index plate, yet it's easily lifted to release the pin and rotate the workpiece.

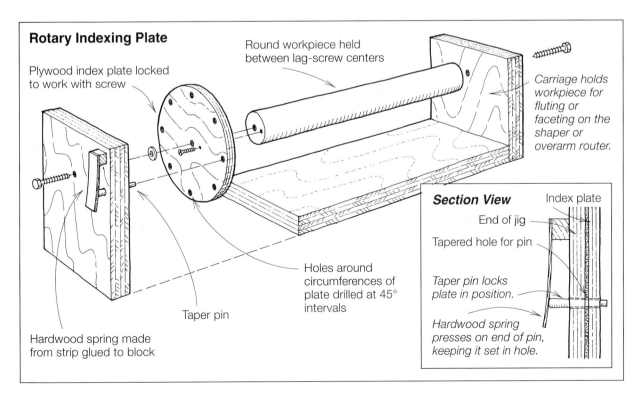

Rotary Indexing Plate

Plywood index plate locked to work with screw

Round workpiece held between lag-screw centers

Carriage holds workpiece for fluting or faceting on the shaper or overarm router.

Holes around circumferences of plate drilled at 45° intervals

Taper pin

Hardwood spring made from strip glued to block

Section View

Index plate

End of jig

Tapered hole for pin

Taper pin locks plate in position.

Hardwood spring presses on end of pin, keeping it set in hole.

Centering stop

It can be frustrating to tinker with fence settings when you're trying to machine a part exactly down the center. A jig made up of a pair of dowels mounted on a base allows you to rout centered grooves with a router table or bore holes with a drill press that are equidistant from the long edges of a workpiece. The advantages of this centering stop, shown in the photo below, is that it's easy to make and works with different stock widths and thicknesses without having to be reset.

In principle, a centering stop works like an inverted version of the router centering sub-base described on p. 37. Two short dowels, maybe $\frac{1}{2}$ in. to 1 in. in diameter, are glued and screwed (from underneath) into holes in a base, which may be part of another jig or an auxiliary table that's fastened to the machine. The dowels can be short or long (for positioning stock on edge) but they must be equidistant from the center of the bit, and on a straight line through the bit center. There are no rules as to how far apart the dowels must be (the dowels in the photo are 14 in. apart) but in general, setting them farther apart allows you to work with wider (or thicker) workpieces. Placing the dowels closer together, however, allows you to rout or drill closer to the end of the workpiece. If you're making the jig for the drill press, add a replaceable backup plate to the center of the base by routing a recess and fitting a scrap of $\frac{1}{4}$-in. plywood or hardboard, as was done on the drill-press tilting table (see pp. 79-80).

Two short dowels set into a base clamped to the drill-press table act as centering stops, which position a long frame member so that holes are drilled along its centerline.

Stops that Limit Travel

Length stops and indexing stops position stationary workpieces so they may be cut, shaped or drilled at precise locations. But many woodworking jigs move the workpiece past the blade or bit. The travel of a part guided along a fence, a carriage sliding on rails or in a miter slot, or the position of a tilting table or an arm pivoting on a jig often needs to be limited to get the results desired. Stops are used with these jigs to regulate the length or depth of saw cuts or holes, the size of mortises or the diameter of round parts.

Stops attached to the fence

Limiting the travel of a workpiece run along the rip fence of a table saw, bandsaw or shaper/router table allows you to cut or shape the work only partway, for half-blind or full-blind rabbets, dadoes and grooves. For example, say you are rabbeting the sides of a box on the table saw but don't want the grooves to show on one end (a half-blind cut). Installing a stop on the rip fence allows you to end the rabbet short of the back end of the part. To cut a full-blind dado or groove, the cut must start beyond the leading end of the part and stop short of the trailing end, a job calling for two stops attached to the fence.

The simplest stops are just blocks clamped to the fence on your machine. But if you do a lot of stopped cutting, you might want to add a sliding rip-fence stop and auxiliary fence, such as the one shown in the photo at right. This system is essentially like the flip-stop system described on pp. 106-107, but with the stop glued and screwed to the sliding block (it doesn't need to flip). One or two stop blocks slide in a T-slot routed into the top of a shop-made wooden fence screwed or clamped to a standard rip fence. The stops are positioned along the fence as needed, then locked in place with T-bolts and hand knobs. Alternatively, you could screw a T-slotted rail to the top of your rip fence, where it could be left in place when not in use. You could also use a ready-made rail-and-stop system, such as FastTrack, described on p. 197.

Two sliding stops, set into a T-slot atop an auxiliary rip fence, allow accurate stopped cuts, such as this rabbet cut on the edge of a box side using a dado blade in the table saw.

Stops attached to the workpiece

In lieu of using sliding stop blocks with a fence or other jig to limit travel, it's sometimes better to attach the stop directly to the workpiece. Such a strategy is called for when a large or long panel that far exceeds the capacity of the rip fence is blind cut. In this case, wood blocks clamped or screwed to the work at the front and/or rear will contact the edges of the machine table to stop the cut at one or both ends of the workpiece.

Stops for carriages

Limiting the travel of a carriage with a stop device has many advantages over doing it manually. For example, adding stops to the rod-type rails of a sliding mortising carriage, such as the one described on pp. 62-63, sets a standard mortise length that the carriage movement will allow, eliminating the need to mark out and oversee the chopping of each mortise individually. Stop collars work very well on rod guides (see the discussion of stop collars on the facing page), one on each side of the carriage to limit its travel in both directions. If you wish to add a more flexible and accurate stop system, a stop bar can be added to the carriage that engages a pair of blocks designed to lock onto the base of the jig below the carriage (see the drawing below). To set an exact amount of carriage movement quickly, you can add a cursor and a scale to the setup, as shown.

Setting the length of travel for a miter-slot-guided carriage will not only allow you to do stopped cuts, but will also make the jig safer by preventing the blade or cutter from exiting from the rear of the jig. A ⅜-in. by ¾-in. wood strip clamped into the miter slot (long enough to reach the edge of the table where it's easier to clamp) acts as a simple stop. Alternatively, many stationary tools have T-shaped slots that accept a miter bar with a safety washer (which keeps the end of the bar from lifting out of the slot). It's easy to make a quick-setting stop that works in these slots, such as the one shown in the drawing on the facing page. Starting with a ⅜-in. by ¾-in. block of hardwood 2½ in. long, drill a ¼-in. dia. hole through the center of the block and press a 10-24

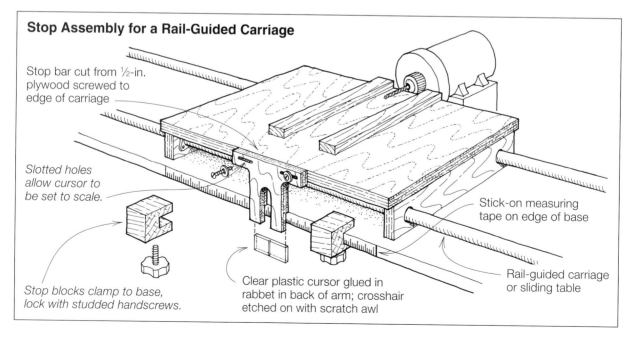

Stop Assembly for a Rail-Guided Carriage

Stop bar cut from ½-in. plywood screwed to edge of carriage

Slotted holes allow cursor to be set to scale.

Stop blocks clamp to base, lock with studded handscrews.

Clear plastic cursor glued in rabbet in back of arm; crosshair etched on with scratch awl

Stick-on measuring tape on edge of base

Rail-guided carriage or sliding table

T-nut into the bottom. Now attach two fender washers (each with an O.D. not exceeding $^{15}/_{16}$ in.) to each end of the bottom of the block with small flat-head screws. Now fit a 10-24, $^3/_4$-in. long studded handscrew into the T-nut through the top of the block. When you slide the stop block into the miter slot, the edges of the washer engage the grooves at the bottom of the miter slot. Position the stop wherever it's needed and gently tighten the handscrew. A longer version of this stop could be used for attaching accessories, such as featherboards and guards, to a machine-table miter slot (see p. 214).

Stop collars

A doughnut-like stop collar is an easy way to limit the travel of any round-rail guided carriage (see pp. 60-62) or sliding table (see pp. 88-90). Round collars fastened directly over the shank of a bit are also perfect for limiting the depth of bored holes, as described below. Stop collars can be sawn or turned from scrap plywood cut like a ring, with a hole that's slightly larger in diameter than the guide rail. A threaded insert installed in the edge of the stop accepts a studded handscrew, which locks the collar on the rail. Commercially made locking collars are also available as drill stops in various diameters.

You can also fasten a stop collar directly to the workpiece itself. Locking the collar to stop the piece against the edge of the jig or machine table will locate the position of the cut. For example, a stop collar locked onto a dowel, positioned for end shaping with a guide block on a router table, limits the depth of shaping done on its end, as shown in the photo on p. 103. A stop collar is also used to set the length of a tenon cut with the sliding V-block carriage described on p. 50. With a scrollsaw or saber saw, you can easily cut out collars that will fit the cross-sectional profile of square, rectangular or geometrical (hexagonal, octagonal, etc.) parts.

Angle stops and detents

Stops built into tilting tables and angled fences are useful because they provide a quick reference to square and commonly used angles, such as 22.5° and 45°. The easiest stops to build into jigs are screw stops that limit the travel of the table or fence at its fully open or fully closed position. For example, see the drawing on p. 120, which shows an adjustable tilting table fitted with screw stops. The 90° stop, a simple wood screw driven into the base, sets the exact distance between the underside of the top and the top of the base to level the top (square it to the bit). A screw stop also allows an angle setting to be fine-tuned, if the jig comes out of adjustment. You can replace the wood screw with a machine screw set into a T-nut in the base, but use a lock nut on the screw to secure the setting. If there isn't enough clearance between base and stop for adjustment, you can mortise the underside of the top slightly.

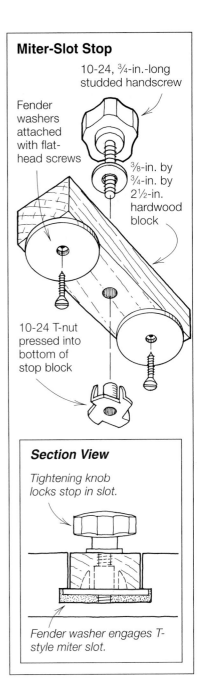

Miter-Slot Stop

10-24, $^3/_4$-in.-long studded handscrew

Fender washers attached with flat-head screws

$^3/_8$-in. by $^3/_4$-in. by $2^1/_2$-in. hardwood block

10-24 T-nut pressed into bottom of stop block

Section View

Tightening knob locks stop in slot.

Fender washer engages T-style miter slot.

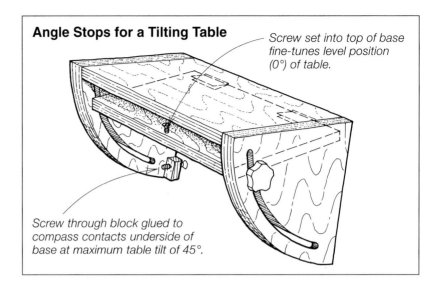

Angle Stops for a Tilting Table

Screw set into top of base fine-tunes level position (0°) of table.

Screw through block glued to compass contacts underside of base at maximum table tilt of 45°.

Another stop screw provides a 45° setting at the other end of the tilting table's travel. This screw is driven through a block that's glued to the inside of the compass; the screw contacts the underside of the base to stop the tilt at exactly 45° (see the drawing above).

Screw-type stops are fine for providing exact settings at the extremes of travel, but what about setting angles in between? One way to reference angles commonly used when cutting mitered joints or crown moldings, such as 35.3° and 31.6°, is to set the table or fence to the desired angle, then drill through the compass and base and fit a taper pin (see p. 194). A even easier-to-use stopping system can be built using detents (pronounced "dee'-tents"). What is a detent? If you have ever adjusted the angle of a power miter saw (chop box), you've heard the little clicks that provide a positive means for quickly finding and accurately setting frequently used angles. These are detents and they work by means of a spring-loaded ball that engages a series of indentations, one for each angle. Once set, the angle is secured by a separate locking device.

A practical way to add a reasonably accurate detent to an adjustable jig is to fit a bullet catch into a stationary part of the jig (usually the base) that clicks into a strike plate set into the adjustable part of the jig (fence, tilt table, etc.) at the desired angle(s). Normally used for latching cabinet doors, a bullet catch has a spring-loaded body that presses into a hole the same diameter as the body; a strike plate with an indent for the bullet mortises into the other component (a shallow hole can also serve as a strike, but it won't be as accurate). For jig detents, I prefer to use brass catches, available from The Woodworker's Store (see Sources of Supply on pp. 224-227), because they are precise and come

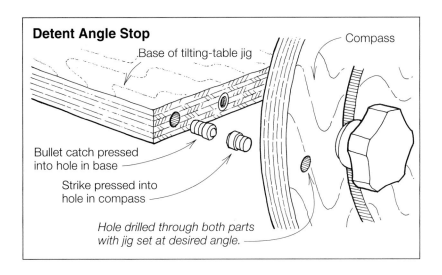

Detent Angle Stop

Base of tilting-table jig

Compass

Bullet catch pressed into hole in base

Strike pressed into hole in compass

Hole drilled through both parts with jig set at desired angle.

with a cylindrical strike that fits in a hole. To fit a detent, using the tilting table as an example (see the drawing above), the jig is first set and locked at the desired angle. A hole is then drilled at 90° through one of the side compasses into the edge of the base. The diameter of this hole should match the diameter of the body of the bullet catch and strike (typically ¼ in. or ⁷⁄₁₆ in.). Holes can be located anywhere on the compass, but the farther from the pivot point of the jig they are, the more accurate they will be (slight errors in placement or catch engagement amount to a lower degree of angular deviation). Since it's very difficult to bore other holes through the compass that match the position of the bullet catch, I recommend using separate holes and bullet catches for subsequent angle detents. Once all the holes are drilled, the tilt table is temporarily removed from the base, the bullet catches are pressed into the base holes and the strikes are pressed into the compass holes (I use an arbor press for this, but a bar clamp with a wood block to protect the catch also works fine). In use, the table is tilted until the catch clicks, then it is locked in place with the handscrews.

Stops for pivoting-arm jigs

The travel of pivoting arms found on jigs such as the pivoting circle jig shown on pp. 64-65) needs to be stopped to control the depth of cut or the regulate the size of parts. If many identical parts are to be made, a simple block screwed to the base of the jig will suffice in stopping the travel of the arm. To set arm travel for several different sizes of parts, a series of holes can be drilled in the jig's base for dowel or taper pin stops. An adjustable stop, such as the compass-style stop (shown on a bandsaw circle jig in the photo at right), will make a pivot-arm jig even more versatile. Such a stop is fully adjustable over a wide range (you can make it as long as necessary), sliding in or out and locking to the desired position to stop the pivot arm's travel. The stop, which

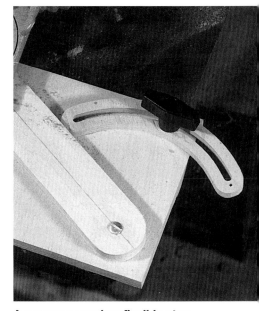

A compass arm is a flexible stop design, useful for limiting the travel of all kinds of swinging or sliding jigs and pivot arms. This compass stop, sawn from ⅜-in. thick plywood, sets the size of discs cut on a bandsaw circle jig. A carriage bolt through the base and hand knob locks the setting.

may be made straight or curved, can be sawn out of just about any strong, stable, thin material: plywood, Masonite, or plastic. Avoid using solid wood though, especially for curved stops. With the stop cut to size, a centered slot is routed. The compass stop can be mounted to the jig's base with a ¼-in. carriage bolt and a hand knob. A washer between the hand knob and the stop will prevent settings from shifting as the hand knob is tightened.

Depth Stops

There are a few strategies for limiting the depth of cut of a drill, hollow-chisel mortising bit or other cutting tool. The simplest jig is a stop block or collar that attaches directly to the tool: A block clamped to a chisel or hand saw will hit the work to prevent the tool from cutting any deeper. For drilling operations, you can make or purchase stop collars that lock onto bits, preventing them from boring any deeper than the collar allows. Stop sleeves are even better insurance against boring too deep of a hole. To make one, choose a dowel at least ⅜ in. larger in diameter than the bit you use, and bore a concentric hole through it lengthwise the same diameter as the bit. Trim the sleeve's length to fit entirely over the chucked bit, allowing only as much of the bit to protrude as the hole should be deep. I use drill sleeves when I mount cleats or other hardware to the underside of tabletops to prevent accidentally plunging through the finished top—an event that can definitely ruin your day.

Depth stop rod

If you're boring holes with a Forstner bit or hole saw that won't accept a stop collar, you can attach the stop to the tool instead. For example, a collar locked onto the neck of a portable hand drill fitted with a sliding stop rod (see the photo at left) will limit drilling depth regardless of the bit that's chucked. The jig consists of a plywood collar with a slit that tightens around the drill with a carriage bolt and wing nut. A lobe on the collar has a hole for a dowel stop rod. Once the stop rod is set and locked in place with a studded handscrew (located to intersect the stop-rod hole), the end of the rod hits the workpiece, preventing the drill from boring any deeper. When working with a stationary machine, you can attach the depth stop to the jig instead of the tool. For instance, a stop block mounted to the fence of a hollow-chisel mortiser can be positioned to contact the chisel housing and limit the penetration of the bit into the workpiece.

Large hole cutters and Forstner bits are difficult to fit with depth stop collars. A jig made from plywood mounted to the neck of an electric hand drill sports a stop rod, which locks in place with a small studded handscrew. Final drilling depth is reached when the end of the rod touches the workpiece.

Plastic fingers on this production spindle-turning jig act as position and depth indicators for grooves turned with a parting tool. The fingers fall through when correct depth of cut is reached, showing that the turning is the right diameter at that location.

Depth and layout jig for multiple turnings

I learned about the stop jig shown in the photo above from Arcata, California, turner Steve Gellman. Although it doesn't actually limit depth of cut, it quickly establishes the location and depth of crucial features on a turning. A jig like this can considerably speed the drudgery of churning out dozens of identical spindles for stairways or furniture. Here's how it works: A simple wooden frame hinged off the back of the lathe holds a dowel rod from which hang a number of short fingers (the ones shown in the photo are made from Lexan plastic, but you could also use wood or aluminum). These "fingers" are positioned to mark the location of crucial elements, such as pummels, coves and beads, along the length of the spindle. Short lengths of PVC tubing act as spacers to keep the fingers in place along the dowel. With the spindle blank turned to a rough cylinder and the fingers riding on the blank, a narrow parting tool is used to cut a groove at each finger. When the proper depth of cut has been reached (meaning the spindle is at the correct diameter there), the finger flips through the groove. After all the grooves are cut and fingers flipped, the spindle is turned to shape.

CHAPTER 5

Templates for Shaped Parts

If you ever helped your mom make sheet cookies during the holidays, you probably used tin cookie cutters to punch out tasty little bells, trees and snowmen. Templates are the cookie cutters of the woodshop: They allow you to produce curved or irregular parts that conform to the original pattern. The most basic templates mimic the shape of the desired part and provide a guide for cutting that part out or trimming a rough-cut part to final size; more sophisticated templates allow perfect inlays or joints between iregularly shaped parts.

In woodshops today, templates are most often used for shaping operations performed with a router or shaper using straight bits and guide bearings, bushings or pins in a process called pattern routing. Templates are also an important part of methods used to create tight-fitting joints such as dovetails, box joints and mortise-and-tenon joints. They also provide a fast and efficient way to mortise recesses for hardware, rout large holes, shape interlocking parts or create intricate designs on the surface of the work. Although templates can be used by themselves, it is often more convenient to incorporate them into some sort of jig or fixture to align and clamp the part as it is shaped. Apart from these shaping applications, templates are also helpful for sawing and sanding pattern parts.

A router fitted with a panel pilot bit creates a pair of complementary templates from the ⅜-in. MDF clamped on top as it follows the master template underneath (pp. 132-134). The ball-bearing piloted router bits in the foreground will be used with the new templates to rout a matching pattern on the edges of the parts to be joined.

Pattern Routing: Three Ways to Guide a Bit

In this book I've generally tried to avoid discussing jigs specifically oriented to only one tool or machine, but in this section the focus will be on template methods for what is perhaps the woodshop's single most versatile tool: the router. Pattern routing is a very powerful and versatile method for making multiple duplicate parts, and worth extensive coverage in this chapter. But before getting into making, mounting and using the templates themselves, let's examine the method used for guiding the bit along the template, since the method chosen affects the way the template is made and used. The three primary guidance methods, illustrated in the drawing on the facing page, are pilot bearings, guide bushings and fixed guide pins. While none of these methods can be used to shape square inside corners, each has advantages that make it better for some applications than for others.

Pilot bearings

A pilot bearing is a sealed ball bearing mounted directly on a router bit. Most woodworkers have used piloted bits without a separate template, with the bearing following the edge of the workpiece itself. Once this edge is established (by sawing, sanding or jointing), the pilot bearing follows it religiously to create a roundover, chamfer, rabbet or other profile. Pilot bearings are also commonly used for pattern routing on the shaper, where they can be mounted on the spindle above or below the cutter. The main disadvantage to using pilot bearings is that ball bearings can foul, especially if the part being routed has been glued up or laminated and excess glue is trimmed by the bit.

Many bit patterns, such as rabbet, roundover and ogee, come as piloted bits. The bearings on these bits are screwed to a small threaded stud on the end of the bit (for clarity, I'll call these end-piloted bits). But almost any standard bit may be piloted as well, with a ball bearing slipped down over the shank of the bit (I'll call these shank-piloted bits). A shank-mounted bearing (which must have the same I.D. as the diameter of the bit's shank) can be left loose—it's essentially trapped between the cutter and router chuck—or secured with a bearing locking collar (see Sources of Supply on pp. 224-227). End- and shank-mounted bearings are shown in the top drawings on the facing page.

Either piloting method can be used to pattern rout the outer contours of parts, but end-piloted bits can't be used for routing inlays or mortises, jobs where the end of the bit doesn't protrude below the work. For these jobs, templates must be mounted above the actual cutter and workpiece. Choosing which side of the workpiece the template is mounted on changes the direction of cut and can affect the smoothness of the cut and the amount of tearout (see the sidebar on p. 128).

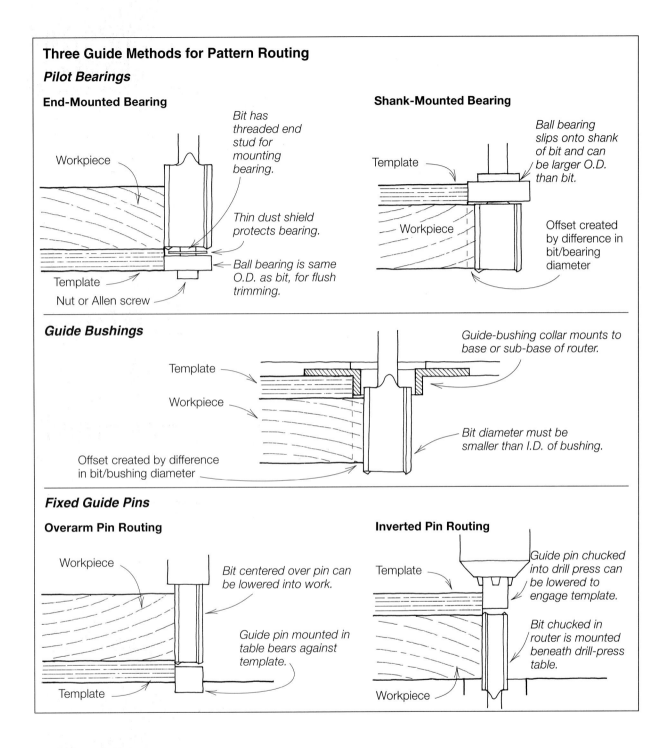

Three Guide Methods for Pattern Routing

Pilot Bearings

End-Mounted Bearing

Workpiece

Bit has threaded end stud for mounting bearing.

Thin dust shield protects bearing.

Ball bearing is same O.D. as bit, for flush trimming.

Template

Nut or Allen screw

Shank-Mounted Bearing

Template

Ball bearing slips onto shank of bit and can be larger O.D. than bit.

Workpiece

Offset created by difference in bit/bearing diameter

Guide Bushings

Template

Workpiece

Offset created by difference in bit/bushing diameter

Guide-bushing collar mounts to base or sub-base of router.

Bit diameter must be smaller than I.D. of bushing.

Fixed Guide Pins

Overarm Pin Routing

Workpiece

Bit centered over pin can be lowered into work.

Guide pin mounted in table bears against template.

Template

Inverted Pin Routing

Template

Guide pin chucked into drill press can be lowered to engage template.

Bit chucked in router is mounted beneath drill-press table.

Workpiece

Straight end-piloted "flush trim" bits are probably the most commonly used bits for pattern routing. These bits have a bearing with the same O.D. as the diameter of the cutter, so they make parts that are exactly the same size as the template. But both shank- and end-piloted bits can

Routing with the Grain

Before attaching a template to any non-symmetrical solid wood part that can be routed either face up or face down, take a moment to consider the direction of the grain in the workpiece. Routers spin at a high rate of speed — 10,000 to 25,000 rpm — and running a router bit with the cutting edge working against the grain can result in a torn-up edge. Areas of short grain can even be split off and thrown by the bit, a hazard to the woodworker. You can sometimes avoid a lot of tearout by flopping the template over and taking the cut so that the bit cuts *with* the grain rather than against it. If you're routing a pattern that requires cutting both with and against the grain, here's a trick to help you avoid excessive edge tearout — the process, shown in the drawing below, is described for a router table, but it can also be done freehand. Use a bit fitted with *both* shank-mounted and end-mounted pilot bearings (both should have the same O.D.). First lower the bit, then set the workpiece "template up" and use the end-mounted bearing to rout the sections that go with the grain. Then flip the assembly over (the template will be on the bottom), raise the bit and use the shank-mounted bearing to guide the remaining work, again routing with the grain.

Avoiding Tearout in a Pattern-Routed Workpiece

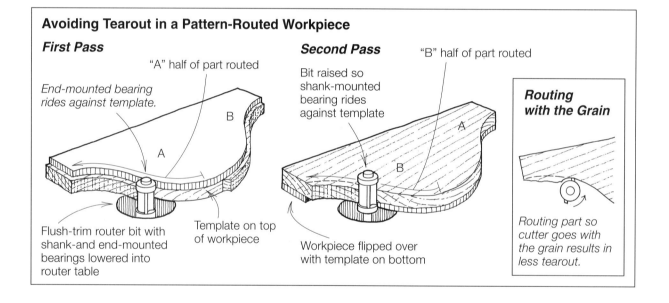

First Pass

"A" half of part routed

End-mounted bearing rides against template.

B

A

Flush-trim router bit with shank-and end-mounted bearings lowered into router table

Template on top of workpiece

Second Pass

"B" half of part routed

Bit raised so shank-mounted bearing rides against template

A

B

Workpiece flipped over with template on bottom

Routing with the Grain

Routing part so cutter goes with the grain results in less tearout.

be fitted with bearings that have an O.D. larger or smaller than the cutting diameter of the bit. Fitting other-size bearings lets you vary the size of the part without changing the template; a larger-diameter bearing produces a larger part, a smaller-diameter bearing a smaller part. Most router-bit sellers offer a wide selection of pilot bearings, some with Delrin or phenolic sleeves to increase their O.D. Although bit/bearing disparity must be carefully considered when sizing templates, there are situations, such as complementary pattern routing (see pp. 132-134), where this difference is used to great advantage.

Guide bushings

Guide bushings, as shown in the drawing on p. 127, mount directly to the base of the router to provide a solid guide that doesn't rotate and can't foul. Guide-bushing systems can be used in many of the same capacities as piloted bits. They are most commonly employed with plunge routers and inside templates used for cutting mortises or finger-style templates for other joints; the bushing contacts the template as the bit is lowered into the work. You can do this with a shank-piloted bit, but it isn't recommended, since you might slip and cut into the template while plunging.

Although guide bushings can be fitted to the insert plate on a router table or shaper, they are most often mounted directly to the router's base or sub-base, concentric with the bit (see the photo on p. 138). Porter-Cable has a standardized system of guide bushings that fit a hole in the router's sub-base; each size bushing slips in and is secured with a threaded ring screwed on from the top. Bosch uses a neat system in its #1613 and #1614 routers: The base has a special built-in holder that quickly locks in different bushings with the flip of a small lever.

Like pilot bearings, guide bushings come with a variety of different outside diameters, ranging typically from $\frac{1}{4}$ in. to $\frac{3}{4}$ in. The biggest limitation to using a guide bushing is that the cutting diameter of the bit must always be smaller than the I.D. of the bushing. This means that you must compensate for bit/bearing offset (see pp. 131-132) even when the shaped part or joint is to be exactly the same size as the template. Further, the template must always be mounted between the workpiece and the router, making guide bushings less versatile than piloted bits.

Fixed guide pins

Guide pins are used in overarm pin routing, a potent technique for the production shaping of parts. An overarm pin router (see the drawing on p. 127) has a guide pin set into its table that follows a template mounted to the bottom of the workpiece; pressing a foot pedal on the machine plunges the spinning bit down from the arm above the workpiece to make the cut. The template can have inside or outside forms as well as complex channels (for routing signs) or highly intricate patterns (for routing maze-like puzzles or inlays). Depending on the routing job, pin size need not correspond to bit size: A $\frac{1}{4}$-in. pin can be used with a $\frac{1}{2}$-in. dia. bit, and so forth.

Unfortunately, few small shops that don't specialize in production work can afford an overarm pin router. An alternative method is to mount a router under the drill-press table and use the drill chuck to hold the guide pin. This method, called inverted pin routing, is shown in the drawing on p. 127 (a kit for converting a standard drill press for inverted pin routing is available from Woodworker's Supply; see Sources of Supply on pp. 224-227). Having the pin on top makes it easier to move the part in the right direction since you can see the pin as it follows the template; however, you can't monitor the quality of the cut. Also, when routing closed forms, such as a lettered sign, you must lower the part down onto the spinning bit as well as lowering the pin to engage the template, which can be tricky.

Templates for Routing

Most templates can be made from any rigid material that can be shaped to a smooth edge. A hard, smooth edge is important because the guide bearing/bushing must ride fluidly along the edge and not hang up. For this reason soft underlayment-grade particleboard and low-grade plywoods likely to have internal voids are not the best template materials. The better materials include medium-density fiberboard (MDF), tempered hardboard (Masonite) and Baltic birch plywood. Many plastics, such as acrylics and solid-surface materials, make excellent, long-wearing templates, but may be more difficult to cut and sand smooth. These materials are discussed more fully on pp. 180-187.

The thickness of templates is typically between $\frac{1}{4}$ in. and $\frac{3}{4}$ in., but your choice will depend on the bit and bearing/bushing combination you use. When using end-piloted bits, the wider the pilot bearing or gap between the bearing and cutter, the thicker the template can be. This is to allow the bearing plenty of purchase on the edge of the template and still have the bit cut through the entire thickness of the work. With shank-piloted bits or with a guide-bushing setup, template thickness should be kept to a minimum so you get the maximum depth of cut from the bit. Also, when edge-routing a part, the farther out toward the end the cutter contacts the work, the more the bit will be subject to deflection.

In designing your template, remember that the radius of the pilot bearing, bushing or pin you plan to use must be equal to or smaller than the smallest radius of inside curves on the template. Otherwise, the guide won't accurately follow the template.

Basic templates

After you've drawn out a pattern for your template and you're ready to cut it out, it's usually faster and more accurate to attach the pattern directly to the template stock, rather than transferring the design with tracing paper. Spray adhesive (available from stationary and art-supply stores) mounts a paper pattern firmly, yet allows it to be peeled off after cutout. If you don't want to cut up your original part drawing, make a photocopy of it and use that. If you have a fairly rigid original part that needs to be duplicated, you can use it as a template to make a production template: Mount the part to the template blank using double-stick tape or adhesive-transfer tape (see pp. 139-140), and use a flush-trim bit to rout the production template out.

When making a template for shaping just one edge of a part or for a part that won't be shaped all the way around, say a curved table leg with one squared end that will join it to its apron, be sure to extend the edge of the template past where the cut will begin and end (see the photo at right). Extending the edge of the template gives the router bearing or bushing a smooth start and finish and results in a cleaner cut at both ends, as well as preventing the bit from accidentally sniping an area you don't wish to shape.

Accounting for offset Making templates for parts that will be shaped with a flush trim bit are easy: You make the template exactly the size of the desired part. But whenever a template is used with a bearing, bushing or guide pin with a diameter different from the cutting diameter of the bit, the size of the template must be adjusted for offset so that the resulting parts will come out to be the desired size.

To help you understand this situation, consider the drawing below. If you attached a 3-in. wide template to a part blank (positioning one edge of the template flush with one edge of the part) and routed with

Templates for parts that aren't shaped all the way around should extend beyond where the shaping starts and ends. This gives a shank-piloted router bit a bearing surface ahead of and after the cut, to prevent sniping on the ends of the part. In this case, the template is attached into the top of the leg with screws through a positioning cleat.

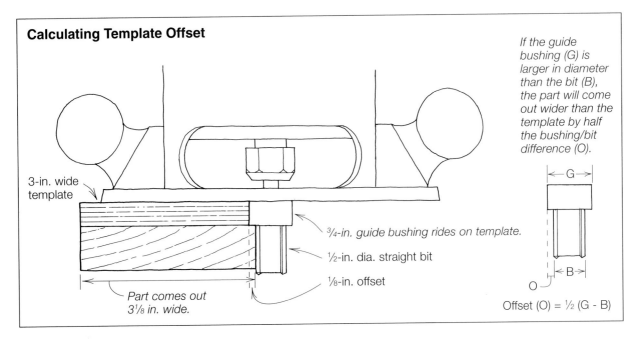

Calculating Template Offset

If the guide bushing (G) is larger in diameter than the bit (B), the part will come out wider than the template by half the bushing/bit difference (O).

3-in. wide template

³⁄₄-in. guide bushing rides on template.

½-in. dia. straight bit

¹⁄₈-in. offset

Part comes out 3¹⁄₈ in. wide.

Offset (O) = ½ (G - B)

a $\frac{1}{2}$-in. dia. straight bit guided by a $\frac{3}{4}$-in. O.D. bushing on the router, the resulting part would be $3\frac{1}{8}$ in. wide. This is because of the $\frac{1}{8}$-in. offset between the bit and the bushing. To yield a 3-in. wide part, the template would need to be $\frac{1}{8}$ in. narrower—$2\frac{7}{8}$ in.—to account for the offset.

The general formula for calculating offset (O) is $O = \frac{1}{2}(G - B)$, where G is the outside diameter of the guide (bearing, bushing or pin) and B is the cutting diameter of the bit. This formula holds true whether the template you're making is for shaped parts, inlays or joinery. Another thing to remember is that whenever you rout both edges of a part or all the way around it, the offset is effectively doubled. That means if you used a 3-in. dia. template with a $\frac{1}{2}$-in. bit and $\frac{3}{4}$-in. bushing and shaped both edges of the part in the example above, you'd end up with a $3\frac{1}{4}$-in. wide part. To end up with a part 3 in. wide you would have to reduce the template width by $\frac{1}{4}$ in.—twice the offset amount.

Making templates with an offset for simple shapes, such as a disc or rectangular mortise, is very straightforward: The line of cut for the template is shifted over from the original pattern line by the amount of the offset. Things get a little trickier when accounting for offset on an irregular pattern, say for a wooden pull toy shaped like a horse or a dinosaur. One common method is to follow along the edge of the pattern with a compass or draftsman's dividers set to the offset and transfer the line of cut for the template. You have to be careful, especially if the pattern is intricate, to keep the compass/dividers perpendicular to the line, or you'll distort the design.

Complicated patterns are much easier to redraw with the right amount of offset using a photocopy machine with variable reduction/enlargement. Start by copying the pattern using an estimated percentage of enlargement or reduction. Check the reduction by overlaying the original pattern and measuring the amount of offset. Change the amount of reduction, check it and try again if necessary (copies are cheap).

Complementary templates for pattern routing

Regular templates are great for shaping parts, but what if you want two parts to fit precisely together for a decorative joint or inlay? Generating a pair of templates that will create a tight-fitting joint line can be fussy and time-consuming using standard methods. There is, however, another way to produce parts that fit together (see the photo on p. 125) that uses only one master template cut to the shape of the desired joint line or inlay to generate a pair of complementary templates. This pair of templates, used with the right combination of straight bits and pilot bearings, can be used to shape the two halves of a joint, or a recess and inlay.

Complementary Pattern Routing

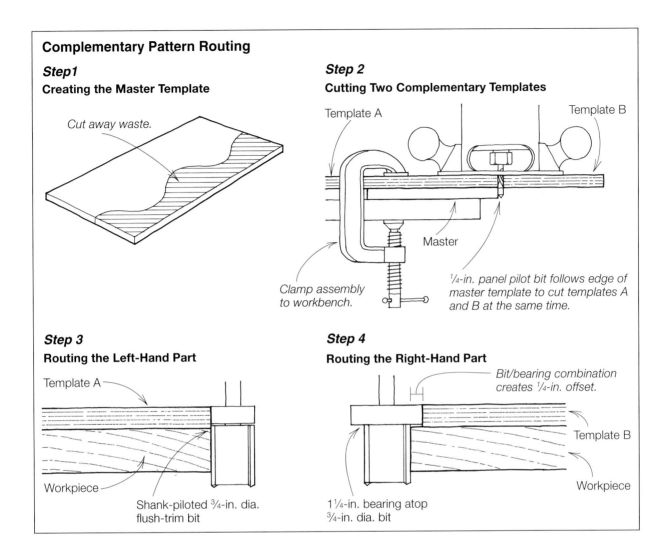

Step 1
Creating the Master Template

Cut away waste.

Step 2
Cutting Two Complementary Templates

Template A

Template B

Clamp assembly
to workbench.

Master

¼-in. panel pilot bit follows edge of
master template to cut templates A
and B at the same time.

Step 3
Routing the Left-Hand Part

Template A

Workpiece

Shank-piloted ¾-in. dia.
flush-trim bit

Step 4
Routing the Right-Hand Part

Bit/bearing combination
creates ¼-in. offset.

Template B

Workpiece

1¼-in. bearing atop
¾-in. dia. bit

The four-step method described below was adapted from a similar technique taught to me by Escondido, California, routing master Pat Warner (see *Fine Woodworking* #75, pp. 59-61). But my method, illustrated in the drawing above, uses a different combination of bits and bearings and requires fewer steps. I've included a description of the kinds of bits to use, but there are dozens of other possible bit and bearing combinations that will work, including tongue and groove cutters for stronger joint lines—I'll leave it to you to figure them out.

Step 1 Draw the line of the joint you wish to rout, then cut out and shape and sand the master template to final form. For inlays, throw out the "hole" (the inner piece) and keep the "doughnut" (the outer portion) for the master template. To work with the bits and bearing combinations described here, no curve on the master template should have a radius of less than ⅜ in.

Step 2 Clamp the master template to the workbench with a piece of ¼-in. or ⅜-in. thick template material about twice as wide as the master template on top, as shown. The complementary templates are cut out of this top piece using a router fitted with a ¼-in. dia. panel pilot bit (such as the CMT #816-064) guided by the edge of the master template. This creates two complementary templates that will be used to rout the two halves of the joint (or to rout out a recess, and shape the inlay that fits into it).

To make the following steps clearer, label the complementary template overlaying the master template "A" and the one overhanging it "B." For inlay templates, label the complementary template for routing the recess "A" and the one for shaping the inlay "B." Also label the upper surface of each complementary template "TOP" and take care not to mount one upside-down inadvertently during the following steps.

Step 3 Mount complementary template A over the workpiece (which has been sawn to rough shape) and rout to shape, using a flush-trim bit with a shank-mounted pilot bearing (such as the Woodhaven #25410 or the CMT 811-690B). For inlay work, use the complementary template A and the flush trim bit to rout around the entire inside perimeter of the recess to the desired depth. Then rout out the center of the area to the same depth.

Step 4 Mount complementary template B over the second workpiece, and rout its edge, using a straight bit with a shank-mounted bearing that provides a ¼-in. offset. For example, a ¾-in. dia. straight bit (CMT #811-690 or Woodhaven #13444) and 1¼-in. O.D. pilot bearing (CMT #791-770 or Woodhaven #9810) yield a bit/bearing combination that offsets the line of cut ¼ in. The offset creates a contour on this workpiece that exactly matches the flush-trimmed edge of the workpiece routed in Step 3. To rout an inlay, attach the complementary template B atop the inlay stock with double-stick tape or adhesive-transfer tape, and rout around its perimeter. For small inlays, it will be safer to flip the stuck-together template/workpiece over and cut them upside-down on the router table, using a push block and great caution.

Finger templates for box joints

Of the many methods for machine-cutting box joints, few are as quick or precise as finger templates. As their name implies, these templates have many evenly spaced fingers projecting along their length. The width of each finger is equal to the width of the space that separates it from the next finger. It is these spaces that are used to make the joint: They guide a router with a guide bearing and a straight bit that cuts the stock clamped beneath the template (a shank-piloted bit can also be used). Templates can be made from Masonite, MDF, high-grade plywood or plastics.

The advantage to using a finger template, rather than a sliding jig or other machine method, is that once the workpiece and template are clamped up, both halves of the joint are cut at the same time, with great speed and accuracy. On the down side, you must make a different template for different-size joints. Worse, if you don't make the template just right, the joint fit will be too tight or loose, and you'll need to remake the template beginning from scratch.

There are a few important points to follow when making a finger template (see the drawing below). Working on a table saw, set the dado-blade thickness so that the width of the slots between fingers is a few thousandths larger than the O.D. of the guide bushing to be used with the template (this is if each slot will be routed in a single pass; smaller bits/bushings can be used if each slot is routed in more than one pass). All slots between fingers must be square to the front edge of the template, and uniform in length. Slot length should be slightly longer than

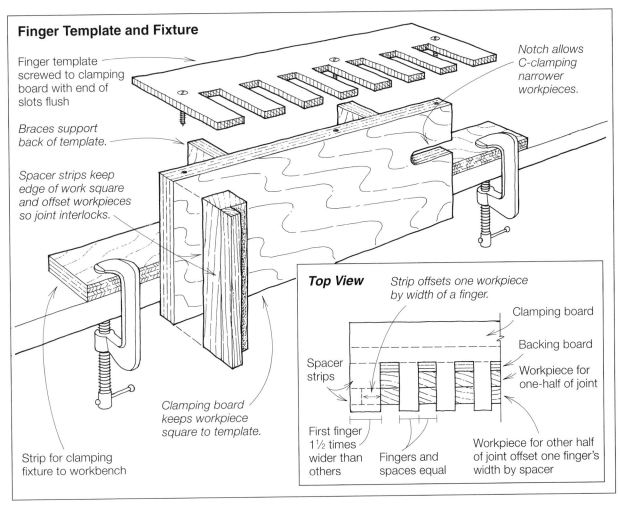

Finger Template and Fixture

Finger template screwed to clamping board with end of slots flush

Notch allows C-clamping narrower workpieces.

Braces support back of template.

Spacer strips keep edge of work square and offset workpieces so joint interlocks.

Clamping board keeps workpiece square to template.

Strip for clamping fixture to workbench

Top View

Strip offsets one workpiece by width of a finger.

Clamping board

Backing board

Workpiece for one-half of joint

Spacer strips

First finger 1½ times wider than others

Fingers and spaces equal

Workpiece for other half of joint offset one finger's width by spacer the thickness of two workpieces, plus the diameter of the guide bushing, plus the thickness of a backing board—a piece of scrap clamped behind the work to prevent tearout. This length gives the bushing purchase at the start of each slot, plus a little runout into the backing board at the end. Fingers at the edges of the template should be 1½ times the width of regular fingers to allow room for the two spacer strips that position the work. It's a good idea to make the template with more slots and fingers than you think you will need, to allow for the odd workpiece that's wider than expected.

The finger template is screwed to the top of a clamping board, which provides a way for workpieces to be aligned and clamped beneath the template (the screws allow different templates to be mounted). The spacer strips, as seen in the top view in the drawing on p. 135, are glued to one edge of the clamping board and serve to create the necessary offset between the two workpieces so that the halves of the joint will interlock. They also help to square the workpieces to the template. Two braces and a wood strip glued and screwed to the back of the clamping board allow the entire jig to be firmly clamped to the edge of the workbench. Stock to be joined (drawer parts, carcase sides, etc.) is secured to the clamping board with a pair of C-clamps or plier clamps. A slot at one end of the board provides access when clamping narrower stock. For high-production fixtures, you could mount a pair of quick-release toggle clamps or rout a T-slot horizontally across the clamping board and use a pair of sliding cleats (see p. 162) or other hold-downs.

Ironically, a sliding fixed-pin box-joint carriage, such as the one described on pp. 47-48, provides a great way to make finger templates that are very precise. By adjusting this jig just as you would for cutting a joint, the spacing of fingers can be adjusted. This also determines the tightness of joints produced by the template cut on the jig. After the box-joint jig has been set, a test joint is cut using a dado blade on the table saw, and joint fit is checked. Blade height is then raised and the finger template is cut the same way that a workpiece would be.

Templates for rectangular mortises

Equipped with a shank-piloted bit or a guide bushing, a router and template are the modern method of choice for chopping out frame mortises. However, routed mortises have rounded corners, so either the corners of the mortise must be squared up with a chisel or the edges of the tenon must be rounded. A better adaptation of this method, which has become extremely popular, is to mortise both halves of the joint and slip in round-edged loose tenons. An appropriately sized mortise-style template can also be used effectively to rout the recesses for hinges and other rectangular hardware.

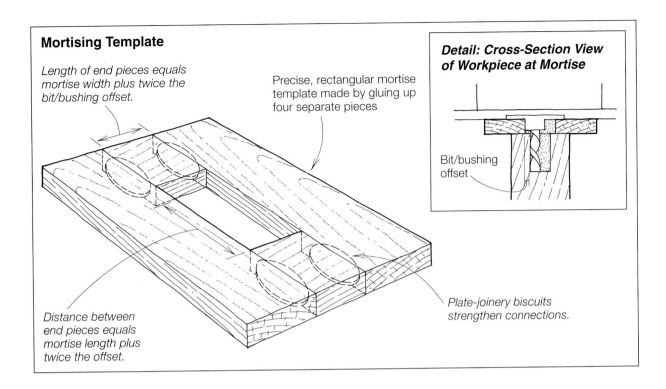

Mortising Template

Length of end pieces equals mortise width plus twice the bit/bushing offset.

Precise, rectangular mortise template made by gluing up four separate pieces

Detail: Cross-Section View of Workpiece at Mortise

Bit/bushing offset

Distance between end pieces equals mortise length plus twice the offset.

Plate-joinery biscuits strengthen connections.

Because you must use a shank-mounted bearing or bushing to guide the bit around the template, you must calculate the offset (see pp. 131-132) and incorporate it into your template. You can simply glue on the paper template pattern and cut it out in the template stock, but you'll get more accurate results by gluing a mortising template up from four separate pieces. As shown in the drawing above, the two side pieces that form the long sides of the mortise should be parallel-edged rectangles as long and wide as needed to create a surface ample enough to support the router. The dimensions of the end pieces are more critical, since their length and distance apart determine the size of the mortise. The length of each end piece should equal the desired mortise width plus twice the bit/bushing offset (see the drawing above). The distance between the two end pieces should equal the desired mortise length plus twice the bit/bushing offset. For strength, rout slots for biscuit joints in all four parts to reinforce the connections. When gluing the template together, make sure the assembly stays flat and that no parts slide out of position as clamping pressure is applied.

With any router mortising setup, I recommend the use of up-cut spiral-fluted, solid carbide mortising bits (see the sidebar on p. 138). If mortises are deep and chips are preventing the guide bushing/bearing from making firm contact with the template, you might consider incorporating dust collection directly into the mortising template, as described on pp. 222-223.

Regardless of whether you use a pilot bearing or a guide bushing for template routing, you need to choose a suitable bit to get the best possible cut. The diameter of the bit should suit both the thickness of the workpiece (or depth of the mortise or inlay) and the intricacy of the template. Deeper, heavier cuts in denser wood species call for larger-diameter bits (with ½-in. shanks). Generally the larger the diameter of the bit, the less likely it will be to tear out; however, smaller-diameter bits are capable of routing more intricate details. Bit diameter should be slightly less than the smallest concave curve found on the template. Long bits for mortising or shaping thick parts are best in solid carbide; these deflect less than HSS (high-speed steel) bits or carbide-tipped bits. Solid carbide, carbide-tipped bits, and titanium-nitride-coated HSS bits all stay sharp longer than regular HSS bits, especially when cutting man-made materials, such as MDF and plywood.

For the cleanest cuts — especially when routing coarse-grained or figured woods — choose a bit with spiral cutting edges rather than straight. The hook and shear angle of a spiral edge cuts with a slicing action, resulting in less tearout. Spiral cutters are available in both in up-cut and down-cut styles. Up-cut bits pull chips out of the kerf and clear them faster, making them the choice for deep mortising and production work. Down-cut bits don't clear chips as readily, but are less likely to tear out the surface of the work, making them better for inlays or delicate work in splintery woods, such as oak, mahogany and Douglas-fir. Woodhaven offers a special up-and-down-cut bit, specially made for routing the edge of plywood. The bit features an opposing pair of spiral cutters and is designed not to chip out delicate veneers on either face of the part (see Sources of Supply on pp. 224-227).

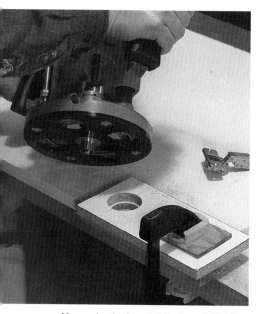

If you lack the right-size drill bit, you can template-rout big holes using a plunge router fitted with a guide bushing and straight bit.

Templates for round mortises

What if you need to bore large round mortises for Euro-style cabinet hinges and you don't have a special metric bit? A great way to create round mortises is to make a template and rout them. The technique will also work for boring large holes, saving you from buying expensive hole saws or Forstner bits. You're limited to routing holes as deep as the length of the bit, but for most carcase work this method is more than adequate.

Make your template from ¼-in. Masonite or MDF, and cut the hole with an adjustable circle cutter (remember to add the necesary bit/bushing offset to the hole's diameter). Circle cutters are designed for boring round holes in thin materials. You must run them in a drill press—never freehand—at a very slow speed—about 250 rpm; clamp the template stock firmly to the table, and keep your hands clear as you bore. The template can be used with a shank-piloted bit (flush-trim style or offset) or a guide bushing, as shown in the photo at left. If you use a template for mounting hardware, such as boring 35mm holes for Euro-style cabinet hinges, adding a positioning cleat will keep the template at the correct distance from the edges of doors and carcase parts.

Mounting Templates

Because the router depends entirely on the template for guidance while cutting the workpiece, the work and the template must be held in rigid alignment. Any movement between the two translates into in-accuracy in the size and contour of the part or joint. However, lots of clamps aren't always a good thing. Clamps can get in the way when routing small parts, or when you're shaping all the way around a part. Also, you don't want to spend all day clamping and unclamping—after all, templates are supposed to speed up production! That is why you need to think carefully about how best to mount a template to a work-piece. There are many different ways to deal with the most common situations you're apt to encounter.

Fastening templates directly

Directly attaching a template to the work by means of clamps, screws or nails provides a firm bond that will resist the forces of routing. C-clamps are an old standby, but for speed, you may wish to use fast-action clamps, such as plier-type toggle clamps, instead (see the photo on p. 49). If you decide to use screws, I recommend using brass, just in case the bit hits one. Adding a positioning cleat to the underside of a template speeds up the process of aligning on the workpiece before securing it. Sometimes, the template can be screwed directly to a part via an aligning strip or positioning cleat; locate these where screw holes will go into an unseen section of the finished part (see the photo on p. 131).

Mounting templates without clamps or fasteners

When you are routing small parts or entirely around the perimeter of a part on a router table or pin router, attaching the template without clamps allows the part to be handled freely, but you may not want to use screws or nails because they leave holes in the workpiece that you usually have to deal with afterwards. There are better alternatives.

Double-stick tape   Until you're tried it, you might not believe that a thin layer of tape can have enough holding power to keep a template in place during the rigors of routing. But there are several types of tape that are relatively inexpensive and perform this task surprisingly well.

Carpet tape is probably the most readily available wide, double-stick tape around. You can find it at many hardware stores, home stores and, of course, carpet dealers. The tape usually comes 2 in. wide, lays down well and peels off after use. One disadvantage of carpet tape is that it takes time to peel the tape off the template and/or the work af-ter routing is complete. Even then, sometimes there is adhesive residue remaining that needs to be cleaned off (VM&P naphtha works well for this).

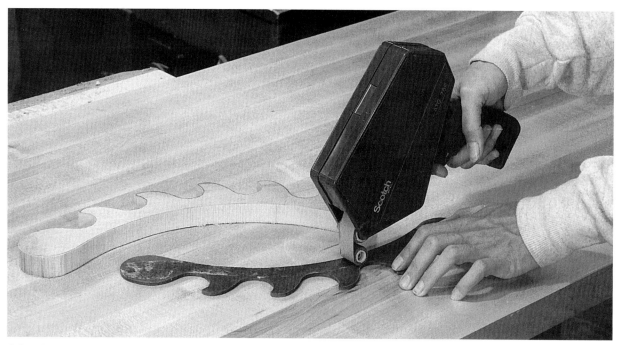

Adhesive transfer tape, applied from a special dispenser gun, provides a speedy means of attaching a template to a workpiece temporarily (here a wooden compass for a tilt-top drafting table).

An even more effective way to attach templates to workpieces is with adhesive transfer tape. This product, available from local stationary suppliers and through 3M (see Sources of Supply on pp. 224-227) isn't really a tape at all. You apply it with a special applicator (see the photo above) that dispenses a layer of adhesive from a backing paper as you roll it over a surface; the used backing paper is collected on a take-up reel inside the applicator. Adhesive transfer tape has a lot more holding power than carpet tape and is also quicker to apply. The only shortcoming is that, since it lacks a tape backing, the adhesive must be "rolled off" with the fingers after routing is done (it does come off cleanly, though).

Vacuum attachment   One of the most elegant ways of mounting templates uses an invisible clamping force: the atmosphere. A basic vacuum valve system, as described on pp. 167-169, is used to harness atmospheric pressure and direct it to lock a template and part firmly together during routing. A flexible plastic hose connects a vacuum valve or pump to a fitting threaded into the center of the template, where it doesn't get in the way of most routing operations. Seal tape or thin weatherstripping around the perimeter of the template creates a seal between template and part to prevent loss of vacuum. This system is terrific for producing scads of identical parts, say for children's toys or Christmas ornaments (see the photo on the facing page).

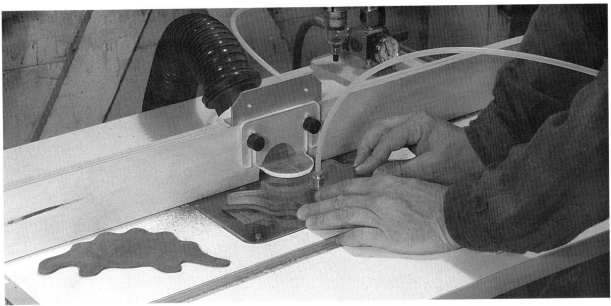

A vacuum valve supplied with compressed air provides the suction used to clamp a clear plastic template to a workpiece. These dinosaur-shaped Christmas ornaments are shaped with an end-piloted bit in the router table.

A vacuum template is incredibly easy to use: Place the template over the part blank and turn the vacuum valve on. After routing, turning the valve off instantly releases the bond, leaving no marks or residue on either part. As with other vacuum clamping setups of this type, templates should be at least 10 sq. in. in area for the atmospheric pressure to provide enough hold. The vacuum technique isn't limited to new templates: You can retrofit existing templates (as long as they're not made from porous materials, such as particleboard) by drilling a center hole and tapping in a hose connection fitting, and pressing on seal tape around the perimeter.

Incorporating templates into fixtures

Mounting a template in a fixture that secures the workpiece and creates the right alignment between template and work eliminates tedious positioning and repositioning when many parts need to be cut. Templates can be built into simple jig boxes, incorporated into existing fixtures or made part of high-volume production jigs that use quick release clamps.

Jig boxes Whenever you wish to machine the end of a frame member or the narrow edge of a carcase side, or rout an angled mortise, it often isn't practical or possible to mount the template directly to the workpiece. In such cases, you can build a jig box (sometimes called a cradle), such as the one shown in the drawing on p. 142, and mount the template on top. Positioning cleats and stops fastened inside the box serve to position the workpiece and orient it at the desired angle relative to the template. The box can also have toggle clamps or other

Template Mounted on a Jig Box

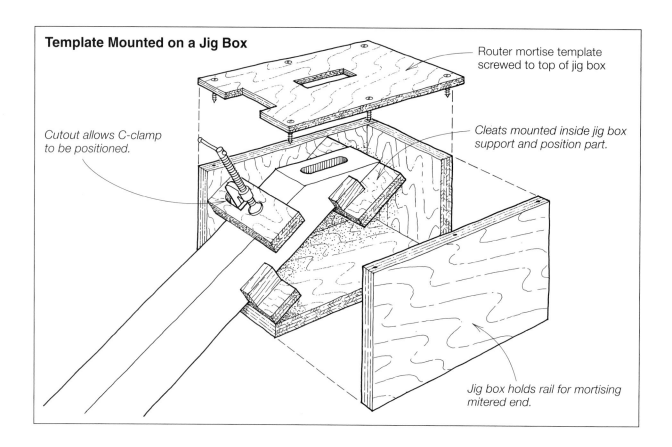

Router mortise template screwed to top of jig box

Cutout allows C-clamp to be positioned.

Cleats mounted inside jig box support and position part.

Jig box holds rail for mortising mitered end.

hold-downs mounted directly inside, or cutouts for more standard clamps that secure the part for routing. The top of the box provides a solid, level surface for the template as well as a sturdy platform for the router.

Mortise templates, which must be aligned with great precision in order for hardware to be properly aligned or joints to fit together correctly, often work best when mounted atop a jig box or incorporated into some kind of fixture. For mortises on the edge or end of stock, a mortise template may be fastened atop a clamping board, similar to the way a finger template is mounted (see the drawing on p. 135). The clamping board squares the workpiece to the template (fence strips or cleats can be used to align it as desired) and also provides a surface to clamp the work to.

Multiple template fixtures   Two or more templates can easily be built into fixtures whose primary purpose may be to clamp those parts together during glue-up or to hold them during other machining operations. This sort of setup can offer an advantage when you need to rout several different mortises for hinges or hardware on a single part; it's easier to clamp the part into a fixture that has all these templates already mounted in the precise locations than to attach a number of separate templates in different steps. For example, say you had a jig that clamped four mitered door-frame members together for glue-up (see the top drawing on p. 174). By incorporating templates along opposite edges, you could rout accurately placed mortises for hinges and latch hardware after the glue has set, before the frame is unclamped.

Quick-release template fixture   If you have a huge stack of parts that need pattern routing, building a template directly into a clamshell-like fixture, as shown in the photo below, provides a lightning-fast way to align and attach the template to each part. I learned about this method from woodworker and musical-instrument technician Michael Dresdner, who uses this system for shaping small cover plates for electric bass guitars. One side of the part bears against a positioning strip that aligns it to the template. The fixture has a quick-release toggle clamp that sandwiches the workpiece between the base and the template itself, which is bolted on the end of the clamp's bar; sandpaper on the template and base keep the workpiece from creeping out of position during routing. The entire contraption is then slid over a router table or shaper and trimmed using an end-piloted bit. Subsequent parts load and unload very quickly.

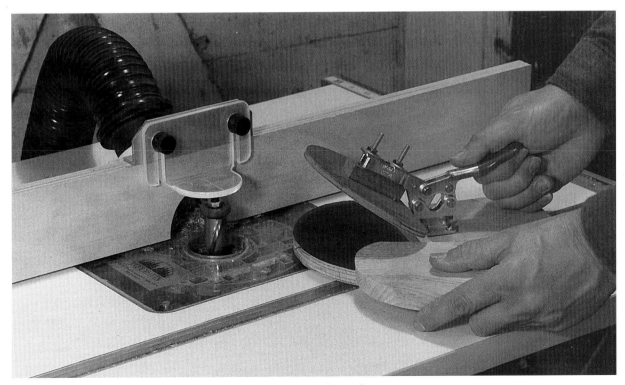

Attaching a template directly to a quick-release toggle-clamp fixture speeds the loading, shaping and unloading of multiple workpieces.

Templates for Sawing and Sanding

While templates provide a versatile way to shape parts with a router, their versatility doesn't end there. Templates can be used in conjunction with other machine tools, such as the table saw, bandsaw and drum sander, to perform tasks such as sawing parts to shape and sanding edges smooth without distorting their contour. Like routing template methods, sawing and sanding template methods are fast and repeatably accurate.

Template for sawing straight parts

A safe, quick way to cut out straight-edged parts on the table saw uses a special fence to guide a part with a template mounted atop it past the sawblade. An L-shaped fence clamped to the table saw's regular rip fence floats above the saw table, just higher than the thickness of the part. The guide edge of this fence is positioned flush with the outside edge of the sawblade teeth. A true-size pattern template can then be tacked or adhesive-transfer-taped to the blank. The pattern can be an irregular polygon, as long as no side is too short (less than 4 in. or 5 in.). Each edge of the template is run against the L-shaped fence, while the workpiece is cut below, as shown in the photo below. To keep hands away from the blade, always use a push block to propel small parts through the cut. The saw should be switched off after every cut, and the cutoff scrap that's trapped under the fence removed (you can cut out a "window" in the fence to make it easier to see what's under it).

Template sawing on the table saw is a powerful technique for quickly cutting many small parts to identical size and shape, especially parts that have sharply angled edges.

Template for sawing curved parts

Another type of template guide can be used for sawing curved parts on a bandsaw. This jig, shown in the drawing below, uses a round-faced template guide with a small notch for a narrow blade (you can use a $1/16$-in., $1/8$-in. or $1/4$-in. wide blade on the saw). The edge of the guide is positioned flush to the outer side of the blade. A template mounted atop the workpiece bears against the guide during the cut. The waste wood passes under the guide, which extends freely beyond a crossmember that allows the guide assembly to be clamped to the saw table. The template can have concave as well as convex curves, as long as the diameter of the concave curves exceeds the diameter of the rounded end of the template guide.

Template for pattern sanding

Once parts have been routed or sawn to shape, they often need their edges sanded. While this can be done freehand, the surest way of maintaining an exact edge contour is to pattern sand the part. This method requires a sanding drum with a spindle, chucked into the drill press. A guide disc—a disc with the same diameter as the O.D. of the drum with sandpaper—is screwed to a base that's clamped to the drill-press table so that the guide disc is concentric with the drum. The

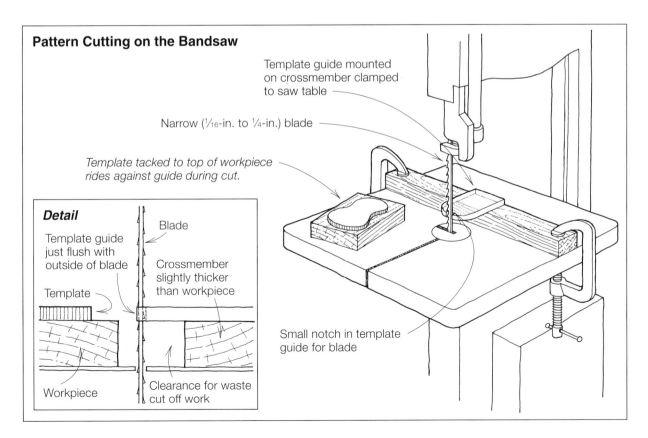

Pattern Cutting on the Bandsaw

Template guide mounted on crossmember clamped to saw table

Narrow ($1/16$-in. to $1/4$-in.) blade

Template tacked to top of workpiece rides against guide during cut.

Detail

Blade

Template guide just flush with outside of blade

Crossmember slightly thicker than workpiece

Template

Workpiece

Clearance for waste cut off work

Small notch in template guide for blade

template (which must not have concave curves smaller than the drum diameter) attaches to the underside of the workpiece and follows the guide disc while the edge of the part is sanded (see the photo below). Because of the small amount of clearance between the end of the sanding drum and the guide disc, the template stock should be about $\frac{1}{16}$ in. thicker than the guide disc (the top edge of the template gets sanded slightly). If you fit the drum with a coarse sandpaper sleeve, this method can actually be used to pattern sand rough-cut parts to final size and shape—though I'd reserve the technique for softwood and the softer hardwoods, such as alder or butternut. If you wish to give a light sanding to parts that have just been pattern routed (most convenient, since the template is still mounted on the part) make the guide disc very slightly smaller in diameter than the drum (about $\frac{1}{32}$ in.) and fit the drum with a fine sandpaper sleeve.

After a part has been template routed, its edges can be cleaned up by pattern sanding on the drill press.

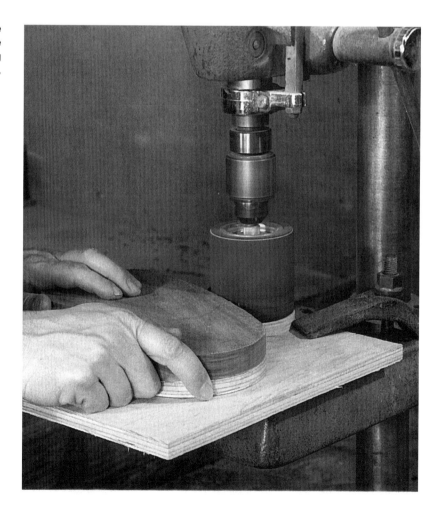

Templates for Drilling

The simplest drilling template is just a block with a hole drilled through it positioned at the desired location. The hole can be drilled square or at an angle. The thicker the template, the more of an aid the template will be in keeping the bit running true. But the problem with simple wood drill templates is that they wear out fairly quickly and lose their accuracy. This is fine if you only have a few holes to drill in a couple of parts. But if you need to drill dozens of holes, it's a good idea to fit the template with guide bushings (see the photo at right). These are basically hollow metal sleeves with the same I.D. as the diameter of the drill bit that press into the template stock (an arbor press is particularly handy for this task). For production jigs, use hardened steel bushings, which are available in a great range of sizes from several woodworking supply catalogs, as well as from most machine tool supply houses. While not cheap, these bushings provide excellent accuracy and can withstand the most rigorous use.

A good alternative to expensive steel bushings for jigs that will see less action is to use brass tubing. It's available at most hobby supply stores in many diameters and lengths. One advantage of using brass tubing is that you can make the bushings as long as need be—steel ones usually come only in shorter lengths. Used with extra-long or aircraft bits (available from machine tool suppliers), long brass bushings will allow you to drill holes in hard-to-reach places or drill at awkward angles accurately. Whichever bushings you use, keep them clean and treat them regularly with a dry lubricant, such as Sandaro DriCote.

Like other templates, drill templates can be fitted with positioning strips or cleats and clamped or simply held in place during drilling. You can also add drill guide bushings to any other template, such as a pattern-routing template. Once this template is mounted to the work, you can shape the part and drill any number of accurately placed holes at one time.

Hardened steel bushings pressed into a template guide a drill bit as it bores holes in a cabinet door for a handle. Fence strips on the edges of the template bear against the edges of the door to position it accurately.

Adjustable track template

If you have to drill a few sets of holes in a particular pattern but the spacing between the sets varies (as for door-hinge screws), you can mount two or more drill templates on a track (see the drawing on p. 148) that allows spacing to be changed as desired. The track can be commercially made pressed-steel T-track (see p. 196) or you can simply rout a T-slot in a strip of wood. Individual templates mounted on T-bolts slide in the track. A hole drilled in each template between the bushing and the T-bolt, with a line drawn through the center, lets you align the template with a stick-on tape measure on the track strip, as shown. This method isn't limited to drill templates—you could also mount pattern-routing templates to a track of this kind.

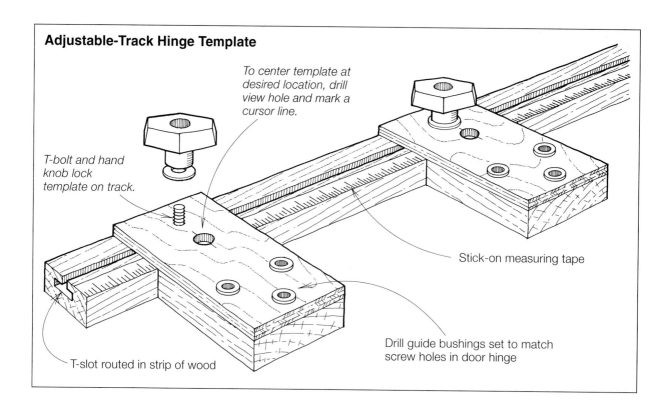

Adjustable-Track Hinge Template

To center template at desired location, drill view hole and mark a cursor line.

T-bolt and hand knob lock template on track.

Stick-on measuring tape

Drill guide bushings set to match screw holes in door hinge

T-slot routed in strip of wood

Multiple-hole template

When you have a great number of holes to drill accurately, such as for shelf pins for adjustable shelves, it's usually impractical to make a drill template with a separate bushing for each hole. Alternatively, the drill template jig shown in the drawing on the facing page positions each separate hole and squares the bit (chucked in a portable electric drill) to the workpiece. The template is made from ⅛-in. or ¼-in. thick Masonite or acrylic plastic with the holes carefully laid out and drilled to final diameter, then countersunk. I use a single-cutter machinist's countersink (see Sources of Supply on pp. 224-227), which cuts extremely cleanly and is much more controllable than the multi-cutter style typically used in woodworking. The countersunk holes act as guides for the tapered tip of a special spring-loaded, self-centering drill called a Vix bit (see Sources of Supply on pp. 224-227). While most Vix bits are smaller sized, intended primarily for drilling small, shallow holes for screws used to mount hardware, a ¼-in. bit is available (from The Woodworker's Store) that's perfect for shelf pins. If larger or deeper holes are needed, you can use a Vix bit to create a pilot hole, then enlarge it with a bigger standard bit.

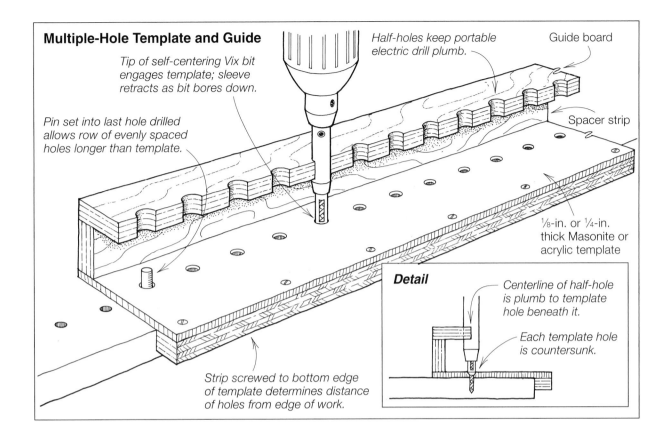

Multiple-Hole Template and Guide

Tip of self-centering Vix bit engages template; sleeve retracts as bit bores down.

Half-holes keep portable electric drill plumb.

Guide board

Pin set into last hole drilled allows row of evenly spaced holes longer than template.

Spacer strip

1/8-in. or 1/4-in. thick Masonite or acrylic template

Detail

Centerline of half-hole is plumb to template hole beneath it.

Each template hole is countersunk.

Strip screwed to bottom edge of template determines distance of holes from edge of work.

As shown in the drawing, the template is screwed to the underside of a spacer strip, which supports a guide board. The front edge of the guide board has a series of half-holes with a radius that matches that of the body of the Vix bit. Each half-hole is positioned exactly over a template hole and serves to keep the bit plumb during drilling, so holes in the workpiece will be square. A strip screwed to the underside of the template helps to align the template to the work and keep all holes a fixed distance from the edge.

In use, the template is clamped to the workpiece, and then the electric drill is used freehand to make the holes. If you need a row of holes longer than the template, simply fit a tapered pin through one of the template's end holes into the last hole drilled in the work, as shown. This kind of drilling jig can be adapted for any number of applications. For example, by altering the angle of the template and guide half-holes, you would be able to drill pilot holes at compound angles in a chair seat for back spindles.

CHAPTER 6

Fixtures that Secure the Work

"Just hold still for a second" is the plea of many amateur photographers attempting to capture a precious moment of family history for posterity. There's abundant proof in our family album that I was unable to follow directions and remain stationary, even for an instant. As a result, my childhood was captured mostly as a blur.

In the woodshop, getting a wooden part to hold steady and in the right position during machining operations is a similar challenge. The part must remain rigid for the cut to be true; if it slips out of position and is miscut, it will end up as kindling for the woodstove. Fixtures are devices that position and hold our workpieces securely for all manner of woodworking from sawing, routing, planing and sanding to assembling and gluing (in contrast, jigs are devices that control the motion of the tool or workpiece). A good fixture works quickly and provides the clamping pressure to grasp the part rigidly or press it together with another part without denting or damaging the wood. Just as important, a good fixture helps you quickly position and align a part so that the cuts will be made exactly where you want them. A fixture with well-designed clamping devices makes woodworking safer, too, since the operator's hands remain farther from the blade or bit.

An eccentrically mounted disc with a handle (p. 163) provides a cam action that can be used to press parts down firmly to the worktable. Here, the eccentric hold-down is mounted to hold down stock next to the blade on a radial-arm saw. An adjustable arm allows the disc to be positioned at various distances from the fence.

Before setting about the task of building a fixture for a a particular job, you should explore these questions: How precisely must the part be positioned? How rigidly must the part be held (will the forces of machining move the part out of position)? Where must the clamps or positioners be located so as not to interfere with machining? Is the fixture for only a few parts or for hundreds? Is rapid loading/unloading of parts important? As we'll see in this chapter, there are a great many different designs for devices that accomplish these goals.

What a Fixture Should Do

A good fixture should serve at least three functions: align the part quickly, resist the forces generated by machining and hold the part rigidly with a minimum of clamps or clamping devices. Let's examine in detail each of these areas of concern before taking a looking at the clamping devices themselves.

Aligning the part before clamping

It does no good to clamp a part down if it's not in the correct position in the fixture before you do so. For an accurate cut, you need a way to position the work in exactly the right spot and at the desired angle to the bit, blade or abrasive. Positioners are simple devices built into fixtures to do just that. Positioners such as fences, blocks or strips of wood work in conjunction with clamping devices to decrease the overall number of clamps needed to hold the work firmly. Although positioners aren't clamps in themselves, there are many circumstances where they are able to keep the stock in place without additional clamping. For example, a couple of positioning strips and light hand pressure are often adequate for keeping parts in place when boring small holes on a drill press, as shown in the top photo at left on the facing page.

Fences, tables and stop blocks   When working with straight, flat stock and parts, components that properly align and orient the workpiece are very often already built into the jig. Fences, strips and lips align the stock edgewise; tables and bases keep the parts horizontal or at the proper degree of tilt; end stops locate the length of the part relative to the blade or bit. All this might seem obvious, but on more than one occasion I've seen woodworkers carefully hand-positioning work before clamping it in place, when the simple addition of a small fence or stop block would have been faster and more reliable.

Contoured blocks   An irregular part is difficult to position using a square-edged block, but it can be accurately positioned using a block that mates to the contour of its edge, which provides a more stable contact with the part. Cutoff scraps can sometimes be used this way.

A base with four stop strips positions a part while drilling four small holes for mounting hardware. The part is pressed into each corner in turn before each hole is made; hand pressure is all that's needed to hold the part down while boring with the small bit.

A positioner and toggle clamp work as a team to locate the workpiece and hold it firmly during machining. The positioner is contoured to fit the negative profile of the workpiece, a leg for a walnut bench.

Depending on the profile of the part and how firmly the part needs to be held to resist the forces of machining, two or three short sections of cutoff scrap are usually enough to limit the part's movement. If the part is elongated, such as a curved bench leg, a contoured block can capture one end, as shown in the photo above right.

V-blocks   A rectangular block with a notch cut lengthwise along its upper face will align round parts (see the photo at right) or position square parts on edge, such as a stool leg for drilling holes for diagonal stretchers. V-blocks can also be incorporated into sliding jigs, such as the table-saw carriage shown on p. 50. Once the V-block is carefully positioned and clamped or screwed down, the perpendicular faces of the V keep parts aligned during most operations, often without need for more clamping pressure than fingertips provide.

Resisting the forces of machining

To work successfully, all components of a fixture should be designed to resist the sometimes considerable forces generated during cutting or machining. At best, cutting pressure can misalign parts and spoil accuracy; at worst, disaster can result: Parts can be hurled from the fixture, or the operator's hands can be dragged into the spinning blade or bit. A basic understanding of the forces of machining will help you make decisions about the location and number of positioners and clamps a fixture needs, as well as their size and strength.

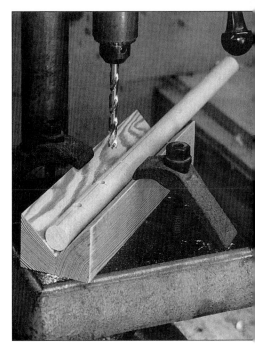

A V-block made from a short length of 4x4 steadies a round stool leg while holes are bored. The block is positioned so that the bottom of the V is centered on the bit.

Direction of machining forces   Cutters, blades, drill bits and powered abrasives (sanding discs, belts and drums) work with a rotary action, rather than a linear one. The leading edge of a rotating device usually works to advantage, by forcing the work down on the table or against the fence—imagine a radial-arm sawblade as it first enters the cut. Unfortunately, the trailing edge of the cutter usually wants to throw the work in the opposite direction (the radial-arm's blade lifts the wood at the back of the cut). You should locate your positioners and clamps accordingly, where they will most directly oppose the cutting forces.

Size and design of cutter   Generally speaking, the larger the bit, blade or abrasive surface, the more cutting pressure it can exert against the workpiece. The design of the cutter or blade—or the coarseness of an abrasive—also affects the amount of force against the workpiece. Router bits with straight flutes create more cutting pressure than spiral cutters. Circular-saw blades with less shear angle to the teeth exert more pressure than blades with high-top-bevel teeth. Coarse-grit abrasives grab the workpiece more than fine-grit abrasives do. In any case, when more pressure is exerted against the work, your setup will require heavier clamps and stronger or more abundant positioners to secure the work against those forces.

Horsepower   Smoother cutting results when the machine has power to overcome knots, areas of reaction wood and differences in density in the stock. But more power also means that the fixture must be built heavier and stronger to absorb higher amounts of pressure, machine vibration and shocks if the cutter suddenly grabs the wood.

Feed rate and direction   The faster the work is fed past a bit, blade or abrasive, the higher the cutting pressure that's generated. Thus, high-production jigs will generally require stronger and/or more clamps than jigs for occasional use because feed rates are higher. Fixtures used for climb cutting (running the stock through the machine with the rotation of the cutter, instead of against it) can also require more rigid clamping to resist the force of the bit self-feeding into the work.

Size and density of part   Small, light workpieces are affected more by cutting forces than large, heavy workpieces, and may require more clamping pressure. For example, imagine routing a narrow groove on the side of a redwood tree trunk that's fallen in your yard. Gravity supplies all the "clamping force" that's needed to resist the pressure of light routing. Now imagine routing a 6-in. sq. part with a large raised-panel cutter—a whole lot more clamping force would be needed to hold the workpiece in place. Also, machining denser woods generates higher cutting pressures than working on less dense species. Hence, more clamping pressure may be needed when cutting rosewood parts than when performing the same cut on a piece of sugar pine.

Locating clamps and positioners on the fixture

It's clear that the forces generated by machinery are capable of pushing against a part with some authority. But when you consider all the possible ways a workpiece can move out of position, clamping it firmly seems to be a daunting task. Every machinist who studies fixturing learns that a workpiece must be kept from moving in 12 possible ways: sliding side to side along three axes—X, Y and Z—and rotating in either direction around those three axes. Machinists call this concept, illustrated in the drawing below, "the 12 degrees of freedom." Fortunately, you don't need a clamp for each degree of freedom; judicious placement and orchestration of clamps and positioners will quickly limit the movement of a part. The idea is to use the minimum number of clamps that will do the job, so the task of clamping and unclamping doesn't get tedious.

One way to reduce the overall number of clamps needed is to locate a positioner, such as a fence or stop block, so that the rotation of the bit or blade presses the stock tighter to that fence or stop block. In many cases, this will eliminate the need for further clamping in the direction that the cutter is applying force. Indeed, we often use the forces applied during machining to limit one or more degrees of freedom of the workpiece. For example, the feed force of a spinning drill bit presses the stock down against the table, and its clockwise rotation tend to press one end of the stock tighter to the fence (see the drawing on p. 156). The only clamp (or clamps) needed should keep the opposite end of the stock from rotating away from the fence, and keep the stock from lifting when the bit is withdrawn.

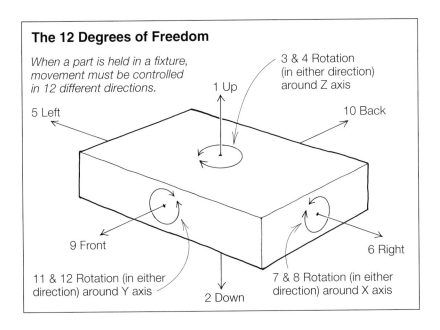

The 12 Degrees of Freedom

When a part is held in a fixture, movement must be controlled in 12 different directions.

1 Up

3 & 4 Rotation (in either direction) around Z axis

5 Left

10 Back

9 Front

6 Right

11 & 12 Rotation (in either direction) around Y axis

2 Down

7 & 8 Rotation (in either direction) around X axis

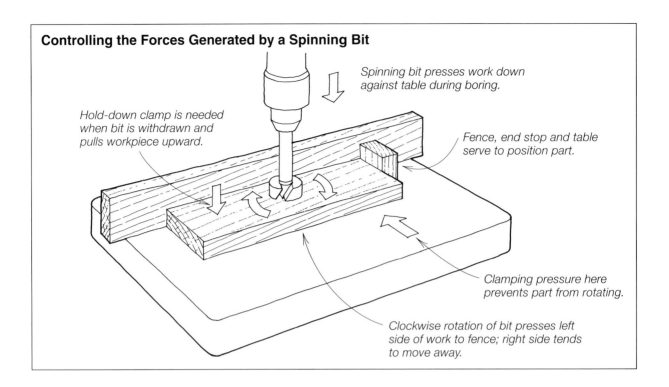

Controlling the Forces Generated by a Spinning Bit

Spinning bit presses work down against table during boring.

Hold-down clamp is needed when bit is withdrawn and pulls workpiece upward.

Fence, end stop and table serve to position part.

Clamping pressure here prevents part from rotating.

Clockwise rotation of bit presses left side of work to fence; right side tends to move away.

Generally speaking, primary clamps and positioners should be placed where they'll support work against the force of the bit or blade, as close as practical to that area. The farther away the clamp is from the machining forces, the more leverage is exerted on the part and the greater the likelihood that the part will creep out of position. Also, a clamping device mounted close to the bit or blade can serve double duty as a guard, since it may serve to block the approach of the hands to the dangerous cutter.

Since one clamp is often not enough to hold a part firmly, a second positioner and clamp should be located as far to the other end of the part as possible. In the drawing on the facing page, you'll see that the positioner and clamp close to the sawblade act as a fulcrum, directing the cutting force to lever the far end of the piece toward the back of the jig. A small block and clamp at that end will hold the piece as firmly as a larger clamp would closer to the center of the part (recall from the principles of physics: A small boy at one end of a seesaw can balance two heavy kids sitting on the other side close to the fulcrum).

Directing clamping pressure Minimize deflection of the workpiece by centering clamping pressure on the part whenever possible. Clamps located too low on a part on edge against a fence may not keep the top half of part from deflecting away from the fence during mortising. At the same time, be careful not to apply force to the part directly where

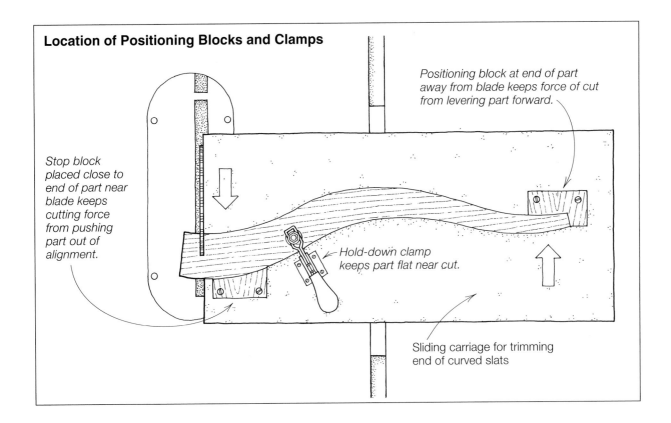

Location of Positioning Blocks and Clamps

Positioning block at end of part away from blade keeps force of cut from levering part forward.

Stop block placed close to end of part near blade keeps cutting force from pushing part out of alignment.

Hold-down clamp keeps part flat near cut.

Sliding carriage for trimming end of curved slats

it will be machined. A plunger-type toggle clamp (described on p. 167) centered over the part of a frame member where the mortising bit must penetrate will make it much more difficult to feed and withdraw the bit.

Evenly distributing clamping pressure is desirable when fewer clamps are used to hold a part in place, especially when thin parts must be held flat; excessive pressure in one spot can cause deflection. Usually, adding a block between the clamp face and part (or increasing the thickness of a clamping block) will correct the problem. If not, try increasing the number of clamps while decreasing the amount of pressure that any one clamp exerts on the work.

Another great way to improve clamping is to tailor the faces of clamps and devices to suit the situation. To distribute clamping pressure more evenly, you can make clamp faces larger. To prevent denting shaped parts, clamp faces can be shaped to fit convex or concave profiles, or even be routed with a negative profile of the workpiece. This sort of shaping would allow a complex softwood molding to be held down very firmly without damaging its delicate details. To prevent part slippage, clamp faces or the area directly beneath the clamp can be covered with sandpaper or high-friction materials (see p. 190).

Simple Clamping Devices

Most of us are used to pulling out a C-clamp or two every time that a part needs to be secured in a jig or on the workbench. But C-clamps are less than ideal for a several reasons. First, they are completely free-floating, and must be hefted and aligned each time they're used. Further, they take some time to tighten and release (especially compared to plier-type toggle clamps and other commercially made quick-locking clamps seen in use in many of the photos in this book). When making any fixture, consider the wealth of other clamping devices that are quick to use that can be elegantly tailored to your application. Many of these are cheap to make and can be attached directly to the fixture or jig you're building, so you won't waste the time it takes to look for and apply a loose clamp.

Wedges

Few clamping devices are as simple, yet as versatile as the basic wedge. Wedges can be used to tighten a mortise-and-tenon joint (for example, foxtail wedges in a blind tenon), and a removable wedge can be used on a through tenon to join the trestle to the base on a trestle-style table. But wedges also can be used in fixtures as clamps.

Fixture wedges can be used individually, in pairs or as components in other clamping setups. Just remember when making wedges that the steeper the slope, the faster a wedge will expand to clamp a part, but the harder it will be to drive, and more apt it will be to loosen. Wedges with shallow angles require more travel for tightening, but are much easier to drive and tend to stay put. Wedge angles between 5° and 15° are about right for most woodworking jobs.

Basic single wedge   A single wedge is one of the easiest clamping devices to use, because it is the sole moving part driven against a stop to hold the part in place. To accommodate the slope of a single wedge, the stop block should either be round in cross section, like a dowel (see the photo on the facing page), or be a square block attached with only one screw, to allow the block to pivot as the wedge is driven. A clamp block that conforms to the profile of the part is often used between the wedge and the work. However, single wedges aren't suitable for all applications, since the force they exert when driven against a part might also drive it out of alignment.

A variation on the single-wedge clamp is the wedge hold-down, which is really a double wedge with one fixed half (see the drawing on the facing page). It uses a stop block with a face tapered to match a single loose wedge. This device makes a good clamp for parts that need to be pressed flat on a carriage base or auxiliary table.

Single wedges work effectively to clamp parts into a fixture or other jig, leaving their top surface clear for any number of machining operations. Here, single wedges driven against dowel posts mounted in a base press against contoured clamping blocks, which distribute clamping pressure evenly. Stop blocks screwed to the base oppose the clamping force.

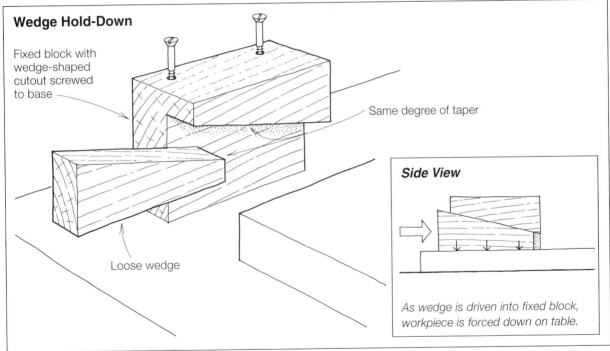

Wedge Hold-Down

Fixed block with wedge-shaped cutout screwed to base

Same degree of taper

Loose wedge

Side View

As wedge is driven into fixed block, workpiece is forced down on table.

Opposing wedges Opposing wedges, also called folding wedges, are very useful for applying even pressure along the edge of a part, rather than just at one point, as with a single wedge. Paired opposing wedges both have the same slope, and they should be long enough to overlap at least a couple of inches before they are driven together. As the wedges' matching slopes slide against each other, they form a parallel-

Paired wedges with identical tapers driven against one another create an expanding parallelogram, providing the pressure necessary to force tambour slats tightly together in a frame before the canvas is applied.

ogram that expands in height. Alternately tapping the wedges, first one, then the other, provides pressure that you can use to clamp together parts for glue-up or to press together tambour slats held in a glue-up fixture, such as the one shown in the photo above. Because they lie flat and occupy relatively little space, opposing wedges are great for fixtures where other clamps would get in the way.

Hold-down cleats

Hold-down cleats are versatile devices that can be adapted to work with a wide range of stock thicknesses, and they are so inexpensive that they can be made by the dozen. A basic hold-down cleat (known to machinists as a "strap clamp") works on the principle of a lever (see the drawing on the facing page). A rear spacer block approximately the same thickness as the workpiece provides a fulcrum for the top-mounted clamping strip. A threaded stud and hand knob or carriage bolt and wing nut located between the fulcrum and the workpiece provides the clamping pressure. Locating the stud or bolt closer to the

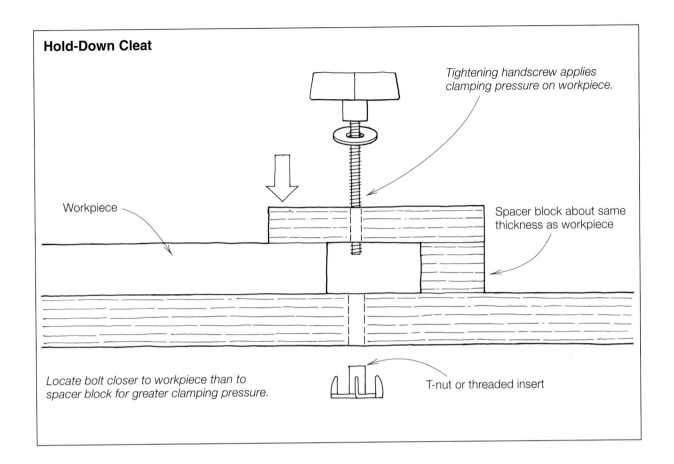

Hold-Down Cleat

Tightening handscrew applies clamping pressure on workpiece.

Workpiece

Spacer block about same thickness as workpiece

Locate bolt closer to workpiece than to spacer block for greater clamping pressure.

T-nut or threaded insert

workpiece (i.e., farther from the rear spacer block) provides more clamping pressure. For applications such as the hold-downs for the belt-sander table described on pp. 100-101), studs for hold-down cleats made from short lengths of threaded rod can be set directly into tapped holes in metal, plastic or composite materials. In plywood and MDF bases and tables, you can tap holes and epoxy the studs in place. If you want the hold-down cleats to be completely removable, bore holes and drive T-nuts or threaded inserts into the base and use studded handscrews with the cleats, as shown above.

If cleats need to be located around the part, make the clamping strip long enough so that each cleat can be loosened and rotated out of the way to provide clearance when loading or removing parts. An even more flexible arrangement for cleats is to mount them on T-bolts that slide in T-slots. This is how the miter-slot auxiliary table shown in the photo on p. 81 is secured to the scrollsaw. T-slot-mounted cleats also provide flexibility for situations where clamping location must be changed to accept workpieces of different dimensions (see the discus-

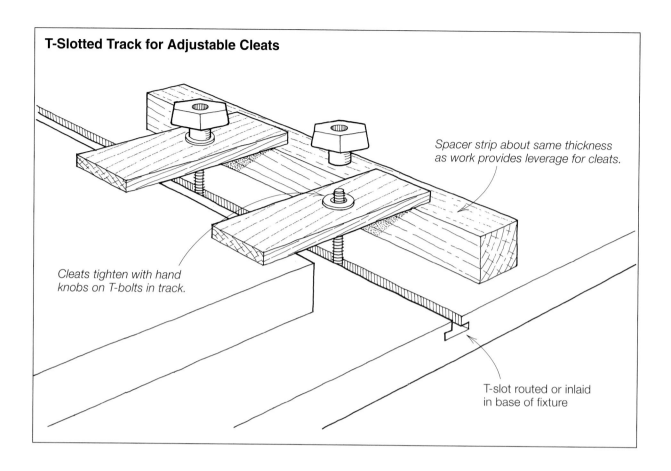

T-Slotted Track for Adjustable Cleats

Spacer strip about same thickness as work provides leverage for cleats.

Cleats tighten with hand knobs on T-bolts in track.

T-slot routed or inlaid in base of fixture

sion of assembly fixtures on pp. 173-176). If many cleats are to be used in a row, in lieu of a rear spacer block on each clamp you can use a single spacer strip that each clamp strip rests on (see the drawing above).

Positioning lugs on the workpiece

A novel but effective way to hold a workpiece is to bolt directly through it into the fixture. Bolting is a great way to hold irregularly shaped or carved three-dimensional parts that would otherwise be very difficult to clamp down. Although it may seem like more trouble than it's worth, this method is terrific when the part must be clamped rock solid, yet no clamping devices can be left in the way.

Obviously, you can't drill the bolt holes where they would show in the finished piece, so the part must be cut out with extra lugs or tabs (or have them glued on) at the ends or around the perimeter wherever they are needed. After the machining, the lugs are trimmed off and those small areas of the part are shaped and sanded smooth. Holes drilled through these lugs take bolts or studs fitted through the fixture. Standard nuts, nylon lock nuts, wing nuts or hand knobs can then be screwed down to hold the part tight.

If you standardize the placement of bolts, you can use the lugs to mount the part on several different fixtures for work on different machines. Further, the part can be easily removed and remounted accurately to the same position in the fixture. If positioning must be drop-dead accurate, say for a positioning fixture for a panel that is routed with an intricate pattern, additional holes through the lugs fitted with taper pins will do the job (see p. 194).

Production Clamping Devices

Speed is clearly one of the foremost concerns in any sort of production shop. And in this case, production need not mean cranking out thousands of identical parts; some pieces of custom furniture require a dozen or more matching components that each need one or more machining or assembly steps. When the task of clamping and unclamping parts takes more time and effort than you want to spend, it's worth the investment of time and money to employ devices that allow parts to be clamped and released with ultimate ease.

Eccentric-cam clamps

Among the fastest of shop-made devices to actuate and release, the eccentric cam lends itself beautifully to clamping. The two designs of eccentric clamps described in this section have a wide range of applications for woodworking fixtures. You can also employ the cam principle to make clamp dogs, as described on pp. 174-175.

Round cam   The round-cam clamp, shown in the photo on p. 151, bears directly on the workpiece. This type of clamp is often seen on horizontal boring machines. The eccentric action not only presses the workpiece firmly down on the table or base of the jig, but also pushes the work forward against a fence or other stop. An advantage of this style of cam clamp is that it handles a pretty good range of stock thicknesses; the farther the handle is rotated forward, the closer the cam gets to the table and the thinner the stock that can be clamped. A dowel handle set into the edge of the disc provides good leverage for strong clamping force. To keep the cam from releasing, the edge of the disc should be covered with a soft yet durable material, such as thick top-grain cowhide (the suede side is glued to the disc). This is a great recycling opportunity if you have any old belts around, or you can buy a strip of cowhide (sold for the purpose of making your own belt) at a hobby store or leather supply shop.

Cam lever   The cam-lever clamp, shown in the drawing on p. 164, has a lever with a cam lobe that bears on a separate strip that also serves as a clamping face. The cam doesn't contact the workpiece directly (it won't mar the surface of the work) and exerts a more neutral pressure on the workpiece than a round cam does, making it more appropriate for jigs where the part needs to be held down and not pressed forward as well. Cam-lever clamps can also be made with very deep throats that apply clamping pressure farther in from the edge of the stock than most other clamps can. You may have seen this sort of cam on wooden luthier's clamps.

Cam-lever clamps should be made from a very hard wood; maple is the cheapest and most commonly available one in America, but hornbeam and other dense species are also fine. The clamp has a single bar with a lengthwise kerf cut with the bandsaw about ⅛ in. to ¼ in. from the edge. The kerf extends one-third to one-half of the way down its length; a small hole drilled at the end of the cut prevents splitting. The cam and lever are a single piece that pivots on a steel spring pin (available at a good hardware store or a machinist's supply) located as

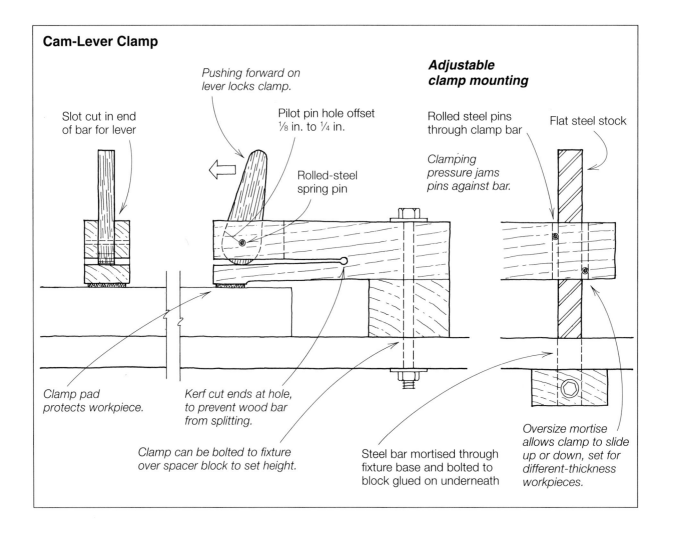

Cam-Lever Clamp

Slot cut in end of bar for lever

Pushing forward on lever locks clamp.

Pilot pin hole offset ⅛ in. to ¼ in.

Rolled-steel spring pin

Clamp pad protects workpiece.

Kerf cut ends at hole, to prevent wood bar from splitting.

Clamp can be bolted to fixture over spacer block to set height.

Steel bar mortised through fixture base and bolted to block glued on underneath

Adjustable clamp mounting

Rolled steel pins through clamp bar

Flat steel stock

Clamping pressure jams pins against bar.

Oversize mortise allows clamp to slide up or down, set for different-thickness workpieces.

shown in the drawing and pressed into an undersized hole. The face of the clamp can be covered with thin neoprene, a cork or felt pad, or even a high-friction material, if need be.

If a cam-lever clamp will be used to secure only parts of uniform thickness, the bar can be screwed or bolted to the base of the fixture over a support block or fence, as shown in the drawing on the facing page. This kind of cam clamp can also be mounted with the cam lever horizontal, as shown on the dedicated clamping board in the top drawing on p. 174. For more flexible clamp positioning, you could mount clamps with T-bolts sliding in a T-slot routed in the fixture. If the clamps will be used to secure workpieces of different thicknesses, the back end of the bar can be mortised to slide down over a vertical post made from flat steel stock. Unlocked, the clamp slides up or down. When the cam is engaged, the clamp bar levers up and two steel spring pins, set into holes in the bar as shown, jam against the post.

When you are making any eccentric cam device, keep this basic guideline in mind: The closer the pivot point is to the true center of the round cam disc, the more gradually clamping pressure will be applied, but the better the setting will hold. The farther the pivot point is from the center of the disc, the larger the range of clamping (and the faster the clamp will lock against the part) but the more easily the clamp will disengage. For most applications, locating the pivot point off the center of the disc one-quarter to one-third the radius of the disc will be about right.

Quick-release toggle clamps

Few clamping devices as useful and versatile to a woodworker as quick-release toggle clamps (I'll call them just "toggle clamps" for brevity). As their name describes, these clamps lock with a toggle action controlled by a handle that's very quick to set or release. Of the many available styles, the lever and plunger styles (see the photo on p. 166) and plier clamps (see the top left photo on p. 49) have the widest applications for direct use in woodworking fixtures. They are available in many sizes, and also as air-powered clamps (see pp. 169-171). When ordering toggle clamps from a catalog, be sure you check the clamp's overall dimensions carefully, or you could easily end up with a model that's much bigger or smaller than what you expected.

Most toggle-clamp bars or plungers accept rubber-tipped, threaded spindles that actually press down on the work. The threads allow you to adjust the amount of clamping pressure and to set clamping depth for workpieces of different thicknesses. The rubber-tipped end is good for general use, though you can always make up a custom spindle with a clamp face designed to suit the application (see p. 157).

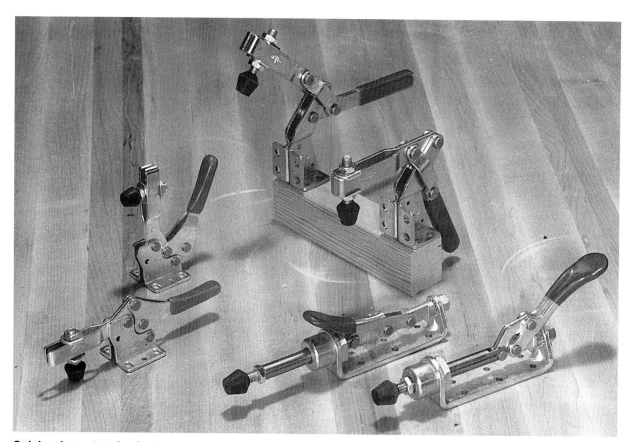

Quick-release toggle clamps are versatile woodworking accessories. Hold-down action clamps (top and left) have a lever arm that swings down to press workpieces flat on a table or base; plunger-style clamps (right) press parts horizontally against a fence or stop.

Toggle clamps can be located on a fixture wherever needed. The smaller models can be mounted with regular wood screws. Machine screws set through the base are best for larger clamps, which are capable of generating pressures of 600 psi to 1000 psi. Spacer blocks can be added under the clamps to increase depth capacity as necessary. The spindle on many lever-style clamps can be shifted along the bar, but closer in will yield maximum clamping pressure.

Lever-style clamps Lever-style toggle clamps, also called hold-down action clamps, have a bar that levers down to exert pressure on the work, usually to press it down flat on the base or table. There are three variations of the basic lever-style clamp, depending on the position of the handle with the clamp locked: vertical, horizontal and pull-down. The vertical handle is a good choice for sliding jigs, where the upright handle can double as a handhold (see the small-parts machining carriage on p. 55). Horizontal handles lie flat, giving the locked clamp a low profile and more working clearance, and pull-down clamps are designed so that the locking bar swings out of the way when opened to make loading and unloading the workpiece easier (see the clamps at top and left in the photo above).

Plunger-style clamps   Plunger-style toggle clamps, also called straight-line action clamps, couple a handle and toggle mechanism to a plunger that moves in the same axis the clamp is mounted in. On most models, the plunger moves forward and locks as the handle is pushed forward (see the photo on the facing page). However, if handle clearance is a problem, models are available that lock the plunger when the handle is pulled back. Plunger-style clamps are usually mounted horizontally to press a part firmly against a fence or stop, but can also be mounted vertically to press the work upward or downward.

Vacuum hold-downs

Besides gravity, one of the most basic forces that surrounds us is the pressure generated by the atmosphere. The reason we don't actively feel this pressure is that it's equalized inside and outside of us, unless there is a vacuum. In a vacuum environment, the atmosphere presses down at about 14 psi, enough force to keep parts secure during many woodworking operations. A vacuum clamping system is a good choice when regular clamps would get in the way. Vacuum clamps are effective for holding parts in place during machining on all manner of jigs and fixtures: on auxiliary tables, such as on the drill-press (see pp. 84-85); on template jigs (see pp. 140-141); on many of the sliding carriages described in Chapter 2; and on assembly fixtures, as described on pp. 173-177.

A vacuum-clamping setup supplies and controls suction between the part and whatever flat surface the part is to be held down on—a base, an auxiliary table, a fence, etc. Suction can be created by a dedicated pump, but there is a compact, economical device called a vacuum venturi valve that's rapidly become the vacuum source of choice for any small woodshop with a compressor.

Several ready-made vacuum-valve systems are currently on the market (see Sources of Supply on pp. 224-227) for under $150. The smaller systems consume only 1 or 2 cfm, so they can be used with compressors as small as $\frac{1}{2}$ hp. The limits of such a system are reasonable: The vacuum hose between the valve and jig should not exceed about 10 ft; the smallest part that can be clamped is about 10 in. square (remember that since the atmosphere clamps the entire surface of the part evenly, the larger the surface area of the part the greater the overall clamping pressure will be).

A schematic of a basic vacuum-valve system is shown in the drawing on p. 168. The small aluminum or plastic vacuum-valve device has several ports, usually threaded for $\frac{1}{4}$-in. or $\frac{1}{8}$-in. NPT (nominal pipe thread) fittings. The input connection is for a standard air compressor. The air rushes through a venturi—essentially a small funnel—inside the device, which speeds up the air's velocity and creates a vacuum as it

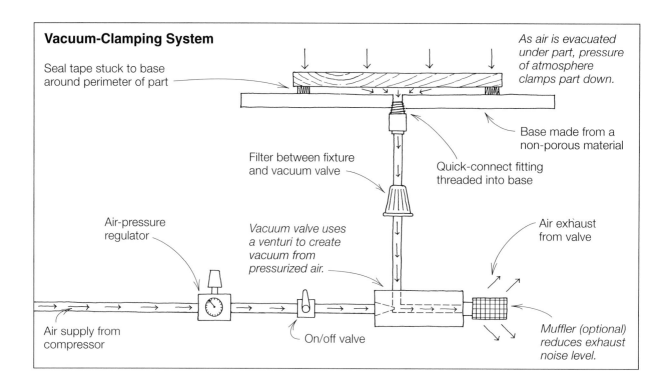

Vacuum-Clamping System

Seal tape stuck to base around perimeter of part

As air is evacuated under part, pressure of atmosphere clamps part down.

Base made from a non-porous material

Quick-connect fitting threaded into base

Filter between fixture and vacuum valve

Air exhaust from valve

Air-pressure regulator

Vacuum valve uses a venturi to create vacuum from pressurized air.

Air supply from compressor

On/off valve

Muffler (optional) reduces exhaust noise level.

rushes through the valve to an exit port, where a muffler may be used to tone down the annoying air blast. The valve's vacuum port is connected via plastic hose to the fixture, with a filter in between to prevent any sucked-up sawdust from fouling the valve. A thin contiguous strip of gasket—special seal tape or regular closed-cell-foam weather-stripping ¼ in. thick—around the perimeter of the part forms the seal between the part and the base of the fixture. A regulator, which keeps input air pressure between 40 and 80 psi, and a simple on-off valve, which engages and disengages the vacuum, complete the system.

To ensure best performance, the base or fixture component the part will be clamped to must not be made of a porous material, lest vacuum be lost. Plastic materials like Plexiglas, Lexan and phenolics are great choices, as are Baltic birch plywood and maple die board. For large surfaces, I particularly like to use solid-surface materials, like Corian and Avonite; they're sturdy and machine well. Avoid using MDF and particleboard: They are the worst choices since they are porous enough to allow a surprising amount of vacuum to escape. If thin parts with a fairly large surface area are to be clamped, the force of the atmospheric pressure may cup the part in the center. To correct this problem, add a few strips of seal tape around the center of the base, making sure they won't block the flow of air between the perimeter and the center hole.

If you have one vacuum system and several jigs, it's a good idea to mount Quickfit connectors (described on p. 172) to the jigs. These fittings work with ¼-in. nylon tubing that allows different jigs to be plugged or unplugged from the vacuum source many times without the assistance of tools. Most materials can be tapped and the Quickfit connector screwed directly in. Use Teflon tape or thread compound on these connections, as well as on all air and vacuum fittings, to ensure a good seal.

Although it doesn't deliver the holding power of a vacuum valve, the suction of a shop vacuum can be used to keep a workpiece put during light machining operations. A fixture base that's built similar to the hold-down table described on pp. 92-93 can secure panels and other large parts for drilling or routing. Small parts can be held safely for freehand sanding by sucking them onto the end of the vacuum's hose, a technique used by woodworker Steven Gray for sanding snowflake-shaped wooden Chrismas-tree ornaments (see his article in *Fine Woodworking* #73).

Air-clamping systems

While usually reserved for production situations, a modest air-clamp setup with a simple on/off valve and one or two clamps isn't outside the reach of small woodshops. Air clamps have endless applications for woodshop fixtures. They can hold parts firmly on a benchtop for routing or other machining, or clamp frame members for boring or mortising operations on a drill press (see the photos on p. 170). Air clamps can also be added to hold workpieces in sliding carriages and other mobile jigs. They're also extremely popular used in glue-up fixtures, as described at the end of the chapter. Air-clamping systems consume air only when they're cycled (clamped and unclamped), so you can run a small air system on a compressor as small as ¾ hp. Most air clamps useful to woodworkers have a maximum inlet pressure of between 80 psi and 120 psi.

Types of clamps   Air-clamping devices include straight air cylinders, which are basically cylinders with a piston, and air clamps, which are air cylinders coupled to quick-release toggle clamps. Air clamps come in lever-action and plunger styles (see pp. 165-167). Air cylinders can be single action or double action. Single-action cylinders use air pressure to engage the piston to create clamping force; when the air is turned off, a spring returns the cylinder. Double-action clamps are of most value to woodworkers. Controlled with a four-way valve, described on p. 171, air pressure is directed to the port at the rear of the cylinder, forcing the piston down to put pressure on the workpiece (see the drawing on p. 172). When the valve is turned to the off position, air pressure is released at the rear port and introduced at the front port, causing the cylinder to retract and release the clamping

One of the fastest way to clamp and unclamp workpieces is with a pair of air-powered toggle clamps connected to a latching foot-controlled four-way valve.

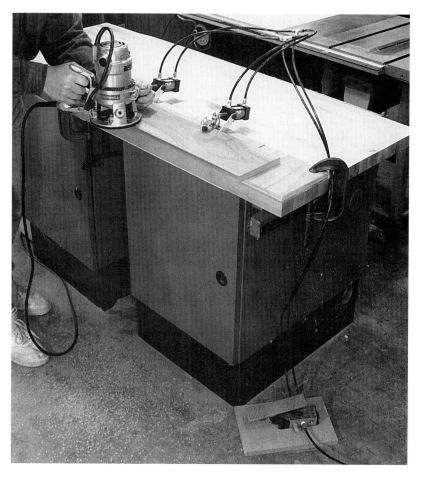

An air-clamping system powering a pair of plunger-action toggle clamps holds a workpiece firmly against the drill-press fence, and prevents the work from lifting when the bit is withdrawn.

pressure. Most double-action air-powered toggle clamps stay locked even after the air supply has been disconnected. This is important if you're using them in a glue-up fixture and want to leave parts clamped overnight without having the compressor running unattended.

When purchasing air clamps, besides design, you must consider the length of stroke and the maximum clamping pressure the device is capable of producing. Clamps with a longer stroke are capable of handling a wider range of work thicknesses; they also retract farther when opened, which might make it easier for you to load and unload work from the fixture. For most woodworking applications, select air clamps that are rated to produce between about 160 lb. and 500 lb. of force (the actual holding pressure of the clamp).

Lever-action and plunger-style air clamps are mounted by through-bolting them to a base, using machine or carriage bolts. As with standard toggle clamps, you often need to use a spacer block to get the thickness clamping capacity you need. Straight air cylinders can be mounted in a variety of ways, depending on the particular brand and model. Many, like the popular Bimba cylinders, are mounted through a large hole in a bracket or other member and secured by a large nut threaded on the end of the cylinder.

Connecting an air system   A basic air-clamping system consists of a compressor, a filter/regulator, one, two or more air-cylinder clamps, a valve and the fittings and tubing that connect them. There are several types of valves that can be used with air cylinders. The simplest has only two positions, on and off. This kind will work with single-action cylinders, but double-action cylinders commonly used in woodworking applications need a more sophisticated four-way valve.

The four-way valve, shown in the drawing on p. 172, has at least four ports: one for the incoming air, two to connect to the air clamp (one to each port, at the front and rear of the cylinder) and an exhaust port (some valves for production applications have two exhaust ports). Four-way valves come in two models: bench-mounted, hand-operated valves and foot-operated valves. Further, foot valves are available in both momentary and latching configurations. Momentary valves engage clamping pressure only while your foot remains on the pedal. This type is great for speedy tasks, where parts are clamped only briefly and the operator must process many parts rapidly. A latching foot valve keeps clamping pressure on, even if your foot is off the pedal. This is good for setups where parts must remain clamped for a long period of time, such as for glue-up, or where the operator needs to move around the machine while the part remains clamped.

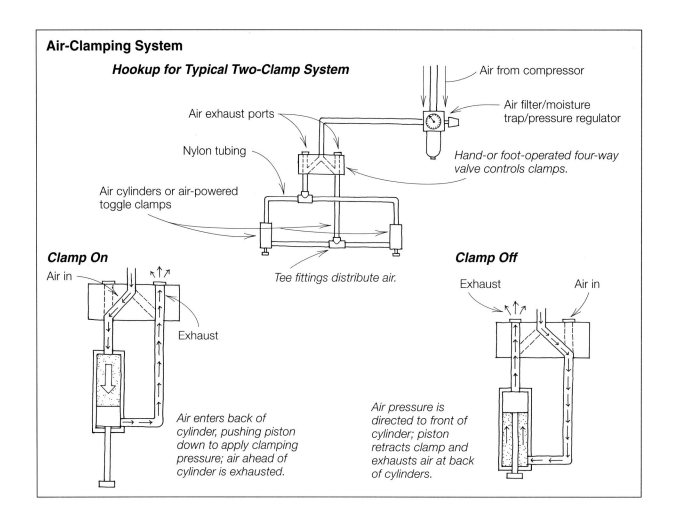

Air-Clamping System

Hookup for Typical Two-Clamp System

Air from compressor

Air filter/moisture trap/pressure regulator

Air exhaust ports

Nylon tubing

Hand-or foot-operated four-way valve controls clamps.

Air cylinders or air-powered toggle clamps

Tee fittings distribute air.

Clamp On

Air in

Exhaust

Air enters back of cylinder, pushing piston down to apply clamping pressure; air ahead of cylinder is exhausted.

Clamp Off

Exhaust

Air in

Air pressure is directed to front of cylinder; piston retracts clamp and exhausts air at back of cylinders.

You can buy standard flexible air hose with standard NPT threaded pipe fittings to connect system components, but the slickest system I've seen uses ¼-in. nylon tubing and special detachable connectors that have O-ring seals. The tubing simply plugs into fittings and seals instantly. Better yet, connections can be plugged and uplugged a few dozen times without wearing out the seal, which makes the system very flexible. The fittings (I use Quickfit brand, available from Woodworker's Supply) are available in ⅛-in. or ¼-in. sizes with male or female threads that screw directly into clamps, control valves, filters, and so on. If two clamps are connected to the same control valve, tee fittings must be installed on both intake and exhaust lines, as shown in the drawing above. If more clamps are used, a pair of manifolds will distribute the air where needed.

Although air clamps can operate without flow controllers, I highly recommend their use. These small, adjustable needle valves mount to the intake and exhaust ports on air clamps to regulate the rate at which air enters and exits, thereby changing the speed with which clamps close and open. A small screw adjusts flow rate; with a little fiddling, you can even adjust multiple clamps to close at slightly different times, to facilitate proper positioning of the workpiece during clamping. Without flow controllers, air clamps operate quite rapidly and could cause injury if operated accidentally. (For this reason, it's a good idea to locate control valves in a safe place away from the jig, where they are not likely to be activated accidentally.)

Assembly Fixtures

Most wooden items are glued together from separate parts that must be pressed against one another and held in place while the glue dries. Another breed of fixture serves this important purpose in the shop, namely, assembly fixtures. These devices provide alignment for parts and the clamping pressure necessary while the glue is setting or while nails or screws are driven. The most common types of assembly fixtures are flat clamping boards for gluing together frames and panels of all kinds. More elaborate assembly fixtures can be used effectively for lamination work or for gluing up three-dimensional constructions.

Clamping boards

Much work that takes place in the shop involves sub-assemblies, such as face frames, door and drawer frames and panels, that are put together flat and then fitted together to make a three-dimensional cabinet. Clamping boards are flat fixtures that position parts precisely and press them together with attached clamps. The positioners must also keep parts from sliding out of alignment as the clamps are tightened (they especially tend to slide when glued) or fasteners are driven. Fixture bases or other components that might get glue on them should be waxed, covered with plastic laminate or made from Melamine-coated fiberboard. From these surfaces, it's easy to clean off glue drips or flake off dried glue.

Dedicated clamping board   For production assembly of parts, nothing beats a fixture designed to handle a particular component, such as a door, window or mirror frame. The example shown in the top drawing on p. 174 is a fixture for assembling a small cabinet door frame with mitered corners. It has eight positioning blocks, two at each corner, mounted to a base. Every other block (one of each opposing pair) contains a built-in cam-lever clamp, made as described on pp. 163-165. Blocks are placed so that each miter receives clamping pressure from two directions. Further, the corner of each block nearest the tip of the

Dedicated Clamping Board for Mitered Frame

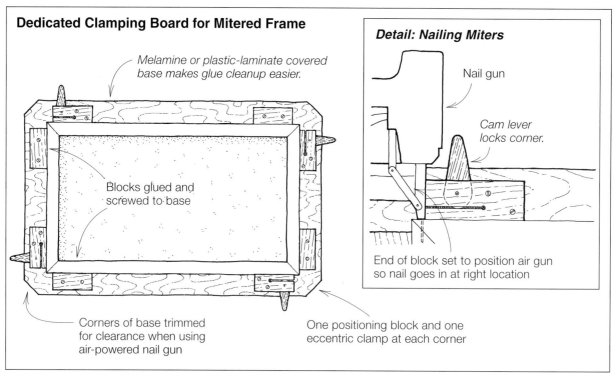

Melamine or plastic-laminate covered base makes glue cleanup easier.

Blocks glued and screwed to base

Corners of base trimmed for clearance when using air-powered nail gun

One positioning block and one eccentric clamp at each corner

Detail: Nailing Miters

Nail gun

Cam lever locks corner.

End of block set to position air gun so nail goes in at right location

Multi-Purpose Clamping Board

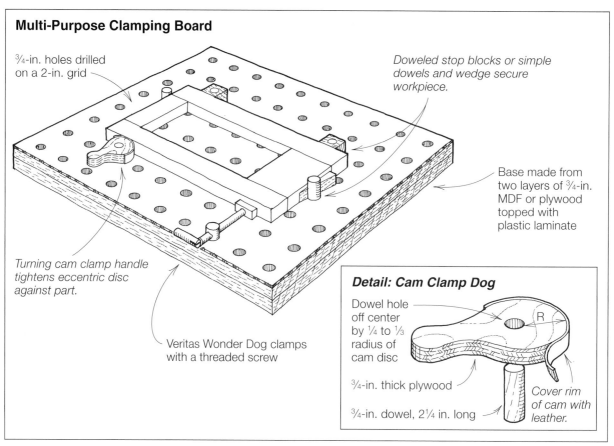

¾-in. holes drilled on a 2-in. grid

Doweled stop blocks or simple dowels and wedge secure workpiece.

Base made from two layers of ¾-in. MDF or plywood topped with plastic laminate

Turning cam clamp handle tightens eccentric disc against part.

Veritas Wonder Dog clamps with a threaded screw

Detail: Cam Clamp Dog

Dowel hole off center by ¼ to ⅓ radius of cam disc

R

¾-in. thick plywood

¾-in. dowel, 2¼ in. long

Cover rim of cam with leather.

miter is positioned to locate the head of an air-powered nail gun at the correct angle to pin each miter from two directions. This fastens the members of a glued-up frame so it can be removed from the jig to dry (see the detail in the top drawing on the facing page). Alternatively, dedicated clamping boards for high-production work, such as cabinet face-frame assembly with pocket screws, can employ air-powered plunger-style toggle clamps to hold parts during glue-up and fastening.

Multi-purpose clamping board   For more generic glue-up applications, the fixture shown in the bottom drawing on the facing page will handle flat assemblies of all shapes and sizes. It can be constructed from two layers of MDF or plywood covered with a layer of plastic laminate. A 2-in. grid pattern of ³⁄₄-in. holes accepts positioning blocks and clamping devices fitted wherever needed to secure parts of any shape. This clamping board isn't limited to glue-up; it can also be used to secure parts for other machining purposes, perhaps to hold work underneath a rail-guided sliding carriage (see pp. 60-62).

To clamp workpieces in place, you can use doweled stop blocks or just plain dowels with wedges. Cam clamp dogs, made as shown in the detail, are easy to make and tighten or loosen rapidly. A more expensive, but very effective alternative to shop-made clamping dogs is to use Veritas Wonder Dogs (see Sources of Supply on pp. 224-227). These are like metal bench dogs with a ³⁄₄-in. round shank with a screw-threaded clamp and swiveling handle.

Clamping forms and frames

Wooden objects such as compound-curved laminations and spiral stairways must often be positioned and assembled in three-dimensional space—a job that flat clamping boards clearly aren't up to. Clamping forms serve to support and orient parts in the correct spacial position for assembly. Forms can have simple concave or convex shapes or complex combinations of compound curves.

Traditionally, forms supply purchase for clamps that hold parts in position during glue-up and/or fastening. However, many woodshops today are using forms to create laminated parts in a vacuum bag. In this process, the glue-covered laminations are placed over the form (or mold), then inserted into a flexible plastic bag. After the bag is sealed, the air is evacuated from it with a vacuum pump. As with vacuum clamping (described on pp. 167-169), the atmosphere effectively provides the force necessary to press the laminations together. For more on vacuum bag lamination, see "Vacuum-Bag Veneering" by Gordon Merrick in *Fine Woodworking* #84. An informative booklet on the subject is "Advanced Vacuum Bagging Techniques," published by Gougeon Brothers, Inc. (see Sources of Supply on pp. 224-227).

Regardless of whether you use clamps or vacuum bags, lamination forms, such as the one shown in the photo below, can be cobbled up using all manner of materials, from particleboard and MDF to construction-grade plywood and lumber. The support surface usually need not be contiguous; sometimes, just a few points of contact between form and workpiece are enough. The shape of the form on the side or sides opposite the work support surface may need to be shaped to provide the right angle and good purchase for clamps (on sharply curved or angled forms, you may have to add cleats or cut notches in the form for firm clamp purchase). Finishing and waxing the form make it easier to flake off dried glue.

Sometimes, a finished assembly can serve as a lamination form. A good example is using the stringers or balusters of a spiral stairway to position and support veneers laminated into a helical handrail. After glue is applied to the laminates, they are bent into place and held with spring clamps. Clamp blocks and C-clamps are then applied along the length of the handrail.

A clamping form constructed from MDF provides a mold for several thin strips of bubinga laminated into a compound-curved rail for a desk. The form also provides purchase for the clamps used to press the laminates together.

If you often face the challenge of gluing up complicated parts, there is an affordable system of fixture fittings, tubing and extrusions available from RK Industries (see Sources of Supply on pp. 224-227). these fittings provide an extremely flexible yet rigid means of creating complex three-dimensional space frames. They can be used for clamping parts for all kinds of complex assemblies prior to fastening or glue-up. The photo below shows a small frame being used with toggle clamps to hold compound-mitered parts in position for gluing.

Commercially made fixture fittings, such as these sold by RK Industries, are useful for creating many types of adjustable assembly and clamping frames. The small frame here holds two parts of a wooden puzzle at a precise compound angle while they are glued together with a cyanoacrylate adhesive.

CHAPTER 7

Materials, Hardware and Construction

Some woodworkers are content to cobble up a jig or fixture out of any old bits and pieces they can find in the scrap box and junk drawer. While it's true that temporary fixtures or one-time jigs usually aren't worth the investment of expensive materials and hardware, jigs designed for everyday use will last longer and retain their accuracy if they are built from high-quality materials following good woodworking construction practices. Well-built jigs are a pleasure to use—a source of great personal pride—and will perhaps become heirlooms you'll want to hand down to another generation of woodworkers.

As with jig designs, there is no one "right" material or construction technique for any given setup. That's why I'll be discussing a variety of materials, general-purpose hardware and construction techniques and tell you what applications they're best suited for. (It seemed more appropriate to discuss some particular hardware items, such as bullet catches, vacuum valves and pneumatic clamps, in the chapters where their use is described.) I've endeavored to include sources for all the hardware and fasteners discussed here and throughout the book, as well as mail-order suppliers for many of the materials. Addresses for these suppliers and some manufacturers are listed in Sources of Supply, which begins on p 224.

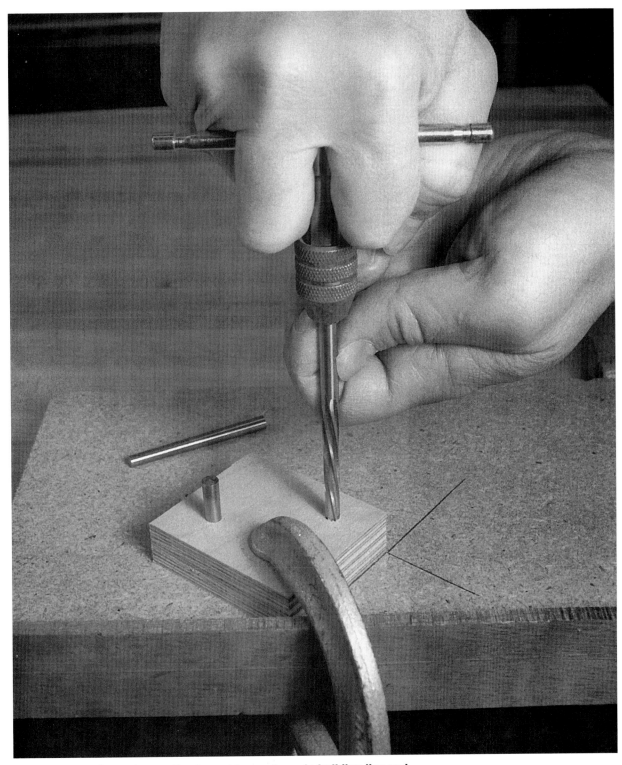

Machinist's equipment can often be put to good use in building jigs and fixtures for woodworking. Here, a spiral reamer (p. 194) is used with a tap handle to prepare holes in a stop block for a pair of #4 taper pins.

Materials

Depending on your needs and preferences, jigs and fixtures can be built from a wide range of wood and wood composite materials, plastics and metals—aluminum in particular. Each has its niche in the jig builder's arsenal of materials. In this section I'll discuss the strengths and weaknesses of most popular jig-building materials, including solid woods and plywoods, as well as some lesser known—but very versatile—materials, such as MDO (medium-density overlay) and polycarbonate plastic. A few specialized materials, such as UHMW glide strips and plastic laminates, will also be presented.

Wood and wood composites

To the average woodworker, solid wood is probably the most obvious choice for building jigs and fixtures. Yet natural wood's eternal responsiveness to atmospheric moisture, resulting in dimensional changes and occasional warpage, makes it less than desirable for jig parts that must maintain crucial tolerances. Large, flat parts, such as sliding carriage bases and auxiliary tables, are better served by composite materials, such as plywood (laminated from thin wood veneers), particleboard (pressed together from wood particles and glue) and MDF and hardboards (made up of fibers consolidated under heat and pressure). Each of these man-made materials has different properties that make it ideal for some jig applications, terrible for others.

Solid wood   Solid stock is a good choice for some jig parts, especially if lightness and strength are issues. I often use kiln-dried, vertical-grained fir (commonly available on the West Coast) for fences, lips and other long, thin components. For stop blocks, cam clamp levers or other parts that must be extra strong and endure abrasion, a dense hardwood like rock maple is a good choice. For parts that slide, such as the guide bars on a crosscut box (see pp. 42-43) or runners on a three-dimensional-shaping carriage (see pp. 69-70), teak is a fine choice because of its natural oiliness, which serves as a lubricant.

Whichever solid woods you employ in your jigs, make sure that they have been properly air- dried or kiln-dried to between 7% and 15% moisture content. If possible, let the lumber sit for a week or two in your shop before building with it, so it may achieve equilibrium moisture content in your indoor environment. For best stability in parts that are more than 4 in. wide, choose boards that have been quarter-sawn (with the annual rings perpendicular to the face of the board), as wood expands and contracts less radially than tangentially.

Plywood   You can cut strong straight or curved parts out of plywood without concern for grain direction because of its dimensionally stable cross-ply construction. For this reason plywood is an ideal jig-

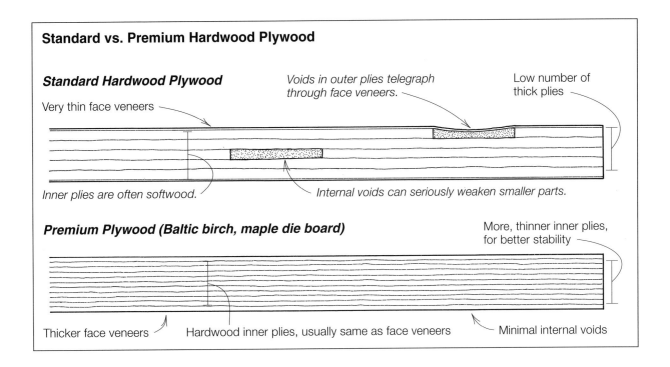

Standard vs. Premium Hardwood Plywood

Standard Hardwood Plywood

Very thin face veneers

Voids in outer plies telegraph through face veneers.

Low number of thick plies

Inner plies are often softwood.

Internal voids can seriously weaken smaller parts.

Premium Plywood (Baltic birch, maple die board)

More, thinner inner plies, for better stability

Thicker face veneers

Hardwood inner plies, usually same as face veneers

Minimal internal voids

building material. However, standard softwood- and hardwood- faced plywoods are usually laminated with internal plies of poor quality softwood containing defects that would weaken cut parts (see the drawing above). Also, these standard lumberyard plywoods may deviate 1/32 in. or more from their specified thicknesses, making it more troublesome to fit tight joints. That is why many woodworkers prefer to use premium plywoods, such as Baltic birch, apple ply and maple die board. Baltic birch (and its neighbors Finnish birch, Russian birch and Polish birch) are found more and more often at hardwood-lumber dealers and sold mail order by some suppliers (see Sources of Supply on pp. 224-227). Apple ply (which, despite its name, doesn't have even a splinter of apple wood in it) is a maple plywood, as is maple die board. Both are very dense plywoods that are often used by die and pattern makers.

Premium plywoods cost more, but are a joy to work with. First, the face plies are nearly the same thickness as internal plies, making them less susceptible to splintering and tearout. Second, the internal plies are made from hardwood veneers (birch or maple) that have a minimum number of voids (holes, loose knots, etc.), making premium plywoods very strong and consistent. Third, premium plywoods are glued up from a larger number of thinner plies than standard plywoods (for example, 3/4 -in. Baltic birch has 11 laminations; standard 3/4-in. plywood has only 7). The more plies, the more stable the material, which is especially important with thinner sheets (i.e., 1/4 in., 3/8 in.).

If you can't locate a source for premium plywoods, you can substitute marine-grade plywood, which typically comes with A- or B-grade faces and no internal voids. It's expensive, but you do get the bonus of an exterior-grade adhesive. The budget-conscious jig maker's standby, shop-grade birch plywood, is also serviceable. It is usually a higher-grade birch plywood that has been downgraded because of banged-up corners or cosmetic blemishes. The bargain pricing is more than worth the slight inconvenience of cutting around these defects when making jig parts.

There are a few other plywood-based materials that are useful for building jigs. Medium-density overlay (MDO) is plywood composed of softwood plies faced with a thermoresin-impregnated paper that gives both sides a very smooth, uniform surface not subject to grain raising. MDO looks very clean, although its surfaces have low scratch and abrasion resistance. Plywood with hardboard surfaces, trade named Plyron, combines the stability of plywood with the smoothness and surface density of hardboard (see the discussion on the facing page). It's useful for jig bases. Your local lumberyard may have to special-order these materials for you.

Particleboard Standard underlayment-grade particleboard, the kind most often sold at lumberyards and home-supply stores, is inexpensive and readily available. While serviceable for jig bases in non-critical applications, its low internal density and mediocre strength make it a poor choice for most other jig parts, the exception being assembly forms where strength and edge quality aren't crucial (see pp. 173-176). Especially avoid using particleboard for templates used with piloted bits—the ball-bearing pilot will likely dig into the edge and ruin the part and template. Also, like solid wood, particleboards (as well as MDF and hardboards, described below) are hygroscopic and can change very slightly in dimension—especially in thickness, up to 5%—with changes in the moisture content of the air. Particleboard is made with formaldehyde-based glues, which can cause adverse reactions in susceptible individuals.

Medium-density fiberboard (MDF) Normally lumped in with particleboard, MDF is actually a hardboard product. MDF is comparable in strength and stability to medium-density particleboard, but made of more finely ground particles with 10% glue as a binder. MDF is a much better-jig building material than underlayment particleboard because MDF's core is at least 85% as dense as its faces. This makes for clean, smooth edges for jig parts. Its dense edges also make it terrific as a template material; piloted router bits don't compress MDF the way they will particleboard. Because of its exceptionally smooth, dependably flat surface, many woodworkers prefer MDF over even premium-grade plywoods for making jig bases or jig table surfaces.

On the down side, MDF weighs roughly 50% more than plywood, which may be an important consideration if lightness is critical to the setup you're building. Under a sustained load, MDF will sag (as will particleboard) so large surfaces should be supported more thoroughly than if they were made from plywood or solid wood. One strategy for making MDF panels more rigid is to cover both sides (as well as the edges) with plastic laminate. Like a torsion box (see pp. 202-203), the laminate skins stiffen the solid MDF core, making the panel surprisingly rigid and useful for auxiliary table tops.

One last caveat: MDF can be messy to work with because of the very fine dust generated when it is cut or shaped. A powerful dust-collection system is almost a must. The fact that most MDF sheet goods are made with formaldehyde-based glues makes matters worse, especially for people who are hypersensitive to formaldehyde. Fortunately, low-formaldehyde MDF (made by Plum Creek) and formaldehyde-free MDF (made by Medite) are available (see Sources of Supply on pp. 224-227). These products are notably more expensive than regular MDF products, but woodworkers I've spoken to don't mind because they find them healthier to work with and a bit tougher and lighter than regular MDF as well.

Hardboard   Hardboards are very versatile fiber-based sheet goods that are used for templates and other jigs with curves because they are typically harder than most solid woods. Hardboards come "screen backed" (smooth on one side with an imprint of the screen pressing process on the other) or smooth on two sides (S2S). Tempered hardboard, such as Masonite, is a high-density hardboard that's been impregnated with resin, then heat cured. Tempering improves the board's hardness, water resistance and strength. Masonite's clean, durable edge makes it a favorite for thin, long-lasting templates for pattern routing. Its abrasion-resistant surface also makes it suitable as a thin base material for sliding carriages.

Clear plastics

No material has proliferated in the modern material world more extensively than plastics. In the woodshop, plastics have not only replaced many of the metal and wood parts in our power and hand tools, but they are also the material of choice for many parts in the jigs that we build. Most common plastics can be worked with standard woodshop tools (see the sidebar on p. 184).

Among all the various types of plastics, few are as useful in jig building as clear plastics. By virtue of their transparency, clear plastics can be used to advantage in many applications: A see-through insert plate on a router table allows better visibility, for easier bit changes; a clear guard protects the user without hindering his or her sight. Acrylics

Working with Plastic Sheet Goods

Plastics, both clear and opaque, are important materials in the jig builder's cache. Most of the plastics described in the main text can be cut, drilled, countersunk, routed and sanded with regular woodworking machines and tools.

When sawing parts to size with circular saws, choose a fine-toothed 10-in. blade in the 60- to 80-tooth range. You can use an inexpensive steel plywood-veneer blade, or if you prefer carbide teeth, a triple-chip grind yields the best results. For extremely clean cuts in plastics up to ¼ in. thick try an 80-tooth sawblade such as the Freud LU98 or the #108-800, made by CMT Tools (see Sources of Supply on pp. 224-227).

When bandsawing curved shapes (as for making templates), choose a coarse-pitch (2 to 4 TPI) blade for plastic sheet goods ½ in. or more thick. For plastic sheet goods in the ⅛-in. to ⅜-in. thick range, use a medium blade (6 to 12 TPI); for plastic sheet goods thinner than ⅛ in., use a fine blade (14 to 32 TPI). With any plastic, blade speed should be slow (800 ft./min.), and so should the feed rate (2 to 4 ft./min.). Acrylic plastic can be scored and snapped like a pane of glass, although snapped edges won't be as clean as sawn ones.

You can clean up the edges of sawn parts by sanding them with a belt, disc or drum sander. Coarse (60-grit to 100-grit) closed-coat abrasives work best (papers finer than 120 grit tend to load up quickly). During sanding, it's important to keep the plastic part moving and not sand any one section too long, lest heat buildup cause the sanded particles to become a gummy slag. If your power sander is variable speed, reducing its rpm will also reduce heat buildup on the sanded edge.

Most plastics can be routed with standard carbide-tipped bits, but ideally with the bit slowed down. This is best accomplished with a variable-speed router, set between 10,000 rpm and 12,000 rpm (you can reduce the rpm of a regular router by plugging it into an electronic speed controller; see Sources of Supply on pp. 224-227). Before drilling plastics (especially acrylics), regrind your drill bits to have a 1/32-in. wide flat on the cutting edges, as shown in the drawing at right. The flat creates a scraping action that prevents the bit from grabbing or gumming up, and you'll get cleaner holes that are less susceptible to cracking. A single-flute machinist's style countersink (see the photo on p. 189) works much cleaner than a multi-flute style countersink.

Clear plastics (especially acrylics) scratch fairly easily and accumulate scratches, so the protective paper should be left on until the part is completely cut and drilled. Should the plastic become scratched, you can sometimes buff out fine scratches with a fine rubbing compound (available from auto-supply stores, for restoring plastic rear windows). You can also try rubbing toothpaste in small circles over the scratched area with a soft, damp cloth.

Regrinding Drill Bits for Acrylic Plastic

Grind or file a small flat on each cutting edge of bit, so it cuts with a scraping action.

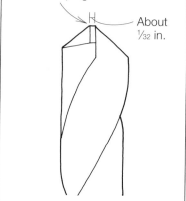

About 1/32 in.

A thin piece of polycarbonate plastic for a custom safety guard is easily bent to shape. A paint-stripping heat gun provides the heat, while plywood cauls clamped to the plastic limit heat to the area of the bend and provide a handle for bending.

and polycarbonates are the two main groups of clear plastics. To tell them apart, look at them edge on, with the protective paper removed. The edge of the polycarbonate will look dark gray; the acrylic will have a yellowish tint to it.

Because they are thermoplastics, thin (⅛-in. to ¼-in.) acrylic or poly-carbonate strips can be heated and bent to shape to form jig parts and safety guards (for some examples, see pgs. 209 and 211). With the pa-per off, parts are clamped between two pairs of plywood cauls, which limit heat to a narrow band (a little wider than the thickness of the part) where the piece will be bent (see the photo above). A paint-strip-ping heat gun is applied alternately to both sides until the plastic is soft enough to bend. The bend must then be held in position until it sets when cool.

Acrylics Acrylics are stiffer than polycarbonates and will not sag or flex as much (see the photos on p. 186). Acrylic plastics, including brand names such as Acrylite and Plexiglas, are easy to cut, sand, rout and glue. On the down side, acrylics can shatter, so I avoid using them for guards or for close-fitting insert plates around a blade or cutter. Acrylics are more susceptible to cracking and splitting than polycar-bonates, both during cutting or drilling and afterwards. It is not un-common to see small cracks develop around holes drilled through acrylic plastic, especially if the screws through such holes are driven

Placing the same weight on top of narrow strips of acrylic (left) and polycarbonate plastic (right) clearly shows that acrylic is stiffer. Acrylics are less likely to sag under heavy loads; however, they are also more brittle and susceptible to shattering.

tightly. Acrylic parts can be edge glued or face glued using special solvent adhesives (available from plastics suppliers), but cyanoacrylates ("super glues") also work very well. Clamp or tape parts into position with joints butted together and wick the thin solvent/glue into the joints, then allow the assembly to dry.

Polycarbonates   Polycarbonate plastics, including brand names such as Cyrolon, Lexan and Tuffak, are less stiff than acrylic plastics but are 30 times more impact resistant and won't shatter into shards. These qualities make them ideal materials for chip deflectors, guards and other safety devices (see pp. 209-211). If you use polycarbonate for insert plates, such as for mounting a router in a table, use thicker stock than you would for a similar acrylic plate to avoid sagging. You can glue polycarbonate with a cement such as Duco.

Opaque plastics

Opaque plastics are generally more durable and scratch resistant than clear plastics, but they also tend to be more expensive and not as easy to find. Phenolics and polyethylene plastics are available in small sheets, which are useful for making insert plates and jig bases. Solid-surface materials can be purchased as scraps or in larger sheets, to use as tops for accessory tables or portable power-tool tables.

Phenolics   Phenolic plastics are about twice as expensive as either acrylic or polycarbonate plastics, but they are stiffer and will take more abuse and repeated wear. This makes them a better choice for insert plates and jigs designed for production woodworking. Phenolics parts can be glued together with epoxy if the mating surfaces are abraded, but the bond isn't good enough for applications where high strength is a factor; fasten parts mechanically instead.

Polyethylene   Polyethylene sheet goods are high-density, fairly costly materials that provide a remarkably slick surface (UHMW glide strips, described on p. 188, are made from dense polyethylene). In addition to being a good fence covering, polyethylene is a great material for carriage glides (see pp. 42-50). This plastic machines easily, doesn't crack or chip and also drills and taps well—just don't try to glue it; even epoxy won't bond to it well. The density and non-porosity of polyethylene also make it particularly good for vacuum hold-down jigs and tables (see pp. 167-169).

Solid-surface materials   With brand names such as Avonite, Corian, Gibraltar and Surell, solid-surface materials are plastics that feel similar to thick polyethylene, except they aren't as slippery. However, you can't usually buy a sheet directly from a dealer. Installers typically sell cutoffs and scraps (check your local Yellow Pages under "Counter Tops"), which will suffice for building most jigs or tops for small portable-power-tool tables.

Solid-surface materials cut and machine well with woodworking tools, but there are a few things to keep in mind. Screwing directly into them with wood screws can cause cracking. Instead, bolt through them or glue wood blocks onto the material and set screws into the blocks. Also, the corners of tables or parts should be rounded, since sharp corners invite cracking. If you wish to glue solid-surface materials together, you must use a special two-part glue made by the manufacturer. When gluing down a large table or base on a frame or substrate, use a flexible adhesive, such as silicone. The flexibility allows the solid surface material to expand and contract with temperature changes.

Plastics for slippery surfaces

Workpieces often need to slide smoothly over fence, table and jig-base surfaces past a cutter or blade. Any jerkiness or unevenness in feed rate can translate into roughness in the cut surface, or even scorching from cutters or bits. A surface can be improved by fine sanding, then finishing and waxing or applying a dry coating, such as Sandaro Top-Cote, but waxes and coatings wear off. It's better to create a permanently slippery surface by covering jig parts with either plastic laminates or special low-friction plastics.

Plastic laminate   Plastic laminates, such as Formica or Wilsonart, are readily available and make terrific smooth, durable surfaces for auxiliary tables or jig bases. They are easy to bond to plywood or composite substrates (such as MDF) with contact cement (you can get away with using regular yellow glue to apply laminates to small surfaces) and provide a hard, relatively slick surface for workpieces to slide on or against. It's highly recommended that you cover assembly tables and glue-up fixtures with plastic laminates; excess adhesive easily peels or scraps off, for fast cleanup.

Low-friction plastics Ultra-high molecular weight (UHMW) plastic glide strips made from dense polyethylene are a tough material that provide a very slick surface. Available in the form of ⅛-in. and ¼-in. thick strips, UHMW plastic can be cut to length or shape easily with a razor knife and screwed or nailed to wood parts to form a surface even more slippery than plastic laminate. Rolls of even thinner UHMW strip are also available with a pressure-sensitive adhesive backing, ready to stick on fence faces (see the photo below). The material also comes in thicker stock (⅜ in. through ¾ in.), which is good for fabricating low-friction fences or guide bars.

Another low-friction product, Nylotape, is a very thin nylon tape; it comes in ½-in. wide and 3-in. wide rolls with a pressure-sensitive peel-and-stick backing. I've used it successfully on the bottom of several miter-slot-guided sliding carriages I've built; the carriage's base contacts the saw table only on these thin strips, so it glides with very little effort. When there isn't enough surface area to attach a glide strip, such as on an outrigger carriage brace, plastic stem bumpers are a good alternative. These small components press into 3⁄16-in. dia. holes to provide small points of low-friction contact.

A thin ultra-high molecular weight (UHMW) polyethylene strip applied to a fence face provides a very slick gliding surface. The paper backing is peeled off a little at a time, and the pressure-sensitive-adhesive backing is stuck down and pressed in place with a rubber veneer roller.

Aluminum

Occasionally, you need a material that's stiffer, stronger and more durable than wood or plastic materials. Aluminum is a good choice because it is affordable and, with a little care, it can be sawn and drilled with regular woodworking machinery. Aluminum is readily available in many forms, including plate, flat stock, rods, tubing and a wide range of extruded shapes (thin plate aluminum is terrific for making insert plates and small jig parts). Check your local Yellow Pages under "Aluminum Suppliers" or "Steel Suppliers," and ask for stock in 2024 T6 or 7075 T6 alloys, which work best; avoid 6061 alloys, which can gum up blades and cutters.

For cutting on the table saw, you should select a carbide-tipped blade with lots of teeth (I'd recommend at least 72 on a 10-in. dia. blade). More important, the blade should have deep gullets between teeth. This is because aluminum swarf (the waste produced by cutting or machining) can gum up teeth. Freud makes a very good blade (the LU89) specifically for cutting aluminum and other non-ferrous metals, such as brass. Cut all parts on the table saw using a miter gauge for crosscutting long parts. Never cut aluminum on the radial-arm saw: The blade can self-feed into the stock, with disastrous consequences. As you cut, keep the blade coated with a fluid lubricant, such as WD-40, or a dry lubricant, such as Sandaro DriCote, and feed the workpiece past the blade slowly.

For cutting curved parts on the bandsaw, choose a standard coarse-pitch blade (pitch refers to the number of teeth per inch, or TPI; a coarse-pitch blade has 3 to 5 TPI). Cutting thin stock (less than ⅛-in. thick sheet or thin-walled tubing) calls for a medium-pitch blade (5 to 7 TPI). For thick plate (¼ in. or more), choose a blade that will have no more than three teeth in the stock at any one time. Set the saw to a slow speed (800 ft./min. or less) and feed the material slowly past the blade. As with circular blades, using a lubricant will prevent the gummy swarf from clogging the blade teeth and gullets. While it is possible to do so, I don't recommend routing aluminum; it's too hard to control the process working freehand.

Construction with aluminum is usually a matter of bolting components together. Machine screws set into tapped holes in the face or edge of the material hold extremely well. The metal can also be glued to itself or wood with epoxy. Aluminum is difficult to braze or weld, but fortunately, it drills and taps very easily. Using a drill press and clamping parts down securely will prevent broken bits, a likely outcome if large holes are drilled freehand. For deep holes, lubricate the bit with a light oil or dishwashing soap. A machinist's style countersink works extremely well in aluminum, as in most plastics, for countersinking holes for flat-head screws, as shown in the photo at right.

A machinist's countersink works clean and chatter-free in wood, aluminum or plastic, countersinking predrilled holes for flat-head screws. Countersinking metal, as shown here, should be done on a drill press, with the part accurately centered and firmly clamped.

High-friction materials

One way to improve the stability of parts that are hand-held against a fence or stop is to apply some kind of high-friction material to keep the workpiece from slipping or creeping. The most popular and readily available material is ordinary paper-backed sandpaper. For most applications, 80-grit to 150-grit sheets work well. Sandpaper can be glued to wood surfaces by applying a spray adhesive to the backing and sticking it in place. Coated abrasives last longer than regular sandpapers. If you use a coarser or thicker-backed abrasive, you should cover the entire fence, lest the thickness of a small patch skew the workpiece relative to the fence (however, thin-backed papers can be applied just to the location under where hand pressure will grip the workpiece). Small patches may also be applied directly to the faces of clamping device. If you need to prevent parts from slipping on clamp faces or stops with small surface area, such as the end stop of the taper jig described on pp. 53-54, apply a non-skid tape, such as 3M Safety Walk, which is normally used on stair treads.

Hardware

Sometimes, finding just the right piece of hardware when building a custom jig or fixture can save a lot of fuss and bother. Some standard hardware items, such as hinges and bullet catches, are readily available and can be most useful in ways they weren't originally meant for (an example: using a cabinetmaker's bullet catch for a detent, as discussed on pp. 120-121). Other special hardware items, such as guide bars, tracks, and micro-adjusters, are designed for woodworking jigs and fixtures. Many hardware items described in this section can be purchased through good hardware stores and supply catalogs; sources for specialized or hard-to-find items are listed on pp. 224-227.

Fasteners

Building strong, versatile jigs often calls for more than simple nails and glue. A stunning array of fasteners, ranging from common screws to specialized threaded inserts, is readily available to suit a whole spectrum of a jig builder's needs. Simple fasteners, such as drywall screws and pneumatically driven staples, allow jigs to be assembled with lightening speed, without sacrificing strength. Other fastening devices, such as screw posts and studded handscrews, provide a means for jig parts to pivot, remain detachable or articulate for adjustment.

Drywall screws   Most serious woodworkers I know eschew standard zinc-plated steel wood screws in favor of hardened-steel drywall screws. Drywall screws are stronger, drive more aggressively, generally have deeper threads (for better holding power) and are far cheaper when bought by the pound at the local building supply. McFeely offers an impressive assortment of square-drive (Robertson) hardened-steel screws (see Sources of Supply on pp. 224-227), including bugle-head screws that are self-countersinking.

Pneumatic staples The Senco Model K pneumatic narrow-crown staple gun (see the photo on p. 202) is an indispensable fastening tool in my shop. Stapling is an extremely quick and easy way to assemble jig parts in a hurry—which is the state many of us are in all too often. The staples, which are only about ¼ in. wide and come in lengths from ⅝ in. to 1½ in., have two dry-adhesive-coated shanks that hold better than simple nails. You can use staples to "clamp" jig parts together that have glue applied to them. But staple carefully, and God help you if parts get stapled together the wrong way: Staples are extremely difficult to remove without mangling the wood parts.

Threaded inserts and T-nuts If your jig parts need to be disassembled at some point, you can install a threaded metal socket for a bolt or machine screw into a solid wood, plywood or composite material (i.e., MDF) by driving a threaded insert or a T-nut (see the drawing below). Threaded inserts are installed on the same face or edge as the part is to be bolted to; this makes threaded inserts suitable for adding threaded sockets on the edges of parts, and on parts too thick to easily bolt through. T-nuts must be installed on the side opposite the insertion of

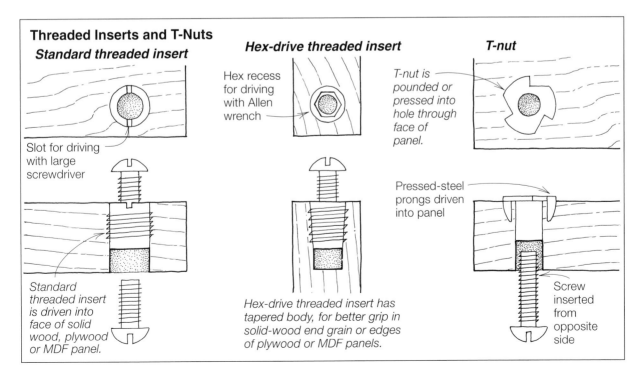

Threaded Inserts and T-Nuts

Standard threaded insert

Slot for driving with large screwdriver

Standard threaded insert is driven into face of solid wood, plywood or MDF panel.

Hex-drive threaded insert

Hex recess for driving with Allen wrench

Hex-drive threaded insert has tapered body, for better grip in solid-wood end grain or edges of plywood or MDF panels.

T-nut

T-nut is pounded or pressed into hole through face of panel.

Pressed-steel prongs driven into panel

Screw inserted from opposite side

the bolt. Both brass and steel inserts are available to fit bolts from 6-32 to ⅜ in. Special hex-drive inserts have coarse teeth and are designed to be driven into end grain, as shown in the drawing. Also, special press-in threaded inserts are available from Reid Tool Supply (see Sources of Supply on pp. 224-227) for adding strong metal threads to plastic parts.

To install a threaded insert, first drill a hole that is the same as the root diameter of the insert (the body minus the teeth). Most styles of inserts have slots on one end that fit a very large screwdriver; some have an Allen fitting. But these tools lend very little control to keep the insert threading straight into the hole. A better way to install them is to run a short bolt with jam nut and washer into the insert and drive it in with a ratcheting socket wrench (see the photo below). The ratchet wrench gives you plenty of downward pressure to keep the insert's threads from stripping in the wood, as well as a more sensitive feel as the insert is driven. The washer helps flatten lifted grain as the insert is seated flush to the surface. A quick snap of the wrench counterclockwise loosens the bolt. You can also buy a special T-handled wrench designed to install threaded inserts that lends a good grip for plenty of torque while driving (the wrench is visible in the foreground of the photo). You must buy a separate wrench for each insert diameter.

Although they are less versatile than threaded inserts, T-nuts are also less expensive and easier to install. T-nuts are commonly available in sizes to handle bolts from 10-24 to ⅜ in. A hole is drilled to match the body diameter of the T-nut, which is pounded into the hole (on the opposite side that the bolt or screw is driven from) with a mallet or pressed in with a small arbor press. Prongs on the T-nut lock it into the wood and keep it from turning.

Threaded inserts can be installed with a special T-handled wrench (shown in the foreground) or by screwing a regular bolt with washer and jam nut into the insert, then driving with a socket wrench.

Hanger bolts Hanger bolts provide a handy way to mount a stud for wing nuts or handscrews on a wooden part. Half of a hanger bolt has a wood-screw-type thread; the other half a standard machine-screw thread. Sizes range from 8-32 to ⅜ in., and lengths range from ⅝ in. to 3 in. Short hanger bolts are a fast, easy way to attach a handle or knob to a carriage or pivoting jig or to mount studs for safety guards or dust-collection fittings. Longer hanger bolts set into a jig base are substantial enough to use for mounting a portable power tool (see the belt-sander table on pp. 100-101).

Like regular screws, hanger bolts require a pilot hole that's the root diameter of the screw part of the bolt (see the photo at right). They are installed by first locking two nuts together on the machine-thread end, then using a socket wrench to drive them in. To keep them from turning once set, I usually put a drop or two of epoxy on the wood-screw end before installation.

Screw posts Screw posts, which are also called post & screw or Chicago screws or bolts, consist of two parts: a hollow post and a screw that threads into it; both have flat heads with screwdriver slots in them. The O.D. of the smooth shank is typically ¼ in., and it fits snugly into a ¼-in. hole drilled through two parts, providing an accurate pivot pin. A thin washer or shim (you can punch or cut one out from flattened aluminum can stock) between wood parts helps them pivot more smoothly (see the drawing below).

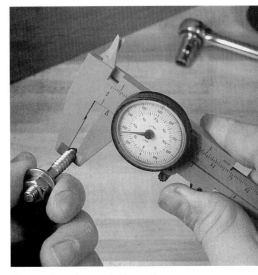

Measuring the root diameter — the size of the shank without the threads — is one way to determine the size of the pilot hole needed to install the wood-screw half of a hanger bolt (or any wood screw). Two nuts and a washer locked onto the hanger bolt's machine screw half provide purchase for a socket wrench to drive it in.

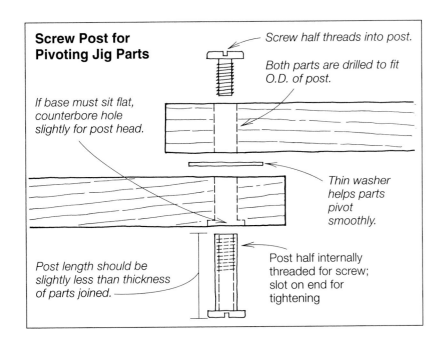

Screw Post for Pivoting Jig Parts

Screw half threads into post.

Both parts are drilled to fit O.D. of post.

If base must sit flat, counterbore hole slightly for post head.

Thin washer helps parts pivot smoothly.

Post half internally threaded for screw; slot on end for tightening

Post length should be slightly less than thickness of parts joined.

Because they can be easily disassembled, screw posts are good for jigs that have interchangeable components or jigs that come apart for storage. If the thickness of parts doesn't suit the stock length of the shank, it can be shortened with a fine-toothed hacksaw or razor saw. Screw posts come in both plastic and aluminum; they are available through well-stocked hardware and hobby stores, leather-tool suppliers, and from The Woodworker's Store. Related fasteners, such as joint connector bolts and cap nuts (from the 32mm system), are like beefy screw posts; these are good for heavier-duty applications.

Taper pins   Taper pins are machinist's devices commonly used for accurately locating rotating or moving parts such as a drill-press table or jointer fence at standard positions, such as square and 45°. The pin fits into a hole drilled through one part and into the other. Taper pins provide a very handy way to locate rotating or removable stops, to fix the angle of fences (see the utility fence on pp. 7-9) or to reference the position of auxiliary tables on stationary machines (see p. 76). They come in many sizes, which are specified by their degree of taper and by their length. Pins used by machinists have tapers that range from #7/0 (the least taper) to #14 (the most taper). I've found the middle-sized pins with #4 and #5 tapers to be most useful for woodworking jigging applications. The friction of a pair of taper pins alone is enough to hold many stops and small parts.

Why use a taper pin rather than regular metal pin or wood dowel? Because with any cylindrical pin, hole size is crucial: Too loose, and the fit won't be accurate; too tight and pins are tough to insert and remove. In contrast, taper pins are self-centering and continue to seat accurately, even if the holes wear slightly larger in diameter, an especially important consideration with wooden jig parts.

To fit parts with taper pins, first align the parts in the desired position and clamp them firmly together. Then drill slightly undersized holes (about the size of the small end of the pin) into both parts (it's preferable to drill through both parts, so pins can be tapped out from the narrow end for removal). Then ream the holes with a special tapered reamer, available from a machinist supply store, mounted in a standard tap handle (see the photo on p. 179).

Hand knobs and studded handscrews   By using hand knobs and studded handscrews in lieu of standard hex- or slot-headed bolts and nuts, you can adjust jigs and fixtures quickly without the use of wrenches or tools. The shapes of the handles, which include three-prong, knurled and star (also called rosette), T and winged, give you plenty of choices for size and leverage for proper tightening. Hand knobs have a built-in threaded insert and tighten onto the end of a T-bolt, regular screw or bolt, or onto a stud. Some hand knobs have nylon inserts, like nylon

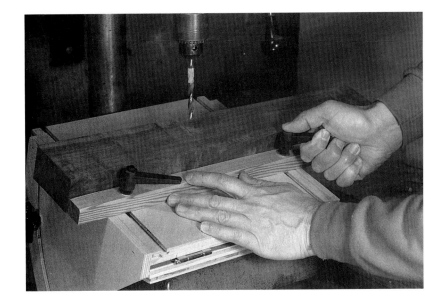

lock nuts. The insert keeps friction on the threads of the bolt so vibration won't loosen it. But hand knobs with nylon inserts are harder to tighten and loosen than hand knobs without them. Before buying, ask your suppliers which kind they stock.

Studded handscrews are like machine screws with plastic hand knobs attached. Locking knobs are another kind of handscrew, with adjustable handles that are spring loaded so that the handle remains engaged unless it is lifted. These work great in tight spaces where you need to change the handle's position to get added clearance or to make an extra turn. They are also useful for tightening adjustable fences or stops where the handle would normally obstruct the workpiece (see the photo above).

Tracks and guide bars

While fasteners provide a means of assembling and articulating jig parts, other special hardware items serve to make jigs more accurate and versatile. Commercially made miter guide bars slide are easier to install on carriage jigs and slide truer than shop-made wood bars. T-track and T-track hardware (such as T-bolts and T-nuts), whether shop-made using a special T-slot bit or purchased as a ready-to-install track, can add tremendous versatility to adjustable jigs or clamping fixtures. And T-track systems, such as FasTTrack, are like erector sets for building all manner of fences, stops and carriages.

T-tracks   One of the handiest methods of joining jig parts that must adjust is to use a T-track and T-bolt fasteners. A T-track can provide a flexible way to mount fences, stops, hold-down clamps or to attach auxiliary tables and more; examples are plentiful throughout the book. You can rout a T-slot into any solid wood, plywood or MDF surface with a special T-slot bit (available from Woodhaven or from the Woodworker's Store). The T-track slot is cut in two passes. The first pass, with a straight bit, makes a plain groove as long as the desired track length. The second pass is taken with the special bit that cuts the T-slot at the bottom of the groove (see the drawing below). The Woodhaven bit requires precutting with a ¼-in. or ⁵⁄₁₆-in. dia. straight bit and cuts a T-slot best suited to ¼-in. dia. T-bolts or toilet bolts. The Woodworker's Store T-slot bit needs a precut ⁵⁄₁₆-in. or ³⁄₈-in. dia. groove and is best for ⁵⁄₁₆-in. dia. T-bolts; the track it makes provides too loose a fit for toilet bolts.

For applications where a more durable slot is needed, The Woodworker's Store offers a pressed-steel track that fits ⁵⁄₁₆-in. dia. T-bolts. The track, which comes in lengths of 40 in. and 60 in., can be cut with a hacksaw and is designed to be epoxied into a ¹³⁄₁₆-in. wide, ¹³⁄₃₂-in. deep slot.

To attach parts or devices to a T-track, T-bolts or T-nuts ride in the track. T-bolts are available in ¼-in. and ⁵⁄₁₆-in. sizes and come in a variety of lengths to suit the thickness of the part. Standard toilet bolts (found in the plumbing department of a hardware store) can also be used, but not in all T-tracks (see above). T-bolts may be secured with a regular nut, wing nut or hand knob. Standard carriage bolts can also be used in T-tracks, but this first requires the depth of the T to be increased with the T-slot bit to clear the head. In my experience, car-

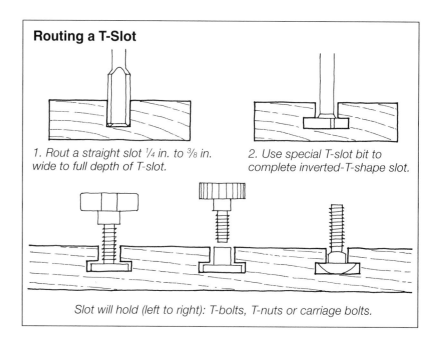

Routing a T-Slot

1. Rout a straight slot ¼ in. to ⅜ in. wide to full depth of T-slot.

2. Use special T-slot bit to complete inverted-T-shape slot.

Slot will hold (left to right): T-bolts, T-nuts or carriage bolts.

riage bolts can't take as much torque as a T-bolts can without stripping the edges of the slot. T-nuts are available to fit several different screw-thread sizes, from 10-24 to ⅜ in. These are secured using a machine screw, a bolt or a studded handscrew.

FasTTrack   A practical alternative to using standard T-slots and hardware is the FasTTrack system, available from Garrett Wade. The centerpiece of this system is an extruded aluminum track that can be screwed to the edge of a fence or other part of a jig or inlaid into a slot. (WoodsmithShop makes a similar T-track system.). The rail, available in lengths from 6 in. to 48 in., has a T-slot to fit the head of a standard ¼-in. hex-head bolt. You can easily bolt all types of stops and devices to this track, including a variety of FasTTrack flip stops and micro-adjusters that allow you to add adjustability to jigs (see pp. 198-199 and the bottom photo on p. 170).

Miter-slot guide bars and track   The trickiest part of building almost any miter-slot guided carriage is making and fitting the guide bars that run in the machine's miter slot(s). Wood bars, even when perfectly sized and aligned, tend to run loose in the dry winter months and tight during humid summers. I've had much better success fitting my shop-made carriages with bars made from UHMW polyethylene (described on p. 188) or commercially made metal guide bars. Although they cost more than shop-made bars, commercial bars are straight, won't swell or shrink like wood, and are adjustable for a tight, accurate fit in the miter slots. I've tried two types, both designed to fit a standard ¾-in. wide, ⅜-in. deep miter slot (see the photos below): solid-steel guide bars, made by FasTTrack, and Incra Miter Sliders, which are extruded aluminum bars made by the same folks who make the Incra Jig. Both guide bars are adjustable for a snug fit in the slot and smooth running.

The extruded aluminum Incra Miter Slider (below left) is checked and adjusted for fit in the miter slot of a table saw before attaching it to a sliding carriage. Two steel FasTTrack miter bars screwed to the bottom of a sliding miter carriage (below right) are tweaked for fit by tightening or loosening four phenolic inserts along the bar.

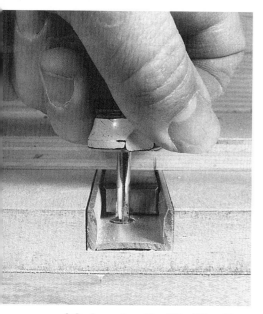

Inlaying a length of FasTTrack's True-Fit Adjustable Miter Track is one way to add a durable miter slot to a plywood or MDF table. Loosening or tightening the screws that hold the track in the slot adjusts the width of the slot to make the guide bar fit snugly and slide smoothly.

The FasTTrack Microadjuster, used with the system's track, makes an accurate and convenient way to fine-set the position of a router-table fence. The Microadjuster is locked into the FasTTrack while an adjuster screw moves the fence in or out.

The 17-in. long FasTTrack bar has four Cool Block inserts (graphite-impregnated phenolic plastic) along the bar that adjust with Allen screws for setting the tightness of the bar in the slot. The 18-in. long Incra Miter Slider bar has two expansion screws that tighten the fit of the bar; these screws can be conveniently accessed through holes drilled in the base of the carriage to fine-tune the bar-to-slot fit.

Regardless of whether you purchase your guide bars or make your own, take care to install them on the bottom of the carriage jig so they'll align to the slots accurately. Trim wood or plastic bars and pre-adjust metal bars first, labeling bars for left and right slots (miter slots aren't always milled exactly the same). Then, apply a little double-stick tape or adhesive transfer tape to the top of each bar and set it into its slot. Place a thin shim underneath each end (a dime works well) to raise the bar slightly proud of the surface. Now square up the edge of the carriage's base with the machine table, center the base to the blade or cutter and lower it carefully onto the guide bars. Press down so the tape sticks, and slide the assembly out and carefully mark the mounting holes for the bars. Unless the base is very thin, use pan-head screws set through counterbored holes in the base down into the guide bars. Drop the guide bars into the miter slots and check that the carriage slides smoothly before tightening the screws fully.

If you wish to use a carriage with guide bars on a machine tool that doesn't have a miter slot, FasTTrack makes an aluminum miter slot track that can be inlaid into a wood or plastic surface. This True-Fit Adjustable Miter Track fits into a 1-in. wide, ½-in. deep dado, easily cut with a router or a dado blade in a table saw. The extruded track has a unique design that allows it to be adjusted to fit the width of the guide bar simply by tightening or loosening the screws that hold it down into its dado (see the top photo at left).

Micro-adjustment devices

While you can build your own micro-adjuster to make adjusting the position of a fence or stop easier (see the sidebar on p. 111), there are also a couple of commercially made devices that are easy to use and affordable. The FasTTrack Microadjuster and the Fastop both provide an accurate, versatile and affordable way to add fine tuning to your jigs.

FasTTrack Microadjuster Made to work with the FasTTrack system, the Microadjuster locks into the aluminum track with a ¼-in. bolt. A machine screw with an easily grasped knurled head threads into a FasTTrack flip stop for tweaking stop position for precise cutoff lengths. The Microadjuster also mounts to a 90° angle bracket and Microbase for use in fine-tuning the position of a router-table fence, as shown in the photo at left. With or without the FasTTrack system, the Microadjuster can add fine tuning to many different types of jigs.

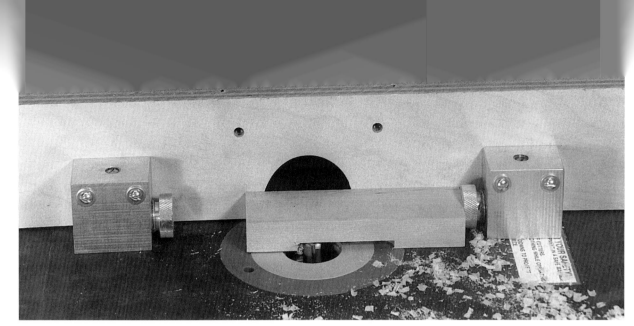

Fastop The Fastop is a detented adjustable stop, machined from a solid block of aluminum, that is designed to be bolted to the fence of a radial-arm saw, miter gauge, etc., in lieu of any regular stop. The business end of the stop has a large knurled knob that acts as the actual stop surface (see the photo above). This knob can be screwed in or out, to change the stop distance; a plunger assembly inside the Fastop has detents that mark quarter-turns of the knob (each equals a $\frac{1}{64}$-in. movement), thereby letting you accurately regulate the position of the stop and hence the length of cut. The body of the Fastop has holes, so it can be temporarily or permanently bolted to a fence or other jig.

Two Fastop micro-adjustment devices screwed to an auxiliary fence on a router table provide accurate, fine-tunable stops to limit the length of a dado or rabbet. Fastops also can be mounted to radial-arm-saw and chopbox fences or stops to fine-adjust cutoff lengths.

Measuring devices

As most parts for cabinets, furniture or other woodworking projects are cut to measured size, you need some way of gauging the distance from a stop or fence to the cutter. While you can always use a ruler or tape measure, it's less time-consuming and more accurate to attach a stick-on tape directly to the jig. And if your need for precision is especially acute, you might want to replace your trusty tape measure with a digital readout device.

Stick-on tape and cursor Thin metal rules with a pressure-sensitive peel-and-stick backing provide a convenient way to add an adjustment scale to any fence or adjustable jig component. Scales are available that read both right-to-left and left-to-right, to suit any application. Reading the position of the movable part can be done by simply mounting the scale underneath the part or by adding a cursor with a

A thin line etched with a scratch awl onto a piece of clear plastic makes the crosshair for a cursor that mounts to a flip stop used on a cutoff saw. A permanent marker is used to color in the etched line for make it easier to see.

fine crosshair to the moving part. To make a cursor, mount a short strip of clear plastic to the jig, then make a test cut to determine the crosshair's exact location. Etch the crosshair on the down-facing side of the plastic, using a scratch awl and a try square (see the photo at left). Color in the crosshair with a thin-point permanent marker pen, applied judiciously, to make it easier to see. If you're using a stop fitted with a cursor on a radial-arm saw that uses dado blades or sawblades of various thicknesses, you can etch additional crosshairs on the cursor, positioned so they will represent the location of the cuts produced by those blades.

Digital readout device The ultimate addition to a jig or fence system is the digital-readout device called the ProScale, made by Accurate Technologies. This device consists of a special scale bar, a read head that slides over the scale to take measurement readings, and a plastic display housing that shows the measurement on a liquid-crystal display (LCD). The read head is mounted to a stationary part of a jig or machine, and the scale is connected to the moving part—a fence, stop or sliding carriage—via a flexible link. A plug-in cable connects the read head to the display housing, which can be mounted in a location where it's convenient to see. The basic ProScale Model 100 can be used to check the settings of fence jigs (see the photo below), joinery jigs, cutoff stops, or the travel distance of sliding carriages.

Setting this bandsaw fence jig for exact resaw thicknesses is a lot easier using a digital measuring device. The read head of the ProScale 100 is fastened to a block screwed to the bandsaw table while the electronic scale, attached to the resaw jig, moves in or out. A cable conveys the measurement to the digital display, where the setting can be read in decimal, metric or fractional units.

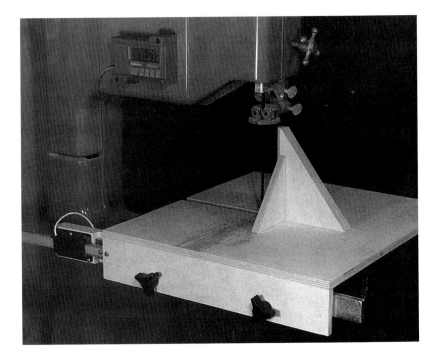

Because it is electronic, the ProScale is easily zeroed to a particular position, to account for blade or bit size. ProScale also offers several measurement displays: decimal, to 0.001 in.; metric, in millimeters; or fractions in increments of $\frac{1}{16}$ in., $\frac{1}{32}$ in. or $\frac{1}{64}$ in. In the $\frac{1}{16}$-in. and $\frac{1}{32}$-in. modes, small bars are displayed for each $\frac{1}{64}$ in. that the measurement is greater than the fraction shown. This feature provides an accurate, practical-to-read display of large fractions: It's easier to grasp that a setting is $\frac{1}{64}$ in. over $\frac{5}{8}$ in. than it is to figure out how what $\frac{41}{64}$ in. means.

Jig Construction Techniques

Most practices for building solid, durable jigs from wood and wood-composite materials are the same as for building quality furniture. However, in many cases jigs must be built to higher tolerances in order for them to be able to guide precise, repeatable operations. Further, they must be durable enough to withstand the forces imposed upon them by powerful machines. This section explores basic woodworking elements, such as joinery, gluing and finishing, with specific regard to jig building. Construction methods for other materials are also touched upon, such as tapping for bolts and screws for metal or plastic parts and assemblies.

Joinery

While throwing a jig together with nails and glue is serviceable (and often necessary), there's no substitute for using solid wood-to-wood joinery to attach parts. Useful joints in jig-building include mortise and tenon, rabbets, dadoes and dowels; plate-joinery biscuits are a particularly easy and expeditious way to add mechanical strength to plywood or MDF parts glued edge to edge or edge to face, as well as to simple butt joints.

For tight-fitting dado joints when using metric-sized imported plywoods, such as Baltic or Finnish birch, metric dado router bits are available in 6mm, 12mm and 18mm diameters. Woodhaven's 12mm and 18mm bits have a "down shear" design which puts a slight downward pressure on the surface of the wood, which results in less tearout when dadoing plywood. For tight-fitting joints when using shop-grade birch or regular hardwood plywoods, which are typically slightly less than their specified thickness, undersized bits are available from Woodcraft as well as several other suppliers. You should use a $\frac{7}{32}$-in. dia. bit for $\frac{1}{4}$-in. plywood, a $\frac{31}{64}$-in. dia. bit for $\frac{1}{2}$-in. plywood, and a $\frac{23}{32}$-in. dia. bit for $\frac{3}{4}$-in. plywood.

An excellent construction method whenever you need a table or other surface that's both extremely rigid and relatively light is the torsion box (see the sidebar below). For an example of how a torsion box may be used, see the air table on pp. 90-93.

Gluing

Fixed jig parts that must maintain alignment, such as non-adjustable stop blocks and fences, should be glued together as well as screwed or nailed. Vibration from machine tools can make most fasteners lose their hold over time, and if that happens the accuracy of the jig is diminished or ruined (see the sidebar on p. 204). For most applications, I use the old shop standby, aliphatic resin (yellow glue). The excellent gap-filling property of quick-setting epoxy is useful for gluing parts that don't fit tightly together or for gluing metal or plastic parts to wood. Cyanoacrylate glues (super glues) are great for securing delicate parts or for holding hardware in alignment while screws are

Torsion Boxes

A torsion box consists of an outer frame and an inner grid covered with thin skins top and bottom (see the drawing on the facing page). Its construction is similar to that of an airplane wing: strong and light. The outer skins can be made of plywood, MDF or hardboard as thin as ⅛ in. The frame and inner grid can be just about anything — plywood, particleboard, No. 2 pine, or any kiln-dried solid wood, typically between ⅜ in. to ¾ in. thick. The depth of the frame and grid can be as little as 1 in., or 6 in. or more. The thinner the skin, the closer the spacing of the grid needs to be to keep the top rigid. For ⅛-in. skins, use about a 2-in. grid; a 3-in. grid is good for ¼-in. skins; a 4-in. to 6-in. is fine for ⅜-in. skins.

Torsion-box construction is a terrific way to build a light, extremely rigid table surface that will stay flat. The inner grid, made of particleboard, is glued and stapled together with a pneumatic narrow-crown staple gun before the top and bottom skins are glued on.

driven. Just as with large case pieces, adding glue blocks or gluing in braces will keep jig assemblies from racking and coming out of square, such as tall fences (see the bottom photo on p. 200 and the tenoning jig on p. 51). In any case, don't forget good woodworking practices and glue wide (4 in. or more) solid-wood parts cross-grain or you'll run into expansion/contraction problems later.

Screwing

Regardless of the type you prefer, here are a few good practices to follow when using screws. Always fasten through the thinner part (usually the base) into the thicker part (fence, stop, etc.). That way the head of the fastener will hold the thin member, and the shank of the fastener will have more purchase in the thicker member to resist withdrawal. When deciding on the length of a screw (or nail), try to get about two-thirds of it into the thicker piece.

Amazingly, no joinery connects the parts of the inner grid — the short components are just glued and stapled (with standard staples ⅜ in. long) to the long ones to hold their edges in a plane until the skins are attached. Lay the assembly on a dead flat bench or machine top and glue the skins on, spreading glue liberally on the edge of every grid member. Rather than trying to apply clamping pressure to the center of the panel, staple the skins in place using a narrow-crown staple gun, or nail it, using fasteners every few inches. For a durable surface, cover the top skin with plastic laminate.

If you're making a router table top, you can frame out an open section in the middle of the torsion box (see the detail drawing at right). Apply the skins, then cut them out top and bottom. A lip routed in the top opening supports an insert plate that mounts the router.

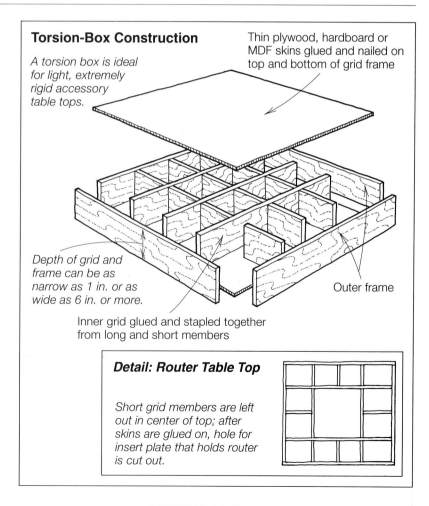

Torsion-Box Construction

A torsion box is ideal for light, extremely rigid accessory table tops.

Thin plywood, hardboard or MDF skins glued and nailed on top and bottom of grid frame

Depth of grid and frame can be as narrow as 1 in. or as wide as 6 in. or more.

Outer frame

Inner grid glued and stapled together from long and short members

Detail: Router Table Top

Short grid members are left out in center of top; after skins are glued on, hole for insert plate that holds router is cut out.

Vibration Problems

Jig components that have been screwed or bolted together can loosen from the vibration of power tools or stationary electric motors. To prevent this, use a pair of jam nuts or nylon lock nuts (sometimes called nylon insert nuts, or aero nuts because of their common usage in the aircraft industry). Another solution is to apply a drop or two of thread lock compound to the bolt's threads. For fasteners that you will want to disassemble, use Locktite thread locker 242; for permanent assemblies, such as studs set into threaded inserts, use Locktite 271.

If excessive vibration is causing adjustable jig parts to creep out of alignment, try adding mass to the jig. The solution to the problem may be as simple as doubling the thickness of the jig's base or building it from a denser material, such as MDF. If vibration causes workpieces to move out of alignment, try adding a high-friction material to positioning or clamping surfaces (see p. 190).

Another tack for attenuating vibration is to reduce its source at the machine: Try fitting your motor with rubber anti-vibration mounts or the arbor with machined-steel or cast-iron pulleys (in lieu of the flimsy die-cast alloy pulleys often fitted). These are available at your local bearing supplier or from W.W. Grainger (see Sources of Supply on pp. 224-227). Also, try replacing the machine's standard V-belt with a PowerTwist belt (available from Woodcraft or Woodworker's Supply), a special flexible drive belt designed to run very smoothly.

To prevent cracks and splits when screwing into solid woods, drill pilot holes that equal the root diameter of the screw (the shank minus the threads). You can usually get away with running drywall screws into the face of plywood or MDF without predrilling, but you must predrill for screws driven into the edges of these materials. For maximum holding power in wood-composite materials, like MDF and particleboard, use special fasteners called Confirmat screws, which are designed for edge-joining composite panels in the European-style 32mm cabinet system.

For an easier time driving screws, lubricate them first with a little beeswax or paste wax. Don't use soap, as it absorbs water and can rust steel screws. When using screws to join an adjustable fence or other component through oversized holes, you can use round-head screws and washers or use special round washer-head screws by themselves (available from McFeely's).

Tapping holes

Many materials, such as plastics, tempered hardboard and aluminum (as well as cast-iron machine tables), are easily tapped to take machine screws directly. For light- and medium-duty applications, you can also tap holes directly into dense woods, such as hard maple or birch, for machine screws and bolts. Direct tapping is often more convenient (and cheaper) than setting a threaded insert, especially if you have a handful of bolts to set. I've even gotten away with tapping plywood by applying a coat of epoxy to the pilot hole and waiting for it to dry before tapping the screw threads.

Standard screw taps and pipe taps are used with a tap handle. Pilot-hole sizes are very important to observe, especially in brittle materials like acrylic plastic. These hole sizes are usually imprinted directly on the tap and often specify number size (1 to 80) or letter size (A to Z) drill bits. If you lack these special sets (available from a machinist's supplier), choose the closest larger fractional-sized bit for metal and brittle plastics and the closest smaller bit for wood or softer plastics. Make sure to use lubrication while tapping.

Finishing

Giving wooden jig parts a quick finish with your favorite varnish or polyurethane will retard the adverse effects of moisture and improve wear resistance. One of the new "environmentally friendly" water-based finishes I've tried and liked is McCloskey's Crystal Clear Polyurethane. It dries very quickly (to the touch in 15 minutes) and has excellent durability.

Adding one last detail to your jig before the finish goes on can save you a lot of head scratching down the road: Petaluma, California, woodworker Jeff Dale taught me to label jigs with pertinent information about them—blades or bits that are used with them, special angles and height/depth settings, and the order to do things in. By writing these details directly on the jig (then protecting the information from wear by top-coating it with finish), you won't have to try to find that scrap of paper you wrote everything down on or remember all the crucial details the next time you need to use the jig.

CHAPTER 8
Safety and Dust Control

It's easy to become complacent about guards when using power tools and machinery, because things go right 99% of the time. Unfortunately, when an accident does happen, one must live with the consequences 100% of the time thereafter. After a close call on the jointer (a minor skirmish, as accidents go, but one that nearly ruined my enjoyment of guitar playing forever) I gave up any macho notions I had about how guards were for pessimists and inattentive woodworkers. When you realize how much protection blade or bit guards, push sticks, hold-downs and other safety devices afford at such a little cost in time or inconvenience, there's just no excuse for not using them.

Whirling cutters aren't the only danger to woodworkers in the shop; sawdust is also a threat. Prolonged breathing of fine dust particles can do real damage to your lungs, spark allergic reactions, or possibly even cause cancer. Adding dust collection directly to your jigs is easy, and keeping sawdust out of the air with a shop vacuum or dust-collection setup has additional benefits, such as keeping annoying chips out of your face and improving the quality of the cut. In fact, dust-collection boxes and shrouds can actually offer protection by themselves by surrounding and covering dangerous cutters.

A clear plastic protective enclosure mounted to a table-saw box-joint jig provides blade protection without interfering with normal operations. The enclosure (pp. 211-212) also deflects chips and improves the saw's built-in dust collection.

Safety Devices

Simple, practical guards can be fitted to nearly all shop-made jigs and setups with very little effort. You'll find that you can also retrofit many of your old jigs and setups to incorporate guards that enhance hand safety without getting in the way. Think of it as a design challenge.

Push sticks and push blocks

Your hands are safest when they are far from the cutter and not in its direct path. Always use push blocks to feed and guide the stock past blades and cutters when fingers would otherwise pass too close to the blade. What's too close? Some woodworkers say 6 in. is safe enough; I prefer not to get my hands any closer than 12 in. to a table-saw blade or large bit or shaper cutter. The push sticks and blocks I use are fairly traditional in design, but with an improvement that increases control over the workpiece: I add a strip of non-skid stair tread tape, such as 3M Safety Walk, to the bottom of my push sticks and push blocks. I find that the added gripping power exerted on the workpiece can keep even a warped part traveling smoothly through a cut.

Knobs, grips and handles

An important line of defense against getting cut is adding well-placed knobs and grips for pushing or articulating a carriage or other jig through the blade or bit. Whenever possible, locate handles away from the line of cut; for an example, see the handsaw-style D-handle on my sliding taper jig shown in the drawing on p. 54. For jigs that don't have separate handles, adding a small lip or block can prevent hands from slipping from their normal gripping location and into the line of cut. For example, adding a collar to the rear member of a sliding tenon jig will keep fingers well away from the two sawblades used with this setup (see the top left photo on the facing page).

Exit guards

Even if you don't want to add a protective guard or enclosure to a sliding carriage (see pp. 211-212), adding an exit guard is an excellent idea. It protects you after the jig has been pushed through the cut, when you're reaching over the saw table and are probably the most vulnerable to blade contact. A simple exit guard, such as the one on the crosscut box in the top right photo on the facing page, is a block of scrap 4x4 glued and screwed to the back of the carriage, where it will sheathe the blade after each cut. If there's any chance of a blade or cutter hitting the fasteners used to attach the guard, use brass screws. Larger blocks provide more protection, but clamping a stop block to the rip fence or fastening a stop in the miter slot (see pp. 117-119) will stop carriage travel short of where the blade would exit the guard.

Adding a wood collar just below the grip on a sliding tenon jig keeps hands from accidentally slipping down into the blades. The clear plastic guard mounted above the blade deflects chips that might otherwise be thrown into the operator's face.

A crosscut box fitted with two simple devices make it safer to use: a protective enclosure made from wood and plastic strips rides above the workpiece and acts as a blade guard; an exit block sheathes the blade after the cut.

Clear plastic guards

Probably the most practical and useful deterrent to woodworking accidents is the clear plastic guard. A simple guard screwed to a stationary fence, sliding carriage or to the machine tool itself can block inadvertent contact with a bit or blade, yet still afford a full view of the operation. Further, guards can serve to deflect chips and improve dust collection. You can make your own guards from clear plastic, drilling, cutting and bending them into shape as needed (see pp. 183-186), and the applications are limitless. Here are some examples of clear guards I've fitted to jigs featured in earlier chapters in this book.

Router-table guards One of the easiest types of guards to add provides protection above a spinning bit on a shaper or router table. This kind of guard works only with cuts where the stock is flat on the table (it must be removed when stock is fed on edge). Nevertheless, it is important to use, especially with big bits, such as panel-raising bits, when there's a lot of cutting-edge exposure. One such guard is shown in the photo at right. This simple guard is a clear plastic rectangle with one end rounded and a 90° bend in it screwed to the fence above the bit. Slotting the mounting holes vertically (with a straight bit in a plunge router) allows you to adjust the height of the guard relative to the thickness of the workpiece. The width of the strip (and diameter of the rounded end) should equal at least half again the diameter of the

A clear guard for a router table is mounted to the fence directly above the bit. The height of the bent-plastic guard is adjusted close to the end-piloted bit (used here for pattern routing a support for a tilt-top drafting table) with clearance allowed for the workpiece.

bit. If shaping a curved workpiece requires more clearance between the bit and the fence, you can extend the horizontal leg of the guard, but use thicker ($\frac{1}{4}$-in. or $\frac{3}{8}$-in.) plastic so it won't break off accidentally (or mount the guard directly to the bit, as described on pp. 212-213). Woodhaven offers several ready-made plastic guards (tinted fluorescent orange for better visibility) that can be used with router-table fences and small shaper setups (see Sources of Supply on pp. 224-227).

Tenon-jig guard The clear guard above the twin blades on the tenon jig shown in the top left photo on p. 209 is nothing more than a 10-in. long, 2$\frac{1}{2}$-in. wide piece of $\frac{1}{8}$-in. thick polycarbonate screwed to the edge of a wood strip. This strip mounts to the face of the jig via slotted holes. The slots allow the guard to be adjusted, front or back, to accommodate the width of the workpiece. The free edges of this guard (as well as the edges of the other guards in this section) have been colored with a wide-tipped permanent marker pen. The red color helps to warn you to steer clear of the guard and the path of danger.

Sliding-miter-carriage guard It's important to use a guard on a sliding miter carriage because you often use your hands to hold the stock against the fence close to the path of the blade. To add protection to my sliding miter jig, shown in the photo below, I cut a triangular block from a short length of 2x4 and glued and screwed it to the jig's base, just behind the fences. This block doubles as an exit guard and a mounting surface for the clear guard. The back end of this guard, made from a 5-in. wide strip of $\frac{1}{8}$-in. polycarbonate, is screwed to the top of the block, while the front end screws to a wood strip attached to the miter carriage's front cross support.

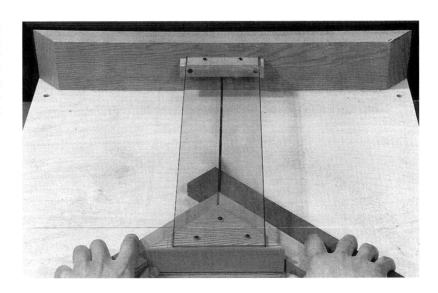

A strip of clear polycarbonate plastic attached to a sliding miter carriage deflects chips and protects the operator's hands from the blade. The back end of the strip is screwed to a triangular block that serves as an exit guard.

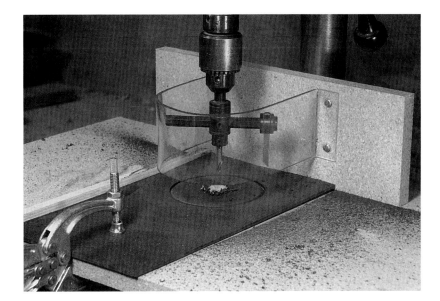

A clear guard prevents knuckles from getting rapped by the long swinging arm of an adjustable circle cutter. The polycarbonate strip was heat bent to a semicircular shape using a coffee can for a form.

Drill-press guard   While usually pretty safe, the drill press can be a mean threat when you use an adjustable circle cutter, which has an arm that swings a wide arc and can smash your knuckles before you know what hit you. A bent strip of clear 1/8-in. thick polycarbonate with flat flanges on each end is drilled and screwed to a backing plate attached to the jig's base (see the photo above). This protects you from the circle cutter, yet allows you to slide the workpiece into position under the bit and clamp and unclamp it without hindrance. I bent the guard using the bending technique described on p. 185. To make the large arc in the guard, I used an empty coffee can for a form to slump the hot plastic over; I then bent up flanges at each end so the guard could be screwed to a fence on the drill-press table.

Protective enclosures

Carriages that slide in the table saw's miter slot almost always require that the stock blade guard be removed. Whether your sliding jig is for box joints, tenons or crosscut dadoes, you can retrofit a large clear protective enclosure that allows you to see what's going on and also keeps you from getting cut. Enclosure-type guards also deflect chips away from you and improve dust collection-efficiency better than the simple types of guards described above.

Box-joint-jig guard   This box-joint-jig guard mounts directly over a standard table-saw box-joint jig, such as the one described on pp. 47-48, to provide protection ahead of the cut (an exit guard, as described on p. 208, protects after the cut). I cobbled up the enclosure-style guard, shown in the photo on p. 207, in about a half-hour from a few scraps of wood and clear plastic. I made the guard's frame wide enough to handle 10-in. drawer sides, but you can adapt the basic design to work with a wider jig. The frame's 2-in. wide wood side rails lend plenty of clearance between the horizontally mounted plastic and the sawblade. I chamfered and waxed the lower edges of these rails to keep them gliding smoothly. I drilled holes in the ⅛-in. thick plastic, then screwed it to the top of the frame. When attaching the plastic, I left about a 1-in. gap to the face of the jig as clearance for the workpiece. The frame attaches to the back side of the box-joint jig with screws through the rear frame member.

Crosscut-box guard   You can add a fixed clear guard across the top of a crosscut box similar to the one fitted to the sliding miter carriage described on p. 210. However, such a guard provides no side protection—a desirable feature, especially if you're cutting thick stock with the blade raised to considerable height. The guard for the crosscut box, shown in the top right photo on p. 209, has an enclosure-type guard that rests on top of the stock over the line of cut, preventing your hands from reaching into the blade.

I started building the guard by cutting two 2¼-in. wide, ⅜-in. thick wood sides, each about ⁵⁄₁₆ in. longer than the inside width of my crosscut box. A 3½-in. wide, ⅛-in. thick clear plastic top, cut slightly shorter than the inside width of my crosscut box, is then screwed to the sides through holes drilled in the plastic. To keep the guard aligned, I glued and nailed two guide strips to the front crossmember, and cut two ⁷⁄₁₆-in. wide, ⅜-in. deep dadoes in the fence (the rear crossmember) to accept the back ends of the wood sides. (Adding guide strips to the fence would prevent the workpiece from lying flat against the fence.)

In use, the workpiece is positioned in the crosscut box, then the guard is dropped down over the top of it. When just the very end of a board is trimmed, the guide strips and dadoes help keep the guard from skewing.

Bit/cutter-mounted disc guards

Jigging setups and operations such as template routing an intricate design using an end-piloted bit in the router table require a lot of clearance around the cutter. You can usually fit some kind of guard above the bit, as described on pp. 209-210. Another strategy is to attach a guard disc directly to the end of the bit or cutter, above the pilot bearing or rub collar that guides the cut (see the photo on the facing page). The disc is cut from a thin (⅛-in. to ¼-in. thick) piece of clear plastic using a hole saw or adjustable circle cutter in the drill press. The diameter of the disc should be at least twice the cutting diameter of the bit. The edges of the disc should be softly rounded and work gloves should be worn, as a rapidly whirling guard disc can still deal a nasty

Mounting a guard disc directly to the end of a router bit provides protection without limiting access, as a conventional fence-mounted guard might. The edge of the clear-plastic disc is rounded, and gloves are worn to protect hands from abrasion in case of contact.

burn or abrasion upon contact with unprotected skin. Coloring the edge of the disc with permanent marker pen is especially important because a spinning guard can be difficult to see.

Mounting the disc is easy on shaper arbors or large router bits that have arbor-mounted cutters, such as kerf cutters or rail and stile (cope and stick) cutters. One or more washers/shims between the pilot bearing and disc provide clearance for the workpiece and allow the bearing to spin freely. You can also mount guard discs on smaller piloted router bits—up to about 1 in. in diameter—by fitting them with an Allen screw long enough to mount both the bearing and the guard. A small-diameter Allen screw isn't strong enough to support guard discs on larger-diameter bits; these must be used with a fixed guard mounted above the bit.

Hold-downs

Although they are not safety guards in the strict sense, hold-downs such as featherboards and wheeled devices can provide many of the same benefits. Hold-downs take the place of precious fingers and hands to keep stock flat on the tool table and keep workpieces fed past a blade or bit traveling smoothly, reducing the chances they'll be kicked back at the operator. And because they are often fastened very close to the cutter, hold-downs can even take the place of guards to block hands and fingers from dangerous contact. Hold-downs apply constant pressure to the workpiece, so they tend to do a better job of flattening the stock than your hands can, leaving them free to feed the workpiece from a safe distance away.

For production work, where the same cut is repeated dozens or hundreds of times, screwing or bolting a hold-down to a machine tool or jig is a good idea. But for most work this isn't the most flexible arrangement. Since hold-downs usually need to be adjusted for position and downward pressure, depending on the operation and the dimensions of the stock, other methods often work better (see the sidebar below). Wheeled hold-downs that simultaneously hold stock flat and against a fence must also be adjusted for angle so the stock is pressed tight to the fence as it is fed.

Featherboards   One of the most popular devices for all kinds of hold-down situations, featherboards have many flexible fingers that apply a steady, even pressure against the stock. The angled tip of each finger (pointing toward the feed direction) also lessens the tendency of the stock to kick back. You can buy ready-made wood or plastic feather-

Mounting Hold-Downs

All manner of clamps can be used to secure hold-downs, but often one needs to locate them near the middle of a machine's table, where clamps can't reach. A more flexible, convenient means of attachment is to use the tool's miter-gauge slot. A wooden strip machined to fit the slot (typically ⅜ in. by ¾ in.) and long enough to span the table serves as a mount for one or more featherboards and/or wheeled hold-downs (see the drawing at right). The 10-24 threaded inserts along the wood strip accept small studded handscrews that secure hold-downs to the strip. Shims are used to raise the height of hold-downs, as needed when working on thicker stock. Slotted holes routed into a featherboard (or

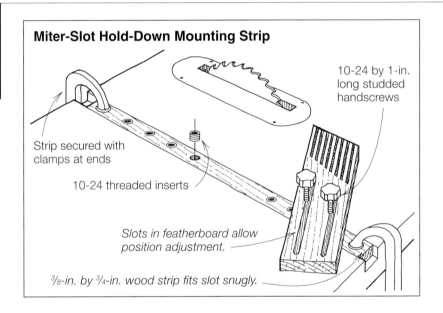

Miter-Slot Hold-Down Mounting Strip

10-24 by 1-in. long studded handscrews

Strip secured with clamps at ends

10-24 threaded inserts

Slots in featherboard allow position adjustment.

⅜-in. by ¾-in. wood strip fits slot snugly.

base of a wheeled hold-down) allow them to be set in or out, for more or less pressure against the workpiece. Once positioned, the wood strip can be clamped into the slot at the ends. Alternatively, if your table has T-style miter-gauge slots, you

could lock the strip into the slot with a T-nut and washers, as described on pp. 118-119.

Another means of attaching hold-downs on a tool table is to mount them to an Incra Miter Slider bar, which can be locked in a miter slot by tightening its

boards from several sources (Woodhaven makes several useful plastic ones), or you can easily make your own, sized to suit the application. Featherboards can be made from many different materials, including solid wood, plywood, plastics, such as polycarbonate and polyethylene, and solid-surface materials, such as Corian and Avonite. For best effect, the featherboard's fingers should be evenly spaced and cut thin—usually between ³⁄₃₂ in. and ⅛ in. thick, depending on the amount of pressure you're after: Thicker fingers make for a stiffer, more forceful hold-down; thinner fingers make for a more flexible, light-action hold-down.

A serviceable multi-purpose featherboard, good for table-saw and router-fence jigs and more, can be cut from a ¾-in. by 3½-in. by 11-in. piece of solid wood with clear, straight grain. Start by cutting a 45° angle on one end and draw two 45° lines parallel to this end on each

A fixture built from commercially available components provides a very flexible means of positioning and adjusting hold-downs. Here, a shop-made wood featherboard is angled to keep a narrow molding down and against a table-saw fence during a cut.

two adjustment screws. There are also commercially available featherboards that are adjustable and mount directly to miter slots (see Sources of Supply on pp. 224-227).

For temporarily mounting small hold-downs to steel or cast-iron machine tables, you might want to try a magnetic base. I made a very handy such base from a magnetic knife-holder rack I bought at my local hardware store. This rack's long bar can be glued into a dado cut into one or more small featherboards. The magnetic base also makes a great temporary attachment for a dust-collection box or shroud (see pp. 220-221).

In more complicated hold-down setups, as for shaping curved moldings, featherboards and wheels must sometimes be set at odd angles to the work. A flexible system of mounting hold-downs is to use fixturing fittings, such as those made by RK Industries (discussed on p. 177). A base flange can be screwed to a base that's clamped to the machine table, with various adjustable fittings used to position and adjust a featherboard or other hold-down. See the photo at left for an example.

side, about 3 in. from the cut end. These lines mark where to stop cutting when you saw each finger. To cut the first finger (centered on the width of the stock), set the fence on the bandsaw so that the finger is made by taking two cuts, flipping the piece side for side between cuts. Check the setting using a scrap of stock that's the same width as the featherboard. After the first finger is cut, reset the fence using the scrap so that the next fingers will be cut the same thickness as the first. Cut two new fingers, one on either side of the center finger, flipping the stock between cuts (see the photo below). Repeat the process until fingers have been cut all the way across the piece. To make two thin featherboards, start with stock that's more than twice as thick, cut all the fingers and then carefully resaw the piece in half, using the bandsaw.

To ease the entry and exit of stock that passes under a featherboard, you can round the ends of the fingers at the edges or saw the profile of all the fingers to a slight radius, as shown on the featherboard for cove cutting in the photo on the facing page.

Featherboards can be positioned either horizontally (to keep stock flat on a surface) or vertically (to keep stock firmly against a fence while it is fed past the cutter or blade). On critical cuts, many woodworkers like to use two or more featherboards. However, never position a featherboard to press stock directly against the side of a blade or cutter; that could pinch the stock and cause kickback. A featherboard can

Cutting the fingers of a featherboard to even thickness is easily done on the bandsaw. After the fence is set using a scrap, two cuts are taken, flipping the featherboard over side for side between cuts.

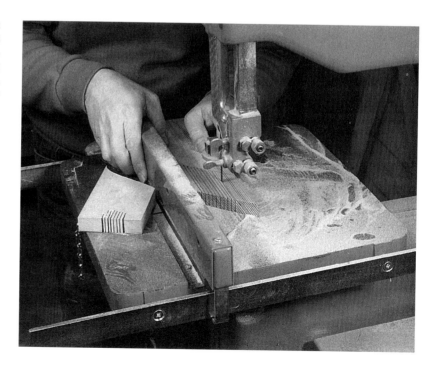

be mounted directly above a small router bit that's used to cut a groove or cove; in that position it will keep stock flat and in steady contact with the bit during the cut.

When cove cutting, it's good to use a featherboard directly above the table-saw blade to hold the stock flat. In this case, a wide featherboard can be bolted to a block that's screwed to the fence used to guide the stock diagonally over the blade (see the photo below). Rounding the end of a featherboard like this makes entry and exit of the workpiece smoother. Another piece of stock, or a scrap the same dimensions as the stock, is used to push the workpiece through the cut.

Wheeled hold-downs Commercial wheeled devices, such as Board Buddies, Shophelpers, Ripstrate wheels and Leichtung anti-kickback hold-downs, can be used with almost any fence or jig for safer feeding of stock. They are usually sold and used in pairs, one just ahead of the bit or blade, one after it (see the top photo on p. 218). Most units clamp or screw to the top of the fence and adjust for different widths and thicknesses of stock. (Board Buddies and Shophelper wheels mount on an extruded aluminum track that screws to the fence or jig; units slide along the track and lock down wherever needed.) Each wheeled unit has a spring-loaded arm that presses the wheel down to keep stock flat on the table. The devices are mounted so the wheels angle slightly relative to the line of cut, which keeps the stock snug against the fence face as it is fed (see the top drawing on p. 219). A ratchet mechanism inside most brands of wheels limits feed direction, preventing the stock from kicking back should it bind on the blade or bit.

A short, wide featherboard mounted to a fence holds stock down as it is cove cut on the table saw. The featherboard's rounded end profile makes it easier to feed stock under it. A secondary fence clamped to the saw table keeps the stock from wandering away from the main fence.

Commercially made wheeled hold-down devices can be mounted to all kinds of jigs to keep stock flat and running true as it is fed, and also to prevent dangerous kickbacks. Here, Shophelper wheeled hold-downs are used on an angled router fence to keep thin stock tight against the bottom lip as it is shaped. A scrap piece is used to push the end of the stock past the bit.

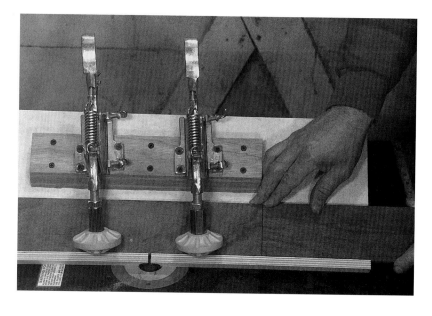

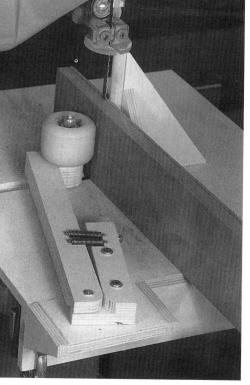

A spring-loaded wheeled device with a urethane plastic skateboard wheel can be shop made to suit many hold-down needs, such as keeping a board flat against a post fence during resawing. Spring tension and wheel position can be adjusted with a screw threaded through the fixed part of the device, which is mounted to the resawing jig's base.

A versatile shop-made hold-down device can be built from plywood, a couple of springs and hardware items and plastic skateboard wheels. Although it won't provide kickback protection, the pivoting-arm wheeled hold-down, shown in the bottom drawing on the facing page, is inexpensive (urethane skateboard wheels cost between $3 to $5 each) and can be used with many different tools and jig setups: on the table saw during ripping, on a shaper or router table during shaping, or on a bandsaw during resawing, as shown in the photo at left. I also have found my pivot-arm wheeled hold-down to be an effective and safe device for keeping stock flat against the fence on my jointer. If you need to hold down narrow stock and moldings, you can easily change the profile of the relatively soft urethane skateboard wheels by reshaping them on a wood lathe using regular turning tools. Narrow wheels from in-line skates (such as Rollerblades) could also be used.

To make the hold-down, cut out the stationary and pivot arms from ½-in. Baltic birch plywood (each arm is glued together from two pieces, as shown in the drawing). The stationary arm is screwed or clamped to the machine or jig base; the pivot arm keeps the wheel against the work. Skateboard wheels are available at skate shops and some sporting-goods stores in sets of two or four wheels. Each wheel requires a pair of sealed ball bearings, which run about $1.75 apiece. Bearings are pressed into wheels, which can be done at a skate store or in your shop with an arbor press. Although the standard bearing I.D. is 8mm, a regular ⁵⁄₁₆-in. bolt works perfectly well as an axle to mount the wheel on the end of the pivot arm (two wheels could be mounted on a longer bolt to handle wider stock). A screw-post pivot pin (see pp. 193-194) hinges the two arms.

Angling Wheeled Hold-Downs

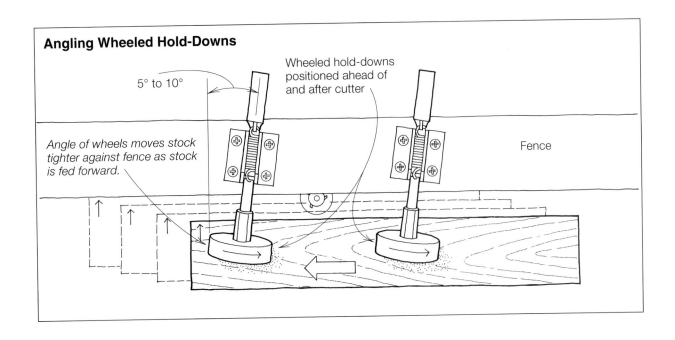

5° to 10°

Wheeled hold-downs positioned ahead of and after cutter

Angle of wheels moves stock tighter against fence as stock is fed forward.

Fence

Pivoting-Arm Wheeled Hold-Down

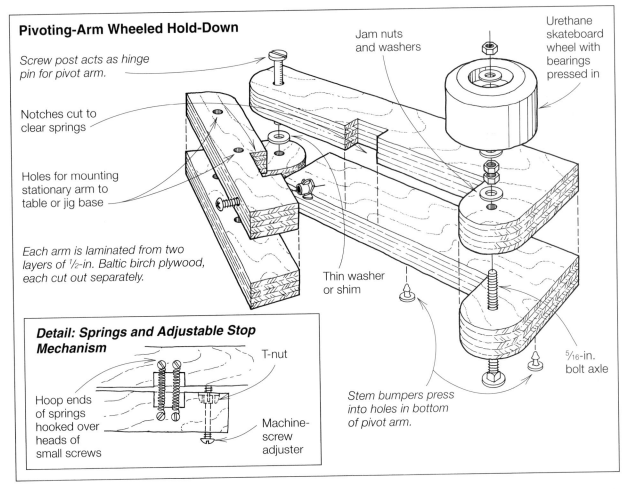

Screw post acts as hinge pin for pivot arm.

Notches cut to clear springs

Holes for mounting stationary arm to table or jig base

Each arm is laminated from two layers of ¹/₂-in. Baltic birch plywood, each cut out separately.

Jam nuts and washers

Urethane skateboard wheel with bearings pressed in

Thin washer or shim

⁵/₁₆-in. bolt axle

Stem bumpers press into holes in bottom of pivot arm.

Detail: Springs and Adjustable Stop Mechanism

T-nut

Hoop ends of springs hooked over heads of small screws

Machine-screw adjuster

Two $\frac{5}{16}$-in. dia., $1\frac{1}{4}$-in. long extension springs hook over the heads of small round-head screws (small headed nails are also fine) to provide the tension that presses the wheel against the stock. If more tension is needed, larger or additional springs can be fitted (you can obtain springs from a well-stocked hardware store or from Reid Tool Supply). Stem bumpers pressed into holes on the underside of the pivoting arm keep it sliding smoothly over the surface the device is mounted to. A small machine screw fitted into a T-nut pressed into the stationary arm acts as an adjustable stop, so the distance between the wheel and the fence or surface can be set. Also, the farther the screw presses the arms apart, the more the springs are pretensioned and the greater the effective hold-down pressure.

Kerf vanes
A kerf vane, also called a kerf splitter, is often incorporated into stock table-saw blade guards to prevent the kerf from closing up (due to the stock warping or reaction wood) and pinching the blade, which usually results in dangerous kickback. You can also incorporate a kerf vane in some jigs both for safety and to keep the workpiece aligned during cutting (see the guide block in the bottom drawing on p. 21).

Dust Collection
While respiratory health might be the most direct motivation for adding dust collection to a jig or machine setup, there are at least three other compelling reasons to install a dust-collection system in your shop. First, shrouds and dust-collection boxes can provide added safety by covering or surrounding cutters and blades, as well as deflecting chips that may strike the operator. Second, chip removal is an important part of improving the quality of the cut and even extending the life of many cutters. Chips that aren't ejected after the initial cut may be recut many times as they tumble about, increasing the work each tooth or cutting edge has to perform. Third, collecting dust and chips before they can fall into a tool's motor or working parts can prolong the life of the machine. This is an especially important consideration with routers used in router tables, since most of these power tools aren't designed to run in an inverted position.

Design and location of the dust box
An efficient means of incorporating dust collection into most jig se-tups is to attach a collection box directly to the jig itself. The collection box will serve to direct the vacuum's suction as close to the source of dust—a whirling bit, blade or abrasive—as possible, as well as to provide a port for connecting the vacuum hose. Further, the collection box can provide a convenient place to mount a hold-down, clear

A dust-collection box mounts to a jig to direct the flow of chips into the vacuum hose mounted to it. Here, a ½-in. plywood box screwed to a biscuit-joinery jig atop a router table provides a connection port for a shop-vacuum hose, as well as a mount for a protective guard mounted above the router bit.

guard or other safety device. Since you can customize the size and shape of the box to suit each setup, collection can be made efficient without the box getting in the way.

A dust-collection box can be built from practically anything: thin plywood and scraps that are nailed and glued together, thin sheet aluminum pieces pop riveted and/or duct-taped together or plastic parts glued or taped together. I've even made temporary boxes from cardboard and duct tape. The photo above shows a simple dust-collection box that screws to the top of my router-table biscuit-joinery jig. To keep the box low profile, I sized it to accept the end of my shop vacuum's accessory crevice tool. The tool is held tight in the box with a little foam weatherstripping. A more common way to connect a vacuum hose to the collector box is to bore a hole as a port. A 2¼-in. to 2⁵⁄₁₆-in. dia. hole provides a good friction fit for the end couplers found on most 2½-in. dia. flexible shop-vacuum hoses.

When designing a dust-collection box, try to make it enclose as much of the area around the blade or bit as is practical in order to capture a reasonable amount of the dust and chips produced. A balance needs to be struck: The more open area, the more clearance for handling the workpiece, but vacuum will need to generate greater suction to capture flying chips. When locating the dust intake port, carefully examine the manner in which the blade or bit hurls sawdust and chips. Your setup will function more efficiently if chips are sucked away in the same direction they are thrown. When in doubt, take some trial cuts without the dust box in place and see where the chips end up. Besides protecting the user, safety guards and chip deflectors around the box can improve the suction around the cutter. The top-mounted clear plastic guard on my router biscuit-joinery jig, shown in the photo above, fulfills all these functions.

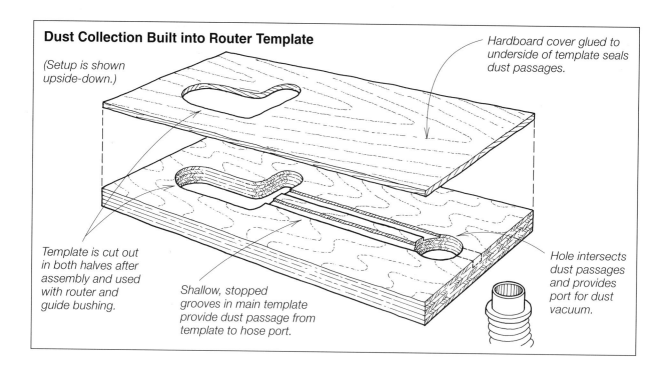

Dust Collection Built into Router Template

(Setup is shown upside-down.)

Hardboard cover glued to underside of template seals dust passages.

Template is cut out in both halves after assembly and used with router and guide bushing.

Shallow, stopped grooves in main template provide dust passage from template to hose port.

Hole intersects dust passages and provides port for dust vacuum.

Dust collection for template jigs

When you are template routing small or intricate inlays or mortising for hardware, chips and debris will often accumulate and prevent the guide bushing or shank-mounted pilot bearing from riding evenly around the template. Instead of trying to vacuum such chips out around the router, you can add dust collection directly to the template. The dust-collecting template shown in the drawing above is made from two layers: a main template and a hardboard cover. The main template, made from MDF or Baltic birch plywood, has dust passages routed into it that connect to a port that accepts a small-diameter vacuum hose. A thin hardboard cover is glued to the bottom of the template to seal the dust passages. The template is made large enough so the hose port can be located away from the template cutout so the router will clear the hose. The dust passages (one, two or more, depending on the size and shape of the template cutout) are stopped grooves that connect the template cutout and dust port—a hole drilled through the template to fit the vacuum hose end connector. The grooves should be shallow enough that the router's guide bushing or bearing will still have a solid surface to contact as it rides around the template cutout (see the drawing on the facing page).

In use, the dust-collecting template is clamped over the workpiece, hardboard side down; the shop vacuum is switched on and template routing (see Chapter 5) proceeds as usual. If the dust passages are too

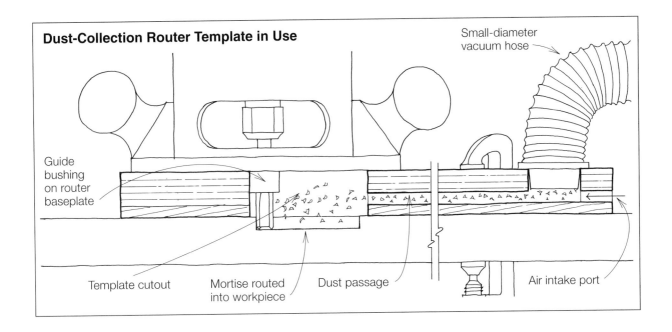

Dust-Collection Router Template in Use

Small-diameter vacuum hose

Guide bushing on router baseplate

Template cutout

Mortise routed into workpiece

Dust passage

Air intake port

restrictive and the vacuum motor sounds taxed, you can extend one or more of the grooves through to the edge of the template, as shown in the drawing, to allow increased air flow to relieve the strain.

Dust-vacuum small-parts collection

Very often, very small parts must be cut in quantity on a machine tool, but the force and wind generated by a whirling sawblade is enough to send these mini-parts flying, often back into the blade, where they get chewed up. You can safely rescue such parts by sucking them up in a portable shop vacuum. First, clean out the vacuum (so you don't have to pick through dirt and sawdust to retrieve your parts). Then, temporarily clamp the vacuum hose to the jig or machine tool, locating the open end so the suction will pull parts away from the blade or cutter immediately after they have been cut off. This method can also be used to remove cutoff scraps generated when trimming the ends of the stock that might otherwise be hurled back at the operator.

Automatic dust-collector switches

It's convenient to switch shop vacuums and dust collectors on and off at the same time as the power tools and machinery they serve. One way to do this is with an automatic electronic switch. Several different models of Automater electronic switch boxes are made by R.F. St. Louis Associates, and they are all very easy to use: The tool and vacuum or dust collector both plug into the switch box. When the tool is activated, the vacuum comes on a short time later, allowing the tool to come up to speed. The vacuum switches off a short time after the tool, a delay that allows dust to be cleared from the hose.

SOURCES OF SUPPLY

Below are listed the parts, devices, materials and hardware described in the text, followed by the names of sources that sell that item. Listings are not exclusive: You might discover other suppliers not mentioned here. The second section, which begins on p. 226, lists the addresses, phone numbers and FAX numbers of the sources cited in the first section. Manufacturers are listed for items that are either hard to get or are widely distributed (by contacting the manufacturer, you can find out if there's a local distributor for the item or if the manufacturer will sell direct). You may also want to contact certain manufacturers for technical information and catalogs of all the items they make.

Most of the companies listed are retail suppliers, and practically all of these have their own mail-order catalogs that they will supply upon request, usually free but some for a modest fee. All listings are current as of Spring 1994, but just as sure as the coming of the seasons, suppliers are bound to change over the course of time.

Items Cited in the Text

Acrylic plastic
Eagle America, Meisel Hardware Specialties, TAP Plastics, Woodcraft, Woodhaven

Adhesive transfer tape (Scotch 934) and applicator
3M (manufacturer)

Adjustable circle cutters
Grizzly Imports, Highland Hardware, Lee Valley Tools, Meisel Hardware Specialties, Trend-lines

"Advanced Vacuum Bagging Techniques" (booklet #002-150)
Gougeon Brothers

Air-clamping systems and accessories
Bimba (manufacturer), De-Sta-Co (manufacturer), Woodworker's Supply

Air-powered quick-release toggle clamps, control valves and accessories
De-Sta-Co (manufacturer), Reid Tool Supply, Woodworker's Supply

Anti-kickback wheeled hold-downs
see Wheeled hold-downs

Arbor presses
Grizzly Imports, Rutland Tool & Supply

Assembly frame fittings, aluminum track extrusions
RK Industries

Automater electronic switch
Highland Hardware, R.F. St. Louis Associates (manufacturer), Woodcraft, Woodworker's Supply

Ball-bearing work rollers
Leichtung Workshops, Woodcraft, Woodworker's Supply

Bullet catches
Reid Tool Supply, The Woodworker's Store, Woodworker's Supply

Captured-ball style rollers
see Roller stands and brackets

Clear plastic guards (for router table)
Woodhaven

Complementary template routing bits and bearings
see Router bits and bearings for complementary template routing

Confirmat (knock-down) screws
Lee Valley Tools, Woodcraft, The Woodworker's Store

Countersinks, machinist's style
AMT, CMT Tools (manufacturer), Enco (manufacturer), Reid Tool Supply, Rutland Tool & Supply, Woodcraft (Weldon)

Curved lid support
Woodcraft, The Woodworker's Store

Cyanoacrylate glues (super glue)
Eagle America, Highland Hardware, Lee Valley Tools, Leichtung Workshops, Woodworker's Supply

Dado router bits
see Router bits for dadoes

Digital measuring devices
see ProScale

Double-stick tape
Constantine's, Eagle America, The Woodworker's Store, Woodworker's Supply

DriCote
see Sandaro

Drill bushings
Reid Tool Supply, Trend-lines, Woodworker's Supply

Drill bits (aircraft style, extra-long)
Rutland Tool & Supply

Drill bits, number size (1 to 80) or letter size (A to Z)
Enco (manufacturer), MSC Industrial Supply, Penn Tool, Reid Tool Supply, Rutland Tool & Supply

Drill-press clamps
see Vise clamps

Dust-collection hoses and fittings
Grizzly Imports, Woodhaven

Electronic speed controller
CMT Tools, Highland Hardware, MLCS, Woodcraft, Woodworker's Supply

Epoxy glue
Highland Hardware, Jamestown Distributors, Gougeon Brothers (manufacturer), Lee Valley Tools, Woodcraft

Extension springs
Reid Tool Supply

Fastop
Witty Inventions (manufacturer)

FasTTrack (all products, including flip stops and micro-adjusters)
Garrett Wade

Featherboards
Grizzly Imports, Highland Hardware, Woodcraft, Woodhaven, The Woodworker's Store, Woodworker's Supply

Flange-mounted bronze bearings
W.W. Grainger (wholesale distributor)

Folding brackets (for extension tables)
The Woodworker's Store

Foot switch, air-actuated electrical
Woodworker's Supply

Foot switch, electrical (and guard housings)
Constantine's, Garrett Wade, Leichtung Workshops, MLCS, Woodcraft, Woodhaven

Glide strips
see UHMW glide strips

Guide bushings, router
Highland Hardware, Lee Valley Tools, MLCS, Woodcraft

Hand knobs and studded handscrews
Reid Tool Supply (extensive selection), Woodcraft, Woodhaven, WoodsmithShop, The Woodworker's Store, Woodworker's Supply

Hold-down clamps (wooden), kit for
WoodsmithShop

Incra Miter Sliders
Eagle America, Grizzly Imports. Woodcraft, Woodworker's Supply

Inlay template-routing kit
CMT Tools, Eagle America, Highland Hardware, Woodcraft, Woodhaven

Inverted pin-router kit for drill press
Woodworker's Supply

Itty Bitty biscuits
Woodhaven

Joint connector bolts and cap nuts
Lee Valley Tools, The Woodworker's Store

Knobs
see Hand knobs and studded handscrews

Lamello #11 round biscuits and special biscuit-router bit
Colonial Saw Machinery, Trend-lines

Lazy Susan bearings
Lee Valley Tools, Meisel Hardware Specialties, Trend-lines, Woodcraft, The Woodworker's Store

Leveling feet (for router tables)
Reid Tool Supply, Woodcraft, The Woodworker's Store

Lexan
see Polycarbonate plastic

Locking collars for shank-mounted pilot bearings on router bits
CMT Tools, Reid Tool Supply, Woodhaven

Magnetic bars
Leichtung Workshops

Medium-density fiberboard (MDF), low formaldehyde
Plum Creek (manufacturer)

Medium-density fiberboard, formaldehyde-free (Medex)
Medite (manufacturer)

Non-skid tape
see Scotch 3M Safety Walk anti-slip tape

Nylotape
The Woodworker's Store

Phenolic plastic
Highland Hardware, Lee Valley Tools, Trend-lines, Woodhaven

Pilot bearings for router bits
CMT Tools, Eagle America, Meisel Hardware Specialties, MLCS, Trend-lines, Woodcraft, Woodhaven

Plywood
Boulter Plywood Corp. (Baltic birch), Constantine's (maple), Meisel Hardware Specialties, The Woodworker's Store (Finnish birch)

Pneumatic staplers (narrow crown)
Senco (manufacturer), Trend-lines, Woodworker's Supply

Pneumatic quick-release toggle clamps
see Quick-release toggle clamps

Polycarbonate plastic
Eagle America, Highland Hardware, TAP Plastics, Trend-lines, Woodworker's Supply, Woodcraft

PowerTwist belt (low-vibration V-belt)
Woodcraft, Woodworker's Supply

Press-in threaded inserts, for plastics
Reid Tool Supply

ProScale
Accurate Technology (manufacturer)

Pulleys, machined steel and cast iron
W.W. Grainger (wholesale distributor), Woodcraft

Quickfit connectors (for pneumatic or vacuum lines)
Woodworker's Supply

Quick-Grip bar clamps
Woodcraft

Quick-release toggle clamps (catalog suppliers)
Grizzly Imports, Highland Hardware, Lee Valley Tools, Reid Tool Supply, Rutland Tool & Supply, The Woodworker's Store, Woodcraft, Woodworker's Supply

Quick-release toggle clamps (manufacturers)
Carr Lane Manufacturing, De-Sta-Co, Te-Co

Roller assemblies and rails
see Sliding table hardware

Roller stands and brackets
AMT, Grizzly Imports, Highland Hardware, Lee Valley Tools, Leichtung Workshops, Trend-lines, Woodcraft, Woodworker's Supply

Round washer-head screws
McFeely's

Router bits and bearings for complementary template routing
CMT Tools, Eagle America, Woodcraft, Woodhaven

Router bits for dadoes in imported plywood (6mm, 12mm, 18mm)
Woodhaven

Router bits for dadoes in undersized plywood
CMT Tools ($^{15}/_{64}$ in., $^{31}/_{64}$ in., $^{23}/_{32}$ in.) Eagle America ($^{7}/_{32}$ in., $^{31}/_{64}$ in., $^{23}/_{32}$ in.), Woodcraft ($^{31}/_{64}$ in., $^{23}/_{32}$ in.)

Router bits, panel pilot
CMT Tools, Eagle America

Router bits, solid carbide spiral
CMT Tools, Eagle America, Highland Hardware, MLCS, Woodcraft, Woodhaven

Router bits, up-cut and down-cut spiral
CMT Tools, Eagle America, Lee Valley Tools (upcut spiral), MLCS, Woodcraft (upcut spiral), Woodhaven

Router bits, up-and-down cut spiral, for plywood
Woodhaven

Router bits, T-slot
Woodcraft, Woodhaven, The Woodworker's Store

Router bit, T-slot wall groover
Eagle America

Router-table insert-plate leveling kit
Woodhaven

Router-table insert plates
CMT Tools, Eagle America, Woodhaven

Safety guards for router table
Woodhaven, WoodsmithShop

Sandaro products (DriCote, TopCote, Bearing Lubricant)
Eagle America, Grizzly Imports, Highland Hardware, Woodcraft

Sawblade for cutting aluminum
Woodworker's Supply (Freud LU89)

Sawblade for cutting thin plastics
CMT Tools (#108-800), Woodworker's Supply (Freud LU98)

Seal tape (for vacuum jigs and tables)
Woodhaven, Vacuum Pressing Systems (manufacturer)

Scotch 3M Safety Walk anti-slip tape
Jamestown Distributors, TAP Plastics

Screw posts
Lee Valley Tools (Chicago bolts), The Woodworker's Store (plastic)

Screws (hardened-steel, square drive)
Lee Valley Tools, McFeely's

Sliding table hardware
RK Industries

Spiral reamers
Reid Tool Supply, Rutland Tool & Supply

Spring pins
Reid Tool Supply, Rutland Tool & Supply

Stem bumpers
The Woodworker's Store

Stick-on (self-stick) measuring tape
Highland Hardware, Lee Valley Tools, Leichtung Workshops, Reid Tool Supply, Rutland Tool & Supply, Woodhaven

Stop collars
Jamestown Distributors

Studded handscrews
see Hand knobs

T-bolts
Reid Tool Supply, Woodhaven, The Woodworker's Store (extra long 3-1/2-in. bolts)

T-nuts
Highland Hardware, Meisel Hardware Specialties, WoodsmithShop, The Woodworker's Store

T-slot nuts
Reid Tool Supply, Woodhaven, WoodsmithShop

T-slot router bits
see Router bits, T-slot

T-track (aluminum)
Garrett Wade (FasTTrack), WoodsmithShop

T-track (steel)
The Woodworker's Store

Taper pins and tapered reamers
Rutland Tool & Supply

Threaded insert T-handle installation tool
Woodcraft

Threaded inserts
Frog Tool, Highland Hardware, Lee Valley Tools, Meisel Hardware Specialties, McFeely's, Reid Tool Supply (also press-in inserts, for plastics), Trend-lines, Woodcraft, The Woodworker's Store (including coarse-thread inserts for end grain)

Toggle clamps
see Quick-release toggle clamps

TopCote
see Sandaro

True-Fit Adjustable Miter Track
Garrett Wade

Universal hold-down clamps
Enco (manufacturer), MSC Industrial Supply, Reid Tool Supply, Rutland Tool & Supply

UHMW glide strips
Meisel Hardware Specialties, Trend-lines, Woodcraft, Woodworker's Supply

Vacuum-valve hold-down systems and acessories
Moon's Saw Shop Supplies (Lil' Oscar), Vacuum Pressing Systems (manufacturer), Woodhaven

Vise clamps (for drill-press table)
AMT, Highland Hardware, Woodcraft, Woodworker's Supply

Vix bits
CMT Tools, Constantine's, Highland Hardware, Jamestown Distributors, Lee Valley Tools, Leichtung Workshops, Trend-lines, Woodcraft, The Woodworker's Store (including ¼ in.), Woodworker's Supply

Wheeled hold-downs
Excalibur Machine & Tool (fits their T-slot saw fence), Grizzly Imports, Lee Valley Tools, Leichtung Workshops, Trend-lines, Woodworker's Supply

Wonder Dogs (Veritas)
Woodcraft, WoodsmithShop, The Woodworker's Store, Woodworker's Supply

Wraparound hinges
Woodworker's Supply, The Woodworker's Store

Accurate Technology (manufacturer)
11533 NE 118th Street, Suite 220
Kirkland, WA 98034
(800) 233-0580
(206) 820-8666
FAX (206) 820-8795

AMT (American Machine & Tool)
PO Box 70
4th Avenue and Spring Street
Royersford, PA 19468
(215) 948-0400

Bimba (manufacturer)
Route 50
Monee, IL 60449
(708) 534-8544
FAX (708) 534-5767

Boulter Plywood Corp.
24 Broadway
Somerville, MA 02145
(617) 666-1340

Carr Lane Manufacturing (manufacturer)
4200 Carr Lane Court
PO Box 191970
St. Louis, MO 63119
(314) 647-6200

CMT Tools (manufacturer)
5425 Beaumont Center Boulevard, Suite 900
Tampa, FL 33634
(800) 531-5559 (orders or information)
(813) 886-1819
FAX (813) 888-6614

Colonial Saw Machinery
100 Pembroke Street
Kingston, MA 02364
(617) 585-4364

Albert Constantine and Son
2050 Eastchester Road
Bronx, NY 10461
(800) 223-8087
(212) 792-1600
FAX (212) 792-2110

De-Sta-Co (manufacturer)
2121 Cole Street
Birmingham, MI 48009
(313) 589-2008
FAX (313) 644-3929

Eagle America
PO Box 1099
Chardon, OH 44024
(800) 872-2511 (orders)
(216) 286-7429
FAX (216) 286-7643

Enco (manufacturer)
5000 West Bloomingdale
Chicago, IL 60639
(800) 645-6094

Excalibur Machine & Tool
29 Passmore Avenue #6
Scarborough, Ontario
Canada M1V 3H5
(800) 387-9789 (United States)
(416) 291-8190 (Canada)
FAX (416) 293-2076

Frog Tool
700 W. Jackson Boulevard
Chicago, IL 60025
(708) 657-7526

Garrett Wade
161 Avenue of the Americas
New York, NY 10013
(800) 221-2942
(212) 807-1757

Gougeon Brothers (manufacturer)
706 Martin Street
Bay City, MI 48706
(517) 684-7286

Grizzly Imports
P.O. Box 2069
Bellingham, WA 98227
(800) 523-4777 (east)
(800) 541-5537 (west)
(206) 647-0801 (customer service)
FAX (800) 225-0021

Highland Hardware
1045 N. Highland Ave., NE
Atlanta, GA 30306
(800) 241-6748 (orders)
(404) 872-4466 (information)
FAX 404 876-1941

Lee Valley Tools
PO Box 6295, Station J
Ottawa, Ontario
Canada K2A 1T4
(800) 267-8767 or (800) 267-8757 (toll-free orders, Canada only)
(613) 596-0350
FAX (613) 596-6030

Leichtung Workshops
4944 Commerce Parkway
Cleveland, OH 44128
(800) 542-4467 (information)
(800) 321-6840 (orders)
FAX (216) 464-6764

McFeely's
712 12th Street
PO Box 3
Lynchburg, VA 24505-0003
(800) 443-7937
FAX (804) 847-7136

Medite (manufacturer)
PO Box 4040
Medford, OR 97501
(503) 773-2522

Meisel Hardware Specialties
PO Box 70
Mound, MN 55364-0700
(800) 441-9870 (orders)
(612) 471-8550
FAX 612 471-8579

MLCS
PO Box 4053 C-13
Rydal, PA 19046
(800) 533-9298 (orders)
(215) 938-5067
FAX 215 938-5070

Moon's Saw Shop Supplies
2531-2539 N. Ashland Avenue
Chicago, IL 60614
(800) 447-7371
(312) 549-7924
FAX (312) 549-7695

MSC Industrial Supply
151 Sunnyside Boulevard
Plainview, NY 11803
(800) 645-7270

Ocemco (manufacturer)
1232 51st. Avenue
Oakland, CA 94601
(415) 532-7669

Penn Tool
1776 Springfield Avenue
Maplewood, NJ 07040
(800) 526-4956
(201) 761-4343 (in New Jersey)
FAX (201) 761-1494

Plum Creek (manufacturer)
PO Box 160
Columbia Falls, MT 59912
(406) 892-6235

Reid Tool Supply
1518 E. Katella Avenue
Anaheim, CA 92805
(800) 367-8056
(714) 634-1961
FAX (800) 367-8050 or (714) 978-3516

R.F. St. Louis Associates (manufacturer)
12 Cove Road
Branchville, NJ 07826
(800) 526-0602

RK Industries
7330 Executive Way
Frederick, MD 21701
(301) 696-9400
FAX (301) 696-9494

Rutland Tool & Supply
16700 E. Gale Avenue
City of Industry, CA 91745
(800) 289-4787
(818) 961-7111
FAX (800) 333-3787

Senco (manufacturer)
8486 Broadwell Road
Cincinnati, OH 45244
(800) 543-4596

TAP Plastics
6475 Sierra Lane
Dublin, CA 94568
(800) 894-0827
(510) 829-4889
FAX (510) 829-6921
No mail order, but has 19 stores in Northern California

Te-Co (manufacturer)
109 Quinter Farm Road
Union, OH 45322
(513) 836-0961

3M (manufacturer)
3M Center
St. Paul, MN 55144
(800) 364-3577 (information)

Trend-lines
375 Beacham Street
Chelsea, MA 02150
(800) 767-9999 (orders)
(800) 877-3338 (automated ordering)
(617) 884-8951 (information)
FAX 617 889-2072

Vacuum Pressing Systems (manufacturer)
553 River Road
Brunswick, ME 04011
(207) 725-0935
FAX (207) 725-0932

W.W. Grainger (wholesale distributor)
333 Knightsbridge Parkway
Lincolnshire, IL 60069-3639
(708) 913-7400 (technical support)
FAX (800) 722-3291 (orders)

Witty Inventions (manufacturer)
PO Box 10807
New Iberia, LA 70562
(318) 367-9962

Woodcraft
7845 Emerson Avenue
Parkersburg, WV 26101
(800) 225-1153 (orders)
(800) 535-4482 (customer service)
FAX (304) 428-8271 (orders)

Woodhaven
5323 W. Kimberly Road
Davenport, IA 52806
(800) 344-6657
(319) 391-2386
FAX (319) 391-1279

WoodsmithShop
2200 Grand Avenue
Des Moines, IA 50312
(800) 444-7002
FAX (515) 283-0447

The Woodworker's Store
21801 Industrial Boulevard
Rogers, MN 55374-9514
(612) 428-2199
(612) 428-2899 (technical service)
FAX (612) 428-8668

Woodworker's Supply
5604 Alameda Place NE
Albuquerque, NM 87113
(800) 645-9292

INDEX

Editor: RUTH DOBSEVAGE

Designer/Layout Artist: JODIE DELOHERY

Illustrator: VINCENT BABAK

Photographer: SANDOR NAGYSZALANCZY

Art Assistants: ILIANA KOEHLER, SUZANNA M. YANNES

Typeface: GARAMOND

Paper: WARREN PATINA MATTE, 70 LB., NEUTRAL pH

Printer: ARCATA GRAPHICS/HAWKINS, NEW CANTON, TENNESSEE